W9-BHP-313

LAWRENCEBURG PUBLIC LIBRARY DISTRICT

THE
MIND
OF A
TERRORIST

THE
MIND
OF A
TERRORIST

David Headley, the Mumbai Massacre, and His European Revenge

KAARE SØRENSEN

Translated from the Danish by Cory Klingsporn

Arcade Publishing • New York

Copyright © 2013, 2016 by Kaare Sørensen and People'sPress
English-language translation copyright © 2016 by Skyhorse Publishing, Inc.

All rights reserved. No part of this book may be reproduced in any manner
without the express written consent of the publisher, except in the case of
brief excerpts in critical reviews or articles. All inquiries should be addressed to
Arcade Publishing, 307 West 36th Street, 11th Floor, New York, NY 10018.

First English-language Edition

First published in Denmark by People'sPress under the title *Halshug*

Arcade Publishing books may be purchased in bulk at special discounts for
sales promotion, corporate gifts, fund-raising, or educational purposes. Special
editions can also be created to specifications. For details, contact the Special
Sales Department, Arcade Publishing, 307 West 36th Street, 11th Floor, New
York, NY 10018 or arcade@skyhorsepublishing.com.

Arcade Publishing® is a registered trademark of Skyhorse Publishing, Inc.®,
a Delaware corporation.

Visit our website at www.arcadepub.com.

10 9 8 7 6 5 4 3 2 1

Library of Congress Cataloging-in-Publication Data

Names: Sørensen, Kaare, author.
Title: The mind of a terrorist: David Headley, the Mumbai massacre, and his
    European revenge / Kaare Sørensen; translated by Cory Klingsporn.
Other titles: Halshug. English
Description: First English-language edition. | New York: Arcade Publishing, [2016]
Identifiers: LCCN 2016005437 | ISBN 978-1-62872-514-8 (hardback) | ISBN
    978-1-62872-545-2 (Ebook)
Subjects: LCSH: Headley, David Coleman. | Terrorists—Biography. | Mumbai
    Terrorist Attacks, Mumbai, India, 2008. | BISAC: POLITICAL SCIENCE /
    Political Freedom & Security / Terrorism.
Classification: LCC HV6430.H43 S6713 2016 | DDC 363.325092—dc23 LC
record available at http://lccn.loc.gov/2016005437

Cover design by Anthony Morais
Cover photo: AP Images

Printed in the United States of Am

YA B HEADLEY
Sorensen, Kaare
The mind of a terrorist :
    David Headley, the Mumbai
    massacre, and his
    European revenge

35340636229659   Jun 16

CONTENTS

Author's Note

This book is a reconstruction of real events.

All dialogue, all the people, meetings, and descriptions are based on a comprehensive collection of documentation.

Central in this context are more than three hundred previously unpublished emails and private letters sent from the man at the center of the story, David Headley, during the period from 2008 to 2009.

In addition, this book builds on the material from several comprehensive interrogation reports, secret audio recordings of the terrorism suspect's discussions in vehicles and offices, comprehensive electronic wiretapping of mobile phones in several countries—including 284 calls from the terrorist attack in Mumbai, from November 26 to November 29, 2008—court transcripts and materials from several trials in the United States, Pakistan, India, and Sweden; internal documents from American embassies, witness statements, military reports and analyses, newspaper articles, recordings from surveillance cameras, hotel receipts, and old boarding passes, passport stamps, journals, martyr videos, and the author's own interviews with eyewitnesses, lawyers, intelligence officers, experts, and others.

Most sources are described in detail at the end of this book, though some wish to remain anonymous, either because they possess confidential information or because they fear for their lives.

PREFACE

Before a terror attack becomes an item on a breaking news ticker or social media, before the first shot is fired, even before the attackers pack their weapons, you will find a guy like David Headley.

He could be the person sitting next to you in the hotel lobby or at a bar in any major city in the world. And he would fit in.

Headley knows the secret about terror. It's not about death. Not even close. Even though that is exactly what we've seen again and again in attacks over the past several years: Tourists with a drink in their hand shot dead at a concert in Paris. Cartoonists in the same city killed at their place of work. Men and women from all over the world blown to pieces with deadly bombs at the airport and in a subway station in Brussels. A British soldier stabbed, then hacked to death while walking on the streets of London.

A fresh incident preceded by the words "mass casualty" and all too often a number so high it is almost impossible to comprehend.

Yet, for modern-day Islamic terrorists the number of dead and wounded doesn't really matter. Killing is part of the mission, of course, but the ultimate goal is something else. It's about the creation of fear. Fear that will spread like an airborne virus from news anchors to the world. And, over time, will force us to change the very nature of our societies.

David Headley is one of these creators of fear. He is the designer.

And Headley is special. He is one of very few Americans who have become involved in Islamic terror at the absolute highest levels and gained access to some of the world's most sought-after men.

This book is a journey through David Headley's chaotic life. It's a journey through his thoughts and ideas. His actions. The killings. And why it all happened. In part, in his own words.

In order to combat fear, we first need to understand. And in order to understand, we need to get inside the mind of a terrorist.

PART 1
MUMBAI

1

A Beginning

Mumbai, India
Saturday, April 12, 2008, 3:00 a.m.

He had wasted his time.

The tourist ferries were packed with two decks of overweight Americans and Brits who had ventured out from their luxury hotels for a few hours before quickly returning to the pool to pour themselves yet another drink.

Pathetic. Just pathetic.

He had taken the ferries twice, but it didn't help much. Harbor cruises couldn't give him the kind of answers he was looking for.

Instead, he now stood on the deck of a little fishing boat as it traveled quickly out into the darkness, the smell of fish and warm seawater filling his senses. He exchanged a few words with the fisherman who had agreed to take him along on this special night cruise in the Arabian Sea, and he sensed that he was on the right path.

Like all the other big modern cities in the world, Mumbai lit the darkness behind him even now, at three in the morning on a random Friday night. They were still partying there. Letting loose. Breaking the rules. Even here, from nearly three miles out, the huge city resembled an impressive, unconquerable fort. Too large to really shake. A city that never went totally dark, though on the ocean darkness was everywhere.

They had no idea.

How did he get here, anyway?

Was it hate for India that had brought him on this deck in the dark of night? That time they bombed his school, more than thirty-five years ago? Was it because of his stint as a drug smuggler? Or as an agent for the Americans? Was it the women? The pictures from Abu Ghraib, the Qur'an thrown into the toilet at Guantánamo, or the cartoons of Muhammad in Denmark?

Or was it something greater?

That day, it was for Allah, the only true God that had ever existed. He had no doubts. He was here because he needed to be right here. He was a soldier in an army assembled by Allah. His life had been a bit of a mess, sure, he knew that, but his mission wouldn't have been possible without his past.

Everything had led up to this trip.

The day before, he had gone down to the fishermen's village and found the fisherman, who lived in a weathered hut near a small Hindu temple. He introduced himself as David Headley. That had been his name for some years now, and he was getting used to it. It sounded American. That was the whole idea.

He'd taken his video camera down to the fisherman's hut and done his best to look like nothing other than an ordinary, adventure-seeking American tourist. He kept his Muslim background, his thoughts about Indians, and his true reasons for the trip to himself.

It was the fisherman who suggested that Headley come back the following night and sail with him, if he wanted a genuine experience of the sea around Mumbai. Headley quickly said yes.

He was searching for the perfect site to make landfall. A place from which everything could be set in motion. And a route there without reefs or other undersea dangers. If there was anybody who knew a safe way through the waters around Mumbai, it had to be this fisherman. He'd give Headley answers without even knowing it. All he had to do was sail.

According to the original plan, the Gateway of India monument, on the eastern side of the peninsula that splits Mumbai from the mainland, was to be the starting point. It sits right across from the majestic Taj Hotel. Headley had to admit that it was an iconic location for beginning a terrorist attack.

To reach the old harbor, though, you have to travel around the southern tip of Mumbai, where the coast guard could be a little too watchful. Headley saw far too many gunboats with uniformed guards on board for that plan to work. The fashionable area along the Cuffe Parade on Mumbai's west side would be better. Much better. The men would be coming from the west, down from Pakistan.

The little fishing village by the beach seemed just right—unlike the rest of the area, it was dirty and often chaotic. There might occasionally be a fair number of people around, but the poor fishermen weren't the kind to complain or call the police if they noticed anything unusual. On the contrary, if there was a crowd, it would be the perfect cover. At the same time, the village was centrally located, and you could quickly go straight up to the main road, hail a taxi, and be wherever in the city you wanted to be within a few minutes.

The outing with the fisherman had convinced Headley: it was possible to go from international waters to the coast and onto land without encountering any significant obstacles.

The men would turn up right in the left atrium of Mumbai's heart, and nobody would realize until it was too late.

He saved the beach's coordinates on his GPS.

It would begin here. Right here.

2

Light the Fire, My Brother

Mumbai, India
Wednesday, November 26, 2008

18° 55' 11.80", 72° 49' 32.30".

The handheld GPS device showed the position on its large screen inside the waterproof rubber case.

They were there.

The black-and-yellow inflatable dinghy reached the shore, and eight of the ten young men quickly jumped out onto the beach with their backpacks. They were silent. The remaining two members of the group fired up the powerful Yamaha outboard motor once more and disappeared into the darkness with the boat, to make landfall elsewhere.

The eight young men stepped over paper, discarded food scraps, and brightly colored old plastic bottles as they made their way up the beach in the poor fishing village.

They split up into four groups of two without a sound.

A few of the vendors were surprised at the sight of men with big backpacks in a place normally frequented only by the local fishermen, but they were told to "mind their own business."

Other witnesses who noticed the young men in T-shirts and worn-out jeans got the same message.

"And what about you? Mind your own business!" said the men, who told other curious bystanders that they were students from a university in Hyderabad, another large Indian city.

In their pockets they carried student IDs with Indian names like Samir, Naresh, Arjunkumar, Dinesh, Raghubir, Arun, and Rohit in case anyone questioned their cover story.

But no one stopped them.

Nazir and Arshad were both twenty-three years old and anything but students. It was years since they'd even opened a book. Apart from the Qur'an, that is.

Walking calmly, they proceeded the short distance from the shore to the busy highway and hailed one of the many taxis available at all hours at the taxi stand.

In the backseat, one of the men fished a little brick of what looked like modeling clay out of his bag. The brick, which weighed about eleven pounds, was connected to a timing device and a stopwatch, and there were instructions in Urdu to ensure that, in the heat of battle, they wouldn't attach the five loose wires incorrectly.

Nazir and Arshad connected the wires and hid the first bomb under a seat in the taxi.

The mission had begun.

In a hotel room less than half a mile away sat a Danish man by the name of Jesper Bornak, phone in hand.

An Indian business contact had first postponed and then canceled a dinner, so Jesper now weighed his options for how to spend the remainder of the evening.

As a thirty-four-year-old independent businessman with his own freight company, a little daughter, and an almost-newborn son back home in Denmark, he always made good use of a free evening. There was always a mountain of emails that needed a reply. And always a considerable sleep deficit to work down.

When was the last time he'd simply thrown himself on the bed, relaxed, and read a book?

The big cities in his travels were just scenery for the long meetings filled with negotiating tactics, shipping containers, and stacks of paper. Singapore, Jakarta, Mumbai. It was all the same.

After a few days of negotiations with Indian customs officers about some containers in various far-flung parts of India, Jesper felt his curiosity about the big city grow.

"Jesper Bornak has returned to 'civilization' in Mumbai," he had written on Facebook page not long before.

He called Gitte at home.

"Everything is great. Yes, I'm headed out to eat. I'll call later. I love you," he said and put on a jacket.

Jesper left his wallet and passport at his hotel, the Oberoi-Trident. He stuffed two credit cards, two hundred dollars, and about two thousand Indian rupees in his pants pocket and, taking his black Nokia N95 out of its charger, left room 2735 for the last time.

Near the popular Leopold Café in central Mumbai, Nazir and Arshad—the group's first two-man team—got out of their taxi. They paid, apparently in American dollars, and were quickly stopped by a merchant who thought they were tourists.

"Want a T-shirt?" he asked.

"No," they replied, and pointed at the café instead. "Is the Leopold Café famous?"

The merchant replied yes.

The two stood for some time with an arm around the other's shoulder, smiling. They both seemed in high spirits.

Perhaps they were remembering the words instilled in them by the men in Pakistan over the past weeks and days:

"This is a struggle between Islam and the unbelievers. We're the people God has chosen to defend our religion against the unbelievers."

Some of the women who happened to be there noticed that the two men were in excellent shape physically and were good-looking too.

Jesper Bornak hopped into a taxi for the short drive to Leopold Café. He paid far too much for the trip, but that didn't matter much to him. It amounted to less than a dollar, and he was in a good mood.

In a corner of the café, he got a seat at a table where four stewardesses and a steward from Lufthansa were enjoying a free evening before they would once again serve drinks and airplane food all the way back to Germany.

Thirty-eight-year-old Thomas ran in his free time, so he and Jesper quickly got on well with each other. They spoke of marathons and Jesper's plans to run, cycle, and swim his way through a triathlon sometime next year. It happened that the group from Lufthansa was staying at the same hotel as Jesper.

"It's a small world," they said with a smile, as Jesper ordered chicken tikka masala, garlic naan, and a much-needed, tall, cold draft beer.

Leopold truly lived up to the description in Gregory David Roberts' cult novel *Shantaram*—a gathering place for Western businesspeople, Indian drug dealers, and happy world travelers with blue Lonely Planet books in hand and credit cards in their pockets.

On the wall hung little messages of greeting from tourists from all over the world, honoring the author.

Behind Jesper sat two Indian men drinking the café's specialty: more than seventy ounces of freshly brewed beer from a sort of glass column with its own tap. To his right sat Line Kristin Woldbeck, a Norwegian woman in an Indian dress and with a prominent nose ring; her husband, Arne Strømme; and their Indian friend, Meetu.

The big TV screen was transmitting live from the large city of Cuttack, about nine hundred miles away, where India was playing the fifth cricket match this month against England. Most of the country was following the match, truly a life-and-death matter. Leopold Café was no exception.

Jesper had finished the spicy chicken and was talking with the Lufthansa group about trips they'd made to Tehran. He was in the middle of a cup of coffee when he first heard the sound of small explosions from the street outside. It lasted just a few seconds and sounded a lot like firecrackers or some other fireworks. Completely normal in that part of Mumbai.

Jesper and Thomas continued talking.

Then, something was tossed through the door into the restaurant.

It was 9:28 p.m. when a young German man, twenty-six-year-old Benjamin Matthijs, saw a small oval-shaped object about the size of a fist roll along the floor to his table, when it unexpectedly made a small jump and rolled off to the right, under the neighboring table where a rugged-looking British man was eating his dinner.

I shouldn't be here right now. Something is very wrong. There shouldn't be a hand grenade in a café, Benjamin managed to think as he reached for his bag.

In the next second, the windows of the café were blown out with a deafening bang.

The explosion left a hole in the floor more than an inch deep, and shrapnel flew through the air, killing several people and boring into Benjamin's leg, foot, and face. He was thrown through the air and landed on the floor four or five yards from his seat, nearly at the other end of the café.

Jesper responded instinctively.

That's an explosion. And this is terrorism, was his immediate thought.

A few years earlier, he and Gitte had been on vacation in Bali. An American tourist had recommended a good restaurant that sounded like a romantic place with a view, but it just happened that they never made it there. The day after they returned home, the restaurant was bombed, and at least twenty people were killed.

That had left a strong impression on both of them.

But Jesper Bornak had military experience. He had been with the Danish forces in Croatia in 1995, where two of his comrades were killed and fourteen injured in a Serbian artillery attack. Jesper was familiar with explosives and had no doubt that the explosion in the café was a controlled one. And thus, most likely a terrorist attack.

Suicide bomb, he thought, instinctively pushing his chair back and throwing himself under the table in case there was another explosion.

Opposite Jesper sat Desiree, the stewardess he had been speaking to just seconds before. He took hold of her legs with both hands and dragged her to cover under the table.

She was screaming loudly. For Desiree had seen what Jesper could not, since he had been sitting with his back to the door: a young man with a backpack, in dark clothing, a tight scarf, and with a raised fire-arm was shooting indiscriminately around the room.

It was either Nazir or Arshad entering the café.

From his cover under the table, Jesper heard several screams and the noise of chairs being overturned and glass breaking. People falling to the ground. The smell of gunpowder was inescapable.

The central railway station in Mumbai, Victoria Terminus, also called Chatrapati Shivaji, is constantly teeming with people.

That Wednesday evening was no exception, with the station filled with travelers returning from weddings, workers on their way home to Mumbai's huge suburbs, and Muslim men still in transit from cele-brating Eid al-Adha, the Feast of the Sacrifice, a few weeks earlier. Two million passengers either board or disembark there from more than 1,200 trains every day.

In the crowd stood two young men with large backpacks, looking like travelers among so many others.

Ismail was the most eye-catching of the two. He was twenty-five years old, tall, and, with his background and experience in Pakistan's northwestern border province, the natural leader for the ten terrorists who had reached the shores of Mumbai just a short while ago.

At his side was his polar opposite: the short, dark-haired twenty-one-year-old Mohammed Ajmal Amir, who would become known as "Kasab," Urdu for "butcher." Kasab came from Faridkot in the Okara district of Pakistan's Punjab province—a small, isolated rural town with only 478 registered voters and an autocratic mayor who issued orders to the inhabitants by means of the loudspeakers in the city mosque.

GO FOR JIHAD, GO FOR JIHAD, said a large sign right outside of Faridkot.

Kasab, though, didn't take the direct route to jihad.

A few years earlier, he often bickered with his poor parents, Amir Shahban and Noor Elahi, and he apparently left home after an argument about some clothing. Kasab found the world outside Faridkot disheartening, though. He could find nothing but difficult, underpaid work and all his efforts met with resistance. He was a young man with too much energy in his body, but without the means to make good use of it.

To make money, he fell into a criminal career: first with a bit of theft, some break-ins, and then armed robberies.

One day, Kasab met a group of Muslim men on the street. They offered to change his life, make him wiser, and free him from everyday misery. They had him watch movies and look at pictures of violent attacks and murders of Muslims all over the world, many of them in the disputed Kashmir region between Pakistan and India. Right around the corner.

Perhaps this was indoctrination, but Kasab was a willing student. He longed for meaning in his life, and here he had found it.

In the following months, Kasab arrived in some of the world's most secret and most feared terrorist camps hidden in the mountains in northern Pakistan. There he was trained in close-quarters combat, the making and use of bombs, swimming, and willpower. And it was there that he was carefully selected to be among the ten who would break and humble India with the attack in Mumbai.

In his backpack, Kasab was carrying an AK-47, six or seven magazines with thirty rounds each, a 9mm pistol with a couple magazines, eight to ten hand grenades, a water bottle, and about five pounds of nuts and dried fruits. He was ready.

The two men entered the station's restrooms together and then returned to the busiest area near line thirteen. At 9:53 p.m., they took their weapons out of their backpacks.

An Indian woman was one of their first victims. She was struck in the head by bullets and fell on the floor, while her husband took the family's children behind a post, where they hid and pretended to be dead.

Bullets and explosions from the hand grenades filled the large building in seconds. When a thirteen-year-old Indian boy by the name of Afroz Ansari regained consciousness, he was in the local hospital. It wasn't until several days later that he came to learn that his father, mother, uncle, two of his cousins, and his brother-in-law had been killed in the attack.

Kasab and Ismail showed no sign of fear. They behaved like children playing a computer game, just firing away and stopping only to reload their AK-47s with fresh ammunition.

A man yelled a few words to an elderly Muslim Indian scholar. When the attackers heard him yell, he was shot on the spot. A baby on the ground began to cry. When his mother went to pick him up, she too was shot.

Somewhere between fifteen and twenty officers were stationed outside the station, but none of them dared to intervene.

"We froze up. We just stood there, petrified," as policeman Sudahm Pandakar later said. When he and his colleagues finally began their counterattack, Pandakar was equipped with only an old rifle with five rounds in it, and it didn't even work.

Others had wooden batons as their only weapons.

Pandakar was struck in the ribs, while his colleagues, Abmadas Pawar and Shashank Shinde, were killed then and there.

The firefights lasted barely an hour before Kasab and Ismail left Victoria Terminus on foot, running out onto the street where they shot officers and random passersby in the dark.

At this point, they had already killed more than fifty. Several of the hundred plus who were injured at the train station later died of their wounds.

Desiree lay underneath Jesper, who had draped himself over her to protect her. Seeking cover, the steward Thomas had then thrown himself on top of Jesper. They lay under the table in a heap. Completely still.

Jesper lay with his head against the wall; he couldn't see much in the café. So he listened intently. And every time Desiree made the slightest sound, Jesper squeezed her side to get her to be quiet.

It was now completely silent in Leopold Café. No screams, no moans, no yells.

There's something very wrong, thought Jesper.

He could hear glass breaking under boots. Tables suddenly being yanked aside. And then came the gunfire. Jesper recognized the sound of automatic weapons fire from his time in Croatia. Two or three shots to make sure the victims were dead, but no more, in order to save ammunition. And then on to the next body. It was every bit a military operation.

Yelling in a language unknown to Jesper could be heard in the room, but the voices were cold and devoid of excitement or fear. It sounded like commands between soldiers.

There must be at least two men, thought Jesper, as the sound of boots on broken glass came closer.

We'll be shot now. I've got one on top of me, and I have my head against the wall, so I'll either be shot in the legs or my lower body. If I can avoid being shot in the head, I can survive. I actually have a chance to survive, thought Jesper as he tensed his abdomen.

And then shots rang out once again.

The exact sequence of events at the Café Leopold is still uncertain, but most of what we know seems to indicate that it was these shots that struck the Indian woman Meetu, who had been sitting near Jesper at the adjacent table, in the back of the head.

The Norwegian woman, Line, lay hiding on the ground holding the hand of twenty-six-year-old Meetu when it happened. She remembers her friend's hand giving a quick jerk before going completely limp. Meetu died instantly.

Meetu had written on Facebook a short time earlier: "Looking forward to meeting Line and Arne. It's gonna be wonderful!"

Line's husband, Arne, was bleeding from his head. He'd raised his hand in front of his face when shots were fired at him a few minutes earlier, and miraculously, the rounds had grazed his forehead and nose without killing him. The shot had broken three of his fingers. There was blood everywhere.

The terrorists had reached the door to the kitchen in their sweep to make sure that everyone in their way was either already dead or would be killed now.

"Run! Run!"

Jesper heard the words in his head as if they were spoken in English, but it was likely the German steward Thomas yelling, *"Raus! Raus!"* Regardless, Jesper knew his life would be determined by what happened in the next few seconds.

He leaped up with the six from Lufthansa. Several of them had bloodied hair and faces, but all of them were able to run.

On his way out, Jesper stepped over several lifeless bodies. His brain wouldn't allow him to see them properly, so he registered only that there were corpses in front of him. Outside the café, an Indian man sat doubled over, the front of his blue shirt drenched in the blood pouring from his stomach.

On the normally very busy main street, Colaba Causeway, everybody else had disappeared.

Desiree ran to the right, along with three of the other Lufthansa stewardesses. Thomas and Rita ran off instinctively to the left. There was no time to gather the group together or agree on a direction.

Jesper followed Thomas and Rita to the left quickly. His legs ran as fast as they possibly could. Past deserted stands, men's clothing stores, and empty cars. They stopped at a street corner and looked at each other.

"Are you okay?" they all asked each other, as they simultaneously nodded and shook their heads. They could hear the sound of gunshots, but they didn't know where it was coming from.

Then they gave each other a good hug.

An hour and a half earlier, Jesper hadn't even known that Thomas and Rita so much as existed. Now he was so happy they weren't among the eleven dead and twenty-eight injured lying on the café floor.

Meanwhile, the two terrorists, Nazir and Arshad, trotted out of the Leopold Café and continued to the next part of their mission on foot.

That evening in November, more than a thousand guests were in the hotel rooms and restaurants at the Taj Mahal Palace and Tower, Mumbai's finest and most famous hotel. Twenty of them were killed in a few minutes, when the barely twenty-year-old Soheb and his age-mate Abu Ali began their part of the attack.

The young men were firing with such abandon that they nearly killed Nazir and Arshad when the two arrived from Leopold a few minutes later.

Now, the four terrorists were gathered at the hotel, the main target of the attack.

On the sixth floor, the men went room to room, questioning the hotel guests with their weapons raised and asking those with a British or American passport to identify themselves. Those who did were either shot immediately or taken hostage.

As the initial assault came to an end, the men took out their phones and called a preprogrammed number.

"Pile up the carpets and mattresses from the room you've opened. Douse them with alcohol and set them alight. Get a couple of floors burning. And when we ring, make sure you answer," said a voice almost five hundred miles away.

"Yeah, yeah," they answered.

The phone rang again later.

"Peace be with you."

"How are you getting on? Have you started the fire yet?"

"No, we haven't started it yet."

"You must start the fire now. Nothing's going to happen until you start the fire. When people see the flames, they'll start to be afraid. And throw some grenades, my brother. There's no harm in throwing a few grenades. How hard can it be to throw a grenade? Just pull the pin and throw it."

Despite having killed so freely just moments ago, the men had a difficult time focusing on the task.

"There is so much light in here. So many buttons. There are computers with thirty-inch screens!" they said on the call back home to Pakistan.

This was the first time the young men had been to a foreign country. None had ever been around so much luxury in their lives. They came from some of the poorest conditions in the world. Before today, only a few of them had experienced anything other than their hometowns, where only the mayor or the local businessman might have a fancy car. Nothing like one of the world's most beautiful hotels.

"Computers? Haven't you set fire to them?"

"We're just about to. You'll be able to see the fire any minute."

"We can't watch if there aren't any flames. Where are they?"

"The entrance to this room is fantastic. The mirrors are really grand. The doors are massive too. It's fabulous. The windows are huge, but it feels very safe. There's a double kitchen at the front, a bathroom and a small shop. And mirrors everywhere," replied one of the four.

Then came another call.

There were still too few flames, said a man who called himself Wasi. The young men apparently couldn't find any axes, but Wasi was well-acquainted with the hotel's layout.

"My brother, there will be an ax hanging next to each fire extinguisher in the hotel. On every floor in every corridor. Now you must start the fire. Nothing will happen until you start the fire. When people see the flames, it will cause fear outside."

Wasi then asked if the men had set fire to the rooms they'd ransacked.

"No, they're right next to each other. We'll set the fire on our way out. We don't want the fire to spread too quickly in case we can't get out."

"No, burn everything as you go along. The bigger the fire, the more pressure you will bring to bear. We're watching it on TV. If you start the fire it will put pressure on the security forces. They won't come up."

"Listen. We don't even walk around our own houses as freely as we do here. We own the third, fourth, and fifth floors, thanks be to God."

"Start the fire, my brother. Start a proper fire, that's the important thing."

The men searched for guests to execute. The doors to more rooms were kicked in; women and men alike were put through painful humiliations before finally being shot. Their naked corpses were later found in contorted positions.

Several seem to have been tortured, for example by shooting them in the genitals.

After some time, in the various rooms where the door had been kicked in, the carpets were soaked with alcohol and were set on fire.

Taj—as the hotel was popularly called—stood in flames. Soon Indian TV was broadcasting images of the smoke-filled, burning icon to the whole nation, and later to most of the world.

"My brother, yours is the most important target. The media are covering your target, the Taj Hotel, more than any other," came the telephone message from Pakistan.

"They're saying that there are many, many killed and injured. They're saying there are fifty gunmen, the whole city has been shot up. Fires are burning everywhere. People are dying all over the place. With God's blessing, you've done a brilliant job!

"You're very close to heaven, brother. Today's the day you'll be remembered for, brother."

Jesper Bornak was keenly aware of his own heartbeat.

In the side streets they could hear more gunfire, and the otherwise safe big city had suddenly become an inferno of fear. Everything had the potential to be a threat. Everyone had the potential to be a terrorist, ready to take a rifle out of a bag at any moment.

Where can we find someplace safe? thought Jesper.

They hadn't run more than seventy or eighty yards from Leopold Café down Colaba Causeway.

A burly, balding Indian man in his forties appeared in a small doorway.

"Come in here," he said in broken English. "Come now, come now."

Jesper and Thomas and Rita from Lufthansa looked at each other, reached a quick decision, and ran after the man toward a rear stairway that smelled of urine. The man's apartment consisted of two rooms: one with bunk beds built from some planks, worn-out mattresses, and a washbasin. In the other room, there were mattresses spread out on the floor, a burner, a refrigerator, and a television. An old woman sat on the floor with a large group of terrified children around her.

Jesper quickly began to inspect the apartment.

If the terrorists come up here, how will we get out? he asked himself.

He found a small hole in the wall where he could see down to the street. The street was still completely empty. Everyone was hiding.

Normally, Jesper charged his mobile phone only at night, but that day he had put his Nokia in the charger while he made a foray down to the hotel pool. It was pure luck that he now had tons of battery life.

He dialed Jens Svendsen's number. A childhood friend from Denmark since the two of them were boys of about twelve or thirteen years old, Jens had also been a soldier in Croatia, and he's one of those guys you can call if your car breaks down, your girlfriend is breaking up with you, or you're going to be a father. Or when you're in the middle of a terrorist attack in a foreign city.

"It's absolutely crazy," Jesper said on the poor connection to Denmark.

He asked Jens to find the number for the Danish consulate in Mumbai so he could get help.

Three thousand miles to the northwest, Jesper's childhood friend was confused.

"I can't hear you well, Jesper. I've got some laundry to do for my parents. Can I call you back later?" Jens asked as he hung up.

Jens didn't think anything of it. He often heard from Jesper when he was traveling in other countries and along with that came a certain amount of experience with bad mobile phone coverage. It was still an hour before news of the attack would make it to mainstream Danish media. And several more hours and days before the attack in Mumbai was known to most everyone.

On the way to his parents' house, Jens received several text messages.

"Will you call soon? It's very important," wrote Jesper.

Once the laundry had been delivered to his parents' house, Jens got hold of Jesper in Mumbai.

"They're firing with handguns. They're throwing grenades." Jens managed to understand despite the terrible connection, and he realized the seriousness of the situation.

"Stay where you are. I'll figure something out," said Jens.

It was about 10:40 p.m. when the first taxi bomb exploded without warning, causing panic in the suburb of Ville Parle, not far from the international airport in Mumbai. The taxi driver and a passenger were killed in the explosion; two others were injured.

Among what remained of the car was the license plate, MH01G779. Some months later, it became clear that this was the airport taxi that had brought Kasab and Ismail to the train station. They had left a time bomb in the taxi. Kasab had slipped it under the driver's seat, while Ismail had distracted the driver with conversation.

Fifty-five-year-old Laxminarayan Goel had taken the taxi from Victoria Terminus en route to the airport, since he had arrived too late for his train to Hyderabad. It ended up costing him his life.

As for the police, news of the bomb led initially to the arrest of the taxi's innocent owner, while various other cars were stopped and people were either detained or arrested on the slightest suspicion.

Everywhere, there seemed to be chaos.

In the media, the situation wasn't any clearer. There were reports of new explosions with exaggerated death tolls, and images of burning buildings gave the sense of one big mess.

"Is this a terrorist attack planned by some large group? We don't know. Was it planned by organized crime? We don't know. What do they want? We don't know," recounted a journalist on one local TV station.

The perpetrators didn't make so much as a single demand or explain why innocent people needed to be killed.

They simply continued their attack.

"The enemy must fear us. When this is over, there will be much more fear in the world."

That was the line from Karachi in Pakistan, where everything was going according to plan in the terrorists' control room. They could make calls to the ten terrorists—who had now formed four teams— without any problem at all and thereby control them, as if they were remote-controlled robots.

The team consisting of Fahadullah and Rahman had taken the inflatable dinghy farther up the Mumbai coast, then headed directly to the Oberoi-Trident hotel complex. Once there, they wasted no time. In the lobby they killed all nine employees and three guests by the same method as their colleagues, hand grenades and bullets.

Esperanza Aguirre, the president of the Spanish region of Madrid, was about to check in at the front desk as she heard shots fired. She threw herself down behind a table, then hid in the kitchen and then in a storage room before she was helped into an office. Finally, she fled, barefoot, out onto the street.

Meanwhile, fear spread throughout the hotel. Several people crawled out windows and clung to the walls, yelling for help.

In a sushi restaurant in the hotel, thirteen were killed. One woman was badly injured but played dead. She lay for sixteen hours before help arrived.

The two men detonated a bomb in a tea room and dragged fifteen hotel guests out into a stairwell. Fahadullah was about to execute the men when one of the wives—Meltem Muezzinoglu—suddenly yelled, "We're from Turkey. We're Muslims."

She and her husband, Seyfi Muezzinoglu, were allowed to live. The other men were shot.

Later, the women in the group were executed too. Among them was the twenty-eight-year-old lawyer Lo Hoei Yen from Singapore, who was in Mumbai for a day trip. She was forced up against a wall and executed.

Out of the entire group of hotel guests taken prisoner, only Meltem and her husband survived—likely because the terrorists heard them reciting a Muslim prayer over the dead. It was the only prayer the married couple knew by heart in Arabic.

"No kill. You brothers. Go in," said Fahadullah to the couple.

A good mile from the Oberoi-Trident, Kasab and Ismail were walking around on the street with their weapons raised. They had apparently gotten lost after the attack on Victoria Terminus and were now simply trying to cause as much havoc as possible.

This was not part of the plan; they improvised.

In several locations, they kicked doors in and killed random people. An elderly man received two cuts to his throat but escaped with his life. Another was shot and killed as he sat eating in a small shed by the side of the road.

They jumped over a fence and made a beeline to a hospital where 450 patients and staff had recently seen the first warnings on TV that there were terrorists in the area.

An Indian woman was in the midst of giving birth, but the doctors and nurses tried to get her to quiet down so she wouldn't attract attention.

She banged her head against the floor in frustration.

"Do something! Do something!" she yelled.

At one point, a group of police officers arrived at that Cama Hospital in a Toyota Qualis. They called for reinforcements by radio, but by that time the command structure of the Mumbai police force had effectively collapsed. Many high-ranking officers and patrolmen had gone home to protect their own families, while others hung back in defeat, not daring to go out to fight the terrorists. They had already lost too many colleagues.

Lacking reinforcements, the officers were attacked, and three of them were immediately killed in the exchange of fire.

Kasab and Ismail probably never discovered that one of their victims was Hemant Karkara, the leader of Mumbai's anti-terrorism unit. His loss did nothing to help the police form a comprehensive picture of the attacks under way.

The two terrorists proceeded to drag some of the corpses out onto the road, where they commandeered the police jeep. In the backseat lay officer Arun Jadhav, shot three times in the left shoulder and twice in the right elbow. He played dead in order to survive.

At one point, a mobile phone rang from a pocket somewhere near Jadhav. Kasab turned toward the backseat and fired at the presumably already dead officer. By pure chance, Jadhav was not hit.

He lay completely still.

They drove around for fifteen to twenty minutes, until the vehicle got a flat tire. The two men then forced three women out of a Škoda Laura and continued on their way. Jadhav was nearly shot when his colleagues later surrounded the abandoned Toyota. But he survived and was able to give the first detailed description of the perpetrators. And where they were off to.

The attack had now been in progress for a few hours.

While the majority of the attacks that night had the purpose of drawing as much attention as possible, one attack was initially conducted in almost complete silence.

In southern Mumbai there was a Jewish studies center known as Chabad—carefully concealed in a five-story building called Nariman House along with, among other things, a synagogue and a few small rooms where mainly young Israeli and American backpackers in India stayed a night before continuing on their journey to Goa or other Indian cities. There was often a sizable crowd of people in the building.

The two young men, Akasha and Umer, were the only ones from the team on the beach who did not take a taxi that evening. Instead, they followed a precisely planned route about five hundred yards from the beach and up to exactly this building. While on the way, they placed a bomb in a gas station.

Using their mobile phone—a simple, cheap Nokia 1200 bought in Pakistan—Akasha and Umer made contact with Karachi.

"As I told you, every person you kill where you are is worth fifty of the ones killed elsewhere," came the message from the other end.

In the house, the twenty-nine-year-old rabbi Gavriel Holtzberg heard shots ring out or something suspicious that caused him to call the Israeli consulate from his mobile. He had been born in Israel, lived many years in New York, and then moved to Mumbai six years earlier to lead the five-thousand-odd Jews in the city.

"The situation is bad," he managed to say before the connection was cut off.

Shortly after that, he and his pregnant wife, Rivka Holtzberg, were overwhelmed and killed by gunfire as they attempted to stop the men from entering the building. Several guests were also killed, while two were taken hostage.

While the men slaughtered everyone around them with abandon, a young girl by the name of Sandra Samuel hid. She didn't lock the door to her room, and that probably saved her life, as the men obviously had no reason to suspect anyone was in a room with an unlocked door. She later left the building carrying the son of the Holtzbergs, who was barely two years old and had found his parents dead on the ground. He was soaked in their blood.

Through his childhood friend Jens, Jesper Bornak had gotten in touch with the consular service in the Danish foreign ministry. They're the people you call if, as a Dane, you've been in some sort of accident while outside Denmark.

The consular service hadn't heard anything about an attack in India.

"Just stay where you are," they said.

But Jesper didn't feel safe in the Indian man's apartment and went down to the street, where the first military jeeps were arriving. A police commander reached the same conclusion: "It's not safe to remain in this area. Get back to your hotel instead and stay there."

None of them knew that the Oberoi-Trident—the hotel where Jesper, Rita, and Thomas were staying—had been under attack for about an hour.

Almost at the same time the three left for the hotel in a taxi, another taxi exploded in Mumbai's Wadi Bunder district. Three were killed and fifteen were injured.

At the Oberoi-Trident, Jesper saw smoke, and now there was a checkpoint that prevented them from going further.

"Leave. The hotel has been attacked. There are terrorists on the street. It's not safe to be here. Head that way," said a soldier in English, pointing toward a park where several hotel guests had gathered.

Not on my life, thought Jesper. *If the terrorists come storming out of the hotel, they'll attack any place where a lot of people have gathered. I just need to get away.*

The three ran down a street that went along the hotel, where a TV crew from the local CNN station, IBN, stopped them.

"What's happened? Have you seen anything?" the journalists asked, still having a hard time keeping track of which places had actually been under attack.

Jesper and Thomas explained to the camera about the attack on Leopold. How they got away. And how they now feared for their lives.

A car drove quickly toward them, and some soldiers raised their weapons. It was a false alarm. But it did nothing to ease the state of paranoia that Jesper was in—everything was a threat, everything was dangerous, and everyone was a terrorist. If he wasn't safe at one of the most distinguished hotels in the city, if he wasn't safe in a taxi, if he wasn't safe on the street—what could he do?

He was about out of ideas and energy. And his cell phone battery was almost dead.

For the first time, it dawned on Jesper that he needed to get hold of his wife, Gitte, at home in Denmark. He had the feeling he might not survive the night.

* * *

It was a little after midnight when the silver-gray Škoda containing Kasab and Ismail reached a police barricade near the popular beach area, Girgaum Chaupati. Ismail tried to turn the car around but ran right into the barricade.

Kasab stepped out of the car as if to surrender and apparently raised his hands in the air. But as the officers approached him, he raised his AK-47.

The forty-eight-year-old officer Tukaram Omble, who had followed the Škoda on his motorcycle, made a split-second fatal decision: he grabbed hold of Kasab's weapon with both hands as Kasab emptied the magazine.

More than twenty rounds ended up in Omble's stomach, but even as Omble collapsed he managed to keep his hold on the gun and thereby prevent Kasab from killing others. The other officers shot Ismail several times. He later died on the way to a local hospital.

Kasab was arrested alive, though the officers wanted more than anything to beat him to death right then and there.

"When we saw that Omble was not letting go of the terrorist's gun, we knew we could not let his sacrifice go in vain. He held on and we completed his unfinished task," one of the officers, Sanjay Govilkar, later explained.

Scared, bruised, and injured, Kasab was interrogated later that night on a flat hospital mattress with a thin, gray blanket over him, in front of rolling cameras. The attacks throughout the city were still in progress, and the investigators were keen to obtain any information that could stop the killings.

But they were also intensely interested in Kasab's story. How did he get here? Who had sent him? And why?

Kasab claimed it was because his father, a poor food merchant from Faridkot in Pakistan, had sold him to some men: "He said, 'These people make loads of money, and so will you. You don't have to do anything difficult. We'll have money. We wouldn't be poor anymore. Your brothers and sisters can get married. Look at these guys living the good life. You can be like them,'" Kasab quoted his father as saying, his voice trembling.

According to the agreement, Kasab's father would receive $1,250 if Kasab were to die as a martyr in battle against the infidel Indian forces.

But that part of the plan had failed. Not only was Kasab alive, but he had been captured by the enemy.

"We were all supposed to die. He said we would go to heaven," cried Kasab, who more than anything else seemed like a little boy as he lay surrounded by the gruff soldiers gathered around his hospital bed.

The young man denied knowing anything in particular about jihad, the Muslim holy war. This wasn't his own personal war, but a war he carried out for a holy man, explained Kasab.

After more than a half hour of interrogation, though, Kasab was ready to reveal the name of the organization that had sent him from his rural town in Pakistan to India, to become a mass murderer.

"They're called Lakshar-e-Taiba," said Kasab.

The army of the righteous.

In a house in a certain residential district of Lahore, Pakistan, a mobile phone vibrated at some point that evening.

"Turn on your TV," said the screen.

The man in the house needed nothing more. Before his hands found the remote control, he knew what was under way in Mumbai, close to a thousand miles away.

Kasab, Ismail, Javed, Shoaib, Nazir, Arshad, Umar, Akasha, Rahman, and Fahadullah must have reached land and managed their initial challenges, and now they were carrying out their lives' most important task. Their final mission.

Allah was great, he was all-powerful, and he was with those ten young men that evening.

David Headley felt he had waited an incredibly long time for this day. Like a photographer who has come home after a long trip, standing in a darkroom and waiting to see his best pictures from the adventure emerge from the developing solution. Excited and hoping that everything will come out as anticipated.

In his dreams, he had envisioned the young men firing wildly; he had heard the screams and tasted satisfaction and pride. Now, those same images would be foisted on the rest of the world.

He had also dreamed of boats capsizing en route, of giving himself away and revealing his mission before it even started. The difference between success and disaster was a matter of inches.

If Mumbai was a success, if everything went according to plan, it would be to his profit. No, he didn't have a weapon in his hands like the ten men at Mumbai's premier hotels. It wasn't him doing the killing. But he had created their actions. He had selected their targets, he had worn his soles thin on the streets of Mumbai making his plans. He had located the beach from which they began their onslaught. He had spent over a year in Mumbai to make this possible.

Kneeling, he had prayed for the last few months, the last few weeks, the last few days, that his efforts would bear fruit. He had prayed that mercy would take leave that day. He had prayed for blood, death, and destruction in India.

Now it had happened, and there was no way back. Not for him.

It was quiet in the big house in Lahore, but not for much longer.

Headley turned on CNN.

3

THE ARMY OF THE RIGHTEOUS

Pakistan
February 2002

The jet of water struck Headley's right hand.

He rinsed his hand, wrist, arm, and elbow three times before repeating the ritual with his left hand. Then he washed his mouth, face, head, ears, and feet.

He knelt facing Mecca. And bent forward, until his forehead, nose, and hands all carefully touched the ground.

"*Allahu akbar.* God is the greatest," said Headley. "I acknowledge that there is no god but Allah."

The cold, dry air hung over the rugs while those around him knelt and took part in the morning prayer at the mosque. Farther off there was a small hospital, a market, farmers' fields, a Qur'an school, and a large main building, all heavily protected behind barbed wire and military guards. On the walls, slogans like INDIA IS AN IMPERIALIST POWER! were painted in large letters.

It was seven years before the attack in Mumbai. Headley was in his early forties, and this was his first stay in what Western intelligence agencies undoubtedly would describe as a training camp for terrorists.

Here, near the city Muridke, about fifteen miles from the big metropolis of Lahore, he felt an extraordinary sense of safety, despite how bitter the cold winter nights could be and despite the talk all around him being about anything but peace. His pulse was slow, his inner voice calm. The days were long, and even the food tasted better.

He had found what he was looking for.

The area with the Qur'an school and the hospital was controlled by Lashkar-e-Taiba, or simply Lashkar in everyday conversation. It was only a month since the group had been declared a terrorist organization by Pakistan's prime minister.

For Headley, Lashkar was a part of a greater Muslim fight for freedom.

It had been less than half a year since the United States was struck by the terrorist attack on September 11 and soon after took control of Kabul in Afghanistan, in an attempt to capture al-Qaeda leader Osama bin Laden and punish the Taliban for failing to extradite him.

"Either you are with us, or you are with the terrorists," as the American president Bush had said.

The war had incited radical Muslims from all over the world to travel to specific locations in Pakistan, Saudi Arabia, and Yemen to report for battle. They had no desire to be "with" the US.

Headley was far from the first American to come to the Lashkar headquarters, Markaz-e-Taiba, but his tall stature and relatively light skin made him an unusual sight among the many Pakistanis in the camp. People knew very well who the tall man was.

In three weeks he was to complete *suffa*, so-called basic training in Salàfism, a fundamentalist movement within Islam. Three weeks of studies, prayer, and lectures in the belief that the perfect version of Islam existed in Muhammad's day, some 1,400 years ago. All developments since that time had been in the wrong direction, explained the imams. All efforts to modernize Islam must be shut down.

In his childhood, Headley had read the Qur'an from beginning to end several times, but there were holes in his knowledge. Holes in his understanding, not in his faith.

He was ready to join Lashkar. The Qur'an was the only truth, and a truth that could not be altered, adjusted, or criticized. Either you were a Muslim, with everything that entails—amputation as the penalty for theft, decapitation of murderers, and stoning for adultery.

"I don't see how anyone can remain a Muslim and challenge it," as Headley said.

Or you were a coward, a heretic, worthless, a lost cause, a useless body, simply waiting to die. No middle ground, thought Headley. There was no room for that when all those American troops were right around the corner in Afghanistan.

It really wasn't all that complicated.

Half a year later, in August 2002, he completed another course—*aama*, they called it—a short ways outside the city of Muzaffarabad, where in addition to Qur'an study there was basic weapons training. Students fired rifles and handguns.

Headley performed well. He passed.

For a time, he could set his Qur'an back on the shelf but certainly not put it away entirely. Headley was driven out to the mountains near Muzaffarabad and taught how to survive in the winter. When March 2003 rolled around, Headley learned to fire the AK-47 and various handguns. He threw grenades and was taught how to attack—vehicles, for example. He passed that course, called *khassa*, as well.

Headley's stays in the various training camps typically lasted from a few weeks to three months. At one point, he was lodged in an apartment with seventeen or eighteen other aspiring terrorists to receive training in the surveillance of potential targets. Other times it was physical training, meant to ensure that the men had both the strength and the will necessary for a long-duration assault.

While Headley was in training camps, the election campaign for India's prime minster was attacked in the city of Srinagar. Not without pride, Headley noted that suicide bombers from these very same training camps that he was attending were behind the attack.

Perhaps that would be him some day? *Inshallah*—if God willed it.

Alongside his training, Headley maintained an everyday life in his father's house in Lahore. He took pains to make sure that he didn't mix the two together. But the everyday faded into indifference when he stayed in the mountains with his friends from Lashkar. They understood the world, thought Headley. If only he could be like them.

The men were fearless, and they neither hesitated nor doubted. At a seminar with the highest-ranking leaders of Lashkar in Abbottabad, one of the leaders spoke of an Indian man who had initially cooperated with Lashkar—a cause for celebration. Later, though, the man reported the group's activities to the Indian authorities. On a screen, the participants now watched a computer animation of the Indian man's murder, which was carried out by Lashkar soldiers. There was no mercy for traitors.

In the evening, they watched martyr videos and hailed those who were slain in the fight for Islam.

Lashkar had hung posters that showed the American Capitol building on fire, with the text: YESTERDAY WE SAW RUSSIA DISINTEGRATE, THEN INDIA, NEXT WE'LL SEE AMERICA AND ISRAEL BURNING.

Over their evening meal, they shared stories. One had a brother who had died honorably in the battle for Kashmir. Another, Abu Anas, had personally met Osama bin Laden in 1987 in Afghanistan. Others said they had heard bin Laden speak in a Lashkar camp in Pakistan in August 2001—right before the attack on the United States. One was the brother of Abu Aiman, who took part in the massacre at Chittisinghpura in India, in March 2000, right before then-president Bill Clinton visited the country.

And they spoke of martyrs who now bathed in a sea of happiness, peace, and virgins.

The men came from all around the world—from Serbia, from England, from cities large and small throughout Pakistan. This confirmed to Headley that they were on the one true path to righteousness.

He was pleased.

* * *

In the Lashkar camps, one would occasionally see a rather odd man walking with quick steps. A man with a large beard, a pistol of Russian manufacture on his hip, and often two bodyguards at his sides.

This was Sajid Mir. He was responsible for the military training of the Western Muslims who came to Lashkar to enlist for battle. He sized them up, sent them off to the relevant training courses, and then decided where the men would end up.

The only known photograph of Sajir Mir shows him with a well-groomed, short beard, combed-back hair, a tight white shirt, and a sharp red tie. But the five-foot-eight-inch-tall man was by no means an office drone.

Already at the age of eighteen, Sajid Mir had completed his military training in Lashkar. After running the local office in Lahore, Mir was charged with managing foreign operations. And now, in his late twenties, he had fought his way up the ranks to a position as one of the most powerful men in the group. This was a remarkable achievement, especially in light of the fact that he had never actually participated in a battle.

Sajid Mir used cover names like Ibrahim and Abraham, Layman, Khalid, Uncle Bill, and Abu Bara, and he occasionally gave last names like Majeed, Majiid, and Majid.

His favorite alias, though, was Wasi, after one of the Lashkar leaders' sons who had been killed in battle in Kashmir.

Sajid Mir apparently also had numerous passports—among them one with a Christian first name and the last name Masih. He used this one for trips to, among other places, Syria, Dubai, Qatar, and Canada in order to raise funds for the terrorism campaign.

For many years, Sajid Mir was something of a ghost for several Western intelligence agencies, who would have been all too happy to get their hands on him. But in Pakistan, he was safe and by all accounts protected by the military and the controversial Pakistani intelligence agency ISI, or Inter-Services Intelligence. One factor contributing to his safety in Pakistan was that Sajid Mir stood by the principle that under no circumstances was Lashkar to attack targets inside Pakistan, but only in India and other places outside the country's borders, where deemed necessary. Perhaps it also helped that Sajid Mir's wife belonged to the family of a high-ranking religious leader with connections to the Pakistani military.

Sajid Mir was excited about Headley, nearly twice his age, whom he met for the first time in one of Lashkar's so-called safe houses in Muzaffarabad. Not only was this man an American citizen, which was a divine gift in and of itself, but he had been born in the US and had Washington, DC, listed as his place of birth on his passport. As an American, he could travel to any country Lashkar needed to get into, and nobody would ever question his citizenship. Headley's passport was worth its weight in gold, Mir concluded excitedly.

The two became friends. Sometimes they'd share a meal in a secret house Mir had near a golf club by the airport in Lahore; at other times they spoke into the night about the global fight for Islamic justice. Sajid Mir had no doubt that it would take blood, tears, and more blood. Evil must be fought with evil.

Mir sent Headley to yet another training course, one that Lashkar had (not without irony) dubbed ATT: anti-terrorist training. He learned to free hostages, break into locations filled with heavily-armed soldiers, and handle explosives as well as common handguns—and to handle himself in a good, old-fashioned fistfight, if all else failed.

In the beginning, the mission was barely more than a loose accumulation of ideas.

New Delhi, Kolkata, Nagpur, Bangalore, Pune, Hyderabad, Gujarat, or maybe Mumbai? Nobody knew.

But among Lashkar's leaders, there was no doubt that an attack on a major Indian city would resonate throughout India, throughout the whole world, even, were it possible. The already irreconcilable relations between Pakistan and India would be further destabilized. And at the same time, revenge on the Indians would be exacted for the many murders of civilians in Kashmir province, which Lashkar's member constantly referred to as "Indian-occupied Kashmir." Hate knew no borders.

Headley had dreamed of being sent to fight in Kashmir, getting the chance to shoot some Indians. That was his personal goal. But he was too old for that, said Lashkar leader Zaki ur-Rehman Lakhvi, who instead asked Sajid Mir to make Headley part of the plans for a large-scale attack in India. Lashkar needed a man who could travel freely in and out of Mumbai over a long period of time with a camera and notebook, and who had a way with people.

Headley was perfect for the mission.

It's still not certain where, exactly, the idea for the attack on Mumbai came from. It is clear, however, that several officers from Pakistan's intelligence agency helped Lashkar with crucial parts of the plan. The question remains as to whether these officers represented a small, militant faction in the agency, acting on their own initiative— or if the planning was sanctioned by very high-ranking officials and therefore an indication of Pakistan moving toward declaring war on India. For Headley, it didn't make much difference. He was on board regardless.

In the spring of 2006, Headley was officially entrusted with the mission. He was to disguise himself as an American on vacation or a business trip in India, so he traveled to America to change his official, very Pakistani name—Daood Gilani—to David Coleman Headley. He got a new passport with his new name.

When he returned to Pakistan, Sajid Mir gave him some advice: "Prostrate yourself during prayers in a gentle way so you won't get a mark on your forehead from its coming in contact with the carpet."

From now on he would conceal his Muslim background and instead pass himself off as a Jewish or Christian American.

In the midst of the preparations for his trip to India, Headley happened to run into someone who would turn out to play a crucial role.

Headley was driven from Lahore to Landi Kotal, west of the large city Peshawar in northern Pakistan, to meet a contact who might be able to help smuggle weapons into India for the mission. Landi Kotal was situated less than three miles from the border with Afghanistan.

Headley was stopped by the local police. Not because he had done anything wrong, but because everything about him seemed rather suspicious: he looked like a Western European, he spoke fluent English, and his only piece of identification was an American passport. In 2006, that sort of person didn't simply travel about in Pakistan's federally administered Tribal Areas.

Headley was taken into custody and locked in a cell in the headquarters of the paramilitary border guard, Khyber Rifles, behind high walls, barbed wire, and armed guards. A major put the question to him: what the hell was he doing in Landi Kotal?

Headley told him everything: about the Lashkar training, the plans for an attack in India, and the hope to find an old acquaintance in the city who would be able to help with part of the mission.

These details didn't alarm the major.

Instead, he smiled: "I think you ought to meet my friend."

With that, he freed Headley and returned the keys to the car.

Somewhat surprised, Headley drove back to Lahore, taking with him the phone number of the major's friend.

Iqbal was the name of the man whom Headley met a few days later in Lahore. He too was a major, he explained, but in the intelligence agency, ISI, which historically has had close ties with militant groups.

He was not immediately recognizable as an intelligence agent. When Headley looked at him, he saw more than anything else a fat man in his thirties with a big head, a deep voice, thick hair, and a mustache. And always dressed in civilian clothes, he later observed.

Headley gave Iqbal the same story he had told in the jail in Landi Kotal.

Iqbal listened, interested, and offered to help Headley with the mission. He had a wish of his own, though: Headley was to attempt to infiltrate the circles of well-known or powerful people in India—actors, politicians, or businesspeople—and gather information about them. You never knew how that sort of information might turn out to be useful.

In contrast to Lashkar's, the Pakistani intelligence agency's interest in India was not grounded solely on religious hatred. Iqbal himself wasn't all that religious. The desire to go to war with India was more about the balance of power between the two countries, which were at loggerheads ever since Pakistan became independent in 1947. It was in Pakistan's interest to hold India down, said Iqbal.

In the next phase, Iqbal got Headley into an advanced training program, apparently run by ISI. Headley often went in for several hours of training at a time—up to half a day, sometimes—in a white, two-story house in a residential district of Lahore. For the most part, Iqbal himself was the instructor. At other times, it was one of his subordinates.

Headley learned to build a cover story, layer by layer. About the small articles of clothing that could increase the chances people would find a cover story believable. A special hat. A chain. A particular tie. Or maybe no tie at all. He learned to fill his stories built of lies with just enough truth to make them meaningful and believable. He learned to surveil targets, to get information about a particular building in a given part of a city. To take safe paths and change clothes while en route, so guards and others wouldn't realize that he had passed by the same spot three or four times in a day. He learned to hide secret messages in an email address by saving the message as a draft, then giving the email address and password to a coconspirator.

And Headley learned to manipulate other people.

"Look for what motivates people and take advantage of it. You can get them to do anything," said Iqbal.

And most importantly: "Never trust anybody."

Iqbal also donated $25,000 toward reconnaissance and other expenses in Mumbai. Headley would make good use of the money.

He visited the house in Lahore at least fifty times in the following period. But he apparently never learned Iqbal's first name, age, or home address. He never saw Iqbal in uniform, and at no time did Iqbal ever actually prove himself to be an ISI major.

It was part of the strategy.

"Need-to-know," Iqbal often told Headley. Give the most central, important details to those who have a need for them. Say nothing to everyone else. Or lie.

When Headley was ready to travel to India, he received a ten-digit phone number from Iqbal. The first three digits were 6-4-6, an American area code for Manhattan. But the number was forwarded to Iqbal's mobile phone in Pakistan.

"Call this number if you really need to contact me," said Iqbal.

Mumbai was humid, flashy, loud, and full of both poor beggars and shrewd businesspeople.

It was a strange city, Headley thought.

This was his first trip to the city, and he landed at the airport as planned, without any hitches, one Thursday in September 2006.

He rented a room on the fifth floor of a property on Bhulabhai Road, a good half hour from the city center by car. The landlord was an older woman, Mrs. Kirplani, and it was nice. He would have all the peace he was looking for.

At home in Pakistan, Headley dressed himself in loose-fitting religious and traditional clothes, abstained from alcohol, and spoke Punjabi or Urdu. In Mumbai, he wore a tailored Armani suit and bought champagne. He was an American now. With an American passport and a home address somewhere in America. He spoke clear, fluent English, more with a British accent than a Pakistani one.

When he sat at a hotel bar at two in the morning, he appeared, with his tall, fair-skinned body, to be neither a Pakistani Muslim nor a teetotaler.

Headley bought a new mobile phone with a new SIM card and began creating his cover story: he was in Mumbai as an immigration consultant, he said. With a false signature under the name of Raymond Joseph Sanders and the $25,000 from Iqbal, he started a business called First World, which was ostensibly to help Indians who had the desire and the skills to work in the United States obtain visas. He opened an office in suites 29 and 31 on the first floor of the AC Market office complex in Mumbai's business district, employed a local Indian as a secretary, and printed advertisements in local papers.

The business gave him a legal reason to stay in Mumbai for long periods of time. Even if he never submitted a single visa application.

At the Five Fitness health club on a random evening, Headley met Vilas Varak, whom he hired to be his personal trainer. Vilas was a so-called *shiv sainik*—a member of the Shiv Sena political party, a right-wing Hindu nationalist movement and thereby one of Lashkar's main enemies.

Headley invited Vilas to breakfasts and dinners. He even held a birthday party for Vilas's thirtieth birthday, and the two became good friends. And through Vilas Headley had access to Shiv Sena's huge headquarters in Mumbai, Shivsena Bhavan. The building was added to Headley's list of possible targets.

It was also through Vilas that Headley met Rahul Bhatt, a young man with a very famous father, the Bollywood producer Mahesh Bhatt, but also with incredibly low self-esteem. Rahul had been chubby as a teenager, but now he'd pumped his body up in the extreme, and at that time his well-toned muscle mass was featured in a commercial for none other than Five Fitness.

Headley gave Rahul both his mobile numbers, and the two exchanged text messages and calls daily or went to the movies to see films like *Vantage Point,* about the carefully-planned murder of an American president. Other times, they simply sat at the Indigo Café in central Mumbai, eating Philly cheesesteaks with apple pie for dessert. Or at one of the local restaurants, where they ate kebabs and drank cans of Diet Coke.

Rahul got his first knife at the age of ten. Ever since, he had been fascinated by weapons, self-defense, spy stories, terrorism, and explosions. He was hoping to get to play the role of a suicide bomber in one of his father's films.

Rahul showed Headley his knife collection, and they discussed the pros and cons of the American M-16 rifle and the Russian AK-47. Or the Glock pistol and the Steyr AUG automatic rifle, both from Austria, compared to weapons from the German manufacturer Heckler & Koch.

To make himself more interesting—and not least to hide the fact that he received his military training from training camps in Pakistan—Headley said that he had been an elite soldier in the American army. He was a former Ranger and that was why he used the email address ranger1david@hotmail.com when writing to Rahul.

He also told Rahul he had trained with Pakistan's elite Special Services Group, known as the Black Storks, after the color of their uniforms. But that was a long time ago, he explained.

At one point, he confided to Rahul that he was considering starting a business to provide important figures in India with bodyguards. He might have use for Rahul then. Rahul, of course, was happy at the prospect of putting his muscles to good use.

Headley also suggested a number of books Rahul might find interesting. For example, *Killing Zone: A Professional's Guide to Preparing and Preventing Ambushes,* a 264-page book that included analyses of more than forty ambushes and attacks on tourists and businesspeople.

Headley's many tales of wild travels, his military knowledge, and his long monologues about justice in the world led Rahul to call him jokingly "Agent Headley." On several occasions, Rahul considered the possibility of his new friend being a secret agent from some intelligence service or other. But he shot those thoughts down.

Headley didn't like the agent nickname. At times he considered maybe recruiting Rahul to fight for Lashkar. He could take Rahul to northern Pakistan for starters, he thought. In the end though, he decided to abandon the idea.

Under the pretense of being a tourist, Headley traveled instead to the capital, New Delhi, and checked out the military academy, National Defence College. He put the coordinates into his sleek, yellow Garmin GPS.

Later he visited a fashion show with a local clothing designer in Mumbai's five hundred-foot-tall World Trade Centre, and this building complex was added to the list too. He photographed the Gateway of India, the famous monument from the colonial period; Maharashtra state's large police headquarters in Mumbai; and a golf course in the Willington district. He bought backpacks for the ten men. He stayed three times at the Taj—and just for fun, stole one of the hotel's towels, which he later gave to Sajid Mir. Headley chose to keep a coffee cup from the Taj for himself, as a souvenir.

Altogether, Headley found more than twenty targets for terrorism in India, which he reported to Lashkar-e-Taiba. And he delivered roughly fifty hours' worth of video from Mumbai.

In Pakistan, Lashkar was beset by division.

One faction of battle-hungry men in the group wanted to join the Taliban's fight against the occupying forces and infidels in Afghanistan. Lashkar could help to step up the fights in the Pakistani border areas in the north and send people, weapons, and money to the Afghans. After all, that was where the real fighting was going on, said the men. That was where Muslims throughout history had defended themselves and fought back against superior forces. Most recently, against the communist Soviet Union.

If the Afghans lost to the capitalist Americans, it would be a catastrophe that would affect all Muslims. The men were deeply impressed and inspired by al-Qaeda, and they spent the evenings watching videos of fresh attacks in Afghanistan and rewatching old videos with lectures from Osama bin Laden.

Another faction wanted to continue the fight against India. That was Lashkar's real main enemy. Lashkar had already solidly established itself in the fight against India, and for a free, independent, Muslim Kashmir. In moving operations to Afghanistan, that fight would basically have to start over from the beginning. That was the objection. Lashkar would have to share in the honor and glory of operations in Afghanistan if they were successful in defeating the Americans. But in India, they more or less had the field to themselves.

Some left Lashkar around this time in order to serve directly with their Muslim brothers in Afghanistan. Since that was where the action was, and to them Lashkar was too much about big plans, big words, and far too little action.

Most of Headley's contacts in the terrorist group belonged to the faction that wanted to reduce India to dust. But if they hoped to retain the banner representing all of Lashkar, they needed to do something that made a resounding bang. Something spectacular that presented itself as an alternative to the fighting in Afghanistan.

The plan for an attack in India was upgraded.

On one of his many trips home to Pakistan to discuss possible targets, Headley noticed progress. There was no longer talk of just two or three men attacking the Taj Hotel in Mumbai, perhaps also killing the participants at a conference. Instead, the plan was now a larger operation to attack several locations simultaneously.

Headley put forth his suggestions, which were listened to.

The lower-ranking Lashkar members noticed that there was a surprising amount of respect for Headley, whom they came to know under the cover name Dawood Khan.

A few days after Christmas in 2007, Headley met Sajid Mir in one of Lashkar's many safe houses. This one was in Ayub Colony in the airport city of Rawalpindi, just outside Pakistan's capital, Islamabad.

In the Liaquat Bagh park not far away, Pakistani politician Benazir Bhutto held a rally during which a man stepped forward, shot two or three rounds toward her white Toyota, and then detonated himself. Twenty-four were killed by the explosion, and for several hours, the perhaps-soon-to-be-president's life was hanging by a thin thread.

In the safe house, Sajid Mir and the others prayed that Bhutto would die of her injuries. That would be best for Pakistan. So there was celebration when the news of her death reached them.

Headley's photographs and videos from Mumbai were studied carefully while the terrorist leaders viewed Google Earth maps in order to get an overview of the mission. They also built a model of the Taj Hotel out of Styrofoam. Though primitive, the model gave them a physical representation of the challenges they faced next in developing their plans. Thoughts slowly became reality.

Sajid Mir praised Headley for the steady results he provided but warned him against becoming too close with people like Rahul Bhatt and Vilas Varak. It was important that he keep his brain sharp with respect to the mission's true purpose.

"Don't make them friends in your heart. They are not the same kind of people as us. They are our enemies."

In the preliminary discussions, work of some detail was done on several plans to get the terrorists out of India after the attack. The young men could, for example, hijack an Indian train or bus and force it to head north, toward Kashmir. Or perhaps they could return to Pakistan by boat under the cover of darkness amid the chaos they had sown. Or hide in an apartment in Mumbai for several weeks to be smuggled out later.

They could also use the mission as an occasion to steal a large quantity of diamonds from the jewelry store Jazdar in Taj, which Headley had studied during one of his stays at the hotel. The jewels could finance future attacks.

Several clues point to the probability that some of the ten men actually believed until the end that they would return to Pakistan. Among other things, they did not—in defiance of a direct order—sink the boat that had taken them most of the way to Mumbai before they had switched to the inflatable dinghy that brought them ashore.

The summer before the attack in Mumbai, though, it was crystal-clear that the plan was for none of the men to survive. It was simply not possible to get them back out without increasing the chances that they would be arrested in the process and thereby risk revealing the people behind the attack. Lashkar was also afraid that their resolve would weaken and they wouldn't kill nearly as many people if they expected to make it out alive. So it was better to simply do away with that element entirely.

One of the Lashkar leaders traveled to Mecca in Saudi Arabia to pray that the mission would be successful. Meanwhile, the young men received some advice for the road: being shot would feel like being stabbed with a needle, blood spots would be like rose petals, and angels would descend from heaven to take their souls back to Paradise.

It was in this late phase of planning that the Jewish center, Nariman House, was added to the list of targets, despite the fact that Lashkar's leadership had reservations about adding Israel as a direct enemy.

But Headley was excited. The attack on Nariman House was his idea. He had eaten at the restaurant Trishna nearby while staking out the house, which was located on a small side street. He had even been inside the house.

* * *

In the heart of Pakistani capital of Islamabad, a garbage truck pulled up to the gate in front of the Hotel Marriott, an American hotel that was the city's most prestigious.

The guards were about to inspect the vehicle when more than thirteen hundred pounds of explosives were detonated. This was on September 20, 2008—two months before Mumbai.

The force of the explosion made a crater several yards deep in the ground in front of the hotel, and afterward, flames could be seen coming out of more than half the windows in the 258 hotel rooms in the enormous building. The rising smoke was visible from almost everywhere in the city. Alarms sounded endlessly, and car alarms wailed throughout the neighborhood.

Among the fifty-four dead was the fifty-three-year-old agent in the Danish intelligence service, PET, Karsten Krabbe, who had been sent to the city as a security advisor to the Danish embassy. Barely an hour earlier, the recently elected president Asif Ali Zardari, widower of Benazir Bhutto, had given his first speech as president in the parliament building near the hotel.

"Terrorism is a cancer in Pakistan. We are determined, God willing, we will rid the country of this cancer," he said after the attack, which he regarded as being so cold and reckless that it was "impossible" for Muslims to have perpetrated it.

But the attack led to intense soul-searching by Pakistan's most senior officials: if one of the few Western hotels with high security could be so easily attacked, with such a powerful bomb, what about the rest of the city? What about the rest of the country?

In India, too, the attack gave rise to serious reflections about the country's security.

Shortly after the attack, Headley took a drive around Mumbai with his friends Rahul and Vilas and talked about the explosion in Islamabad.

"You know guys, you're going to see things like that happening in this country soon," he said, encouraging the two to "be careful" and "keep an eye out for" any dangerous elements in Mumbai.

"How do you know this?" asked Rahul.

"On the Internet, you know."

The same month, Headley received a message from Sajid Mir: the attack was to take place on the twenty-seventh night of Ramadan. In 2008, that was September 29.

Around this time, Headley received a text message from Sajid Mir: "The die has been cast," came the message.

But when the team of ten young men—"the boys"—began their trip to Mumbai, their ship ran aground and sank. They survived only because of some life vests that happened to be on board. A few weeks later, they tried again with a new ship and new weapons, but when "the boys" tried to board an Indian ship, it led to a firefight, and the mission had to be aborted. All this was relayed to Headley later by Sajid Mir.

Headley was ready to give up hope. Perhaps it had all been a waste.

Perhaps these unsuccessful attempts were a sign from some higher power? Not to give up the project, but maybe that Lashkar wasn't the right place for Headley.

For the first time, he considered joining an entirely different terrorist group. He was always ready to take a risk if there was some indication that his efforts would lead to results.

But in the middle of November came a new message from Sajid Mir: a third attempt would soon take place. And then came the text message the evening of November 26. The attack was under way.

Headley spent next three days in front of his TV, following CNN and the Pakistani channel GEO. He also went online and read whatever he could about the attack.

He wanted to know everything.

4

IN THE CONTROL ROOM

Mumbai, India
Thursday, November 27, 2008

At the Taj Hotel in Mumbai, at 1:08 a.m., a satellite telephone rang.

"How many hostages?" came the query from the terrorists' control room in Pakistan.

"One Belgian. We killed him. One from Bangalore, who had to be controlled with great effort," replied one of the ten hostage takers.

"I hope there were no Muslims."

"None."

The battle had been going on for barely five hours, but already the ten men had killed more than a hundred people, injured at least twice as many, and achieved their ultimate goal. There was fear and chaos all over Mumbai.

Klaus Seiersen, a medical doctor from Aarhus University Hospital in Denmark, who was in the city for a conference on radiation treatments, was staying at the five-star American Hotel Marriott in northern Mumbai. After midnight, he heard several loud bangs through the window, and on Indian CNN there were reports that three armed terrorists had broken into the lobby of none other than the Marriott Hotel and were now searching for Western tourists to take hostage.

Many hotel guests panicked. Where could they hide?

After some time, Klaus Seiersen learned that the bangs had come from a long-planned fireworks show to celebrate the Indian national cricket team's victory over England. He called the front desk, which calmly told him that the entire CNN story was fiction. There were no terrorists at the hotel.

However, exaggerated reports of terrorist attacks in the media of both East and West were nothing in comparison to the authorities' incomplete grasp of what was going on. Nobody fully understood what was actually happening. And instead of mobilizing all their military and civilian resources, the government ended up doing essentially nothing at all. Shivraj Patil—India's interior minister, who was responsible for domestic security—first heard of the attacks after an hour and a half, when a relative happened to tell him to turn on the TV. Crucial top-level meetings in the Indian government were deferred hour after hour, because several ministers were out and couldn't be reached. The leader of Indian special forces, NSG, was at a private party in New Delhi.

When it was finally decided to dispatch the country's best soldiers from the capital to Mumbai, there were no planes available that could hold that many men and their equipment.

It was not until 2:10 a.m. that the two hundred heavily armed and armored men boarded a slow transport plane, an Ilyushin Il-76, that had landed in New Delhi. Barely an hour later, they began on the seven hundred-mile-long flight to Mumbai.

Seven more hours would pass before the soldiers were ready to go in.

From the outside, the building looked like a fishing business.

There were life vests, fishnets, and pieces of a boat on the ground. It was from here—a building in the Malir district, at the eastern end of Karachi in Pakistan—that the attack was conducted.

In this place, Sajid Mir sat with a group of his best men. Mir was the one moving the attackers around Mumbai as though they were chess pieces in a huge game. He sacrificed them when it accomplished some higher purpose. He was the voice who called himself Wasi.

He was in complete control.

Several TV stations were broadcasting direct from the location of hostage situations and burning buildings, and on the control room's small TV screens and laptops Sajid Mir and his men could follow the police's advances and evacuations, as well as military reinforcements. The delay in the arrival of the special forces was noted in the control room. This gave them all the more time to inflict damage, set buildings on fire, and kill hostages.

The men in that room were able to maintain contact with the young attackers by means of an advanced IP telephony system that could, among other things, route the calls from India through New Jersey and then to Pakistan. They hardly cared whether they left digital tracks, so long as the killings would continue without interference from the authorities. And if the IP system failed, the team in Mumbai was equipped with a number of satellite telephones. Even the cell phones of several of the hostages were used to connect with the control room during the operation.

Over the telephones, the young men in Mumbai were reminded again and again that they were on a holy mission, and that Allah would honor their courage with all kinds of beautiful women in Paradise. They received advice with regard to food, survival, and sleep.

"If you get tired, give each other massages," came the word from the control room.

After those first hours, it was time to take stock of the situation. The team had lost two of the original ten men in Mumbai: one had been killed, and one had been taken prisoner.

Two were in the Jewish center in Nariman House with two female hostages. Two had taken hostages in the Oberoi-Trident Hotel. And four were gathered at the enormous Taj Hotel, where they continued setting fire to the rooms.

All eight were still heavily armed. And it was now clear to all of them that they would be fighting to the death. No matter what they would claim in telephone interviews with TV stations in the hours to come, there would be no real talk of surrender. Never.

Jesper Bornak thought the attack would undoubtedly make the evening news in Denmark. Everyone would hear about it then. He called Gitte after midnight on Thursday, Indian time. For the first time, he realized that he was on the verge of losing control over the situation and himself.

"Hi, dear, don't worry, but there's been a terrorist attack here. There have been many deaths," said Jesper.

Gitte was at home in Hornbæk with their almost two-year-old daughter, an infant boy of two and a half months, and Jesper's mother. Neither Gitte nor Jesper's mother had heard about the attack in Mumbai.

"I'm almost to safety. We're trying to find a place where we can stay. I want to save some battery power, so I'll text you later. I love you," said Jesper.

A bald man in a white coat stopped Jesper on the street. He was a journalist from the *Asia Times* newspaper and had an office nearby with clean water, a sofa, and chocolate bars.

"You can wait there until you can make it out of the city," said the man.

In the little office, they watched IBN, the Indian CNN, where the attack was called a "Mumbai invasion" on the crawl at the bottom of the screen. Jesper saw it more as war.

But an entirely different war than the one he had taken part in as a UN soldier, thirteen years earlier.

"Tonight was more terrifying because I had no gun to defend myself. Soldiers firing on soldiers in a war is easier to understand than civilians firing at other civilians," said Jesper to the *Asia Times* journalist.

The journalist stayed awake all night in order to write his story for the paper.

"When I met Thomas, Rita, and Jesper near the Air India building facing the Arabian Sea, Marine Drive had turned into a Hollywood disaster movie set: ambulances, police vehicles, satellite TV vans, trucks of heavily armed soldiers rumbling into the zone, and reporters screaming into their cell phones. Thomas and Rita were desperately trying to contact three missing crew members, not yet sure whether one of them had escaped alive out of the Leopold Café," wrote the journalist in his article.

Jesper had but one wish: to return home. Now.

In Nariman House, one of the hostages, the fifty-year-old Mexican Norma Shvarzblat Rabinovich, had called the Israeli embassy in India to relay some demands on behalf of the hostage takers. Norma picked up another handset to speak with the anonymous men in Karachi.

"I was talking to the consulate just a few seconds ago, and they are making the phone call. They said to leave the line free. They are calling the prime minister and the army in India from the embassy in Delhi," she said.

Norma had been staying at the Jewish center in India for the past two months. She had a plane ticket to Israel for just a few days later, December 1, 2008, where she was to celebrate her son's eighteenth birthday.

From Pakistan, the terrorist leaders tried to calm her down. They promised her that she would most likely survive.

Sajid Mir was speaking. He spoke slowly:

"Don't worry, Norma. Just sit back and relax and don't worry, and just wait for them to contact. Okay?"

From the recordings of the call, it is clear that Norma was crying.

"And save your energy for good days. If they make contact right now, maybe you're gonna celebrate your Sabbath with your family," said Sajid Mir, who continued to identify himself as Wasi.

Next, he got one of the young terrorists on the line.

"The Indian authorities will call you on this number and ask what you want. Just say, release our guy to us with his weapons within half an hour."

The terrorist was also clearly instructed not to reveal that they had already killed four of the hostages in the Jewish center—among others, the twenty-eight-year-old Bentzion Kruman from Israel.

"You mustn't say you'll release the two hostages. You must say that you'll release all the hostages."

"Yes."

"And you tell them they can negotiate with us."

At Oberoi-Trident, some hostages were let go.

They ran out to freedom and were escorted away by the Indian authorities, who wanted to make sure that none of the released hostages were actually terrorists trying to leave the hotel disguised as victims.

But the majority of the people at the hotel continued to try to barricade their doors with chairs, desks, and suitcases and then hide in closets, under beds, or in bathrooms while clutching their cell phones.

Meanwhile, several explosions went off. The fourth floor was a sea of flames.

Fahadullah's phone rang. Sajid Mir, from the control room in Pakistan, attempted to spur on the two terrorists to fight to the last bullet: "The manner of your death will instill fear in the unbelievers. This is a battle between Islam and the unbelievers. Keep looking for a place to die. Keep moving," said Sajid Mir.

"*Inshallah*," replied Fahadullah.

"You're very close to heaven now. One way or another, we've all got to go there. You will be remembered for what you've done here. Fight till the end. Stretch it out as long as possible."

Jesper Bornak had been awake for more than an entire day.

He had made it to the Hyatt Hotel at the airport along with the Lufthansa crew, when a man in a suit and a yellow security vest came up to him. "Denmark" was written on the back.

"Hello, Jesper. You look like someone who could really use a beer," said the Danish consul, patting Jesper on the shoulder.

Jesper collapsed. He knew he was lucky to be alive, and the pictures still imprinted his retinas were difficult to process. Even for a former soldier.

For the first time, Jesper realized that his pants were soaked in blood. He had noticed they were wet after the attack at the Leopold Café, but at first thought it was coffee. Now he saw that his dark-blue jeans were covered with large, dark-red splotches.

One of the young women from the Lufthansa crew had blood in her hair, too, but none of the crew had been struck by bullets. All of them had survived the Leopold Café attack.

The consul took Jesper down to a market to have a photo taken for a temporary passport and to buy some clothes, but all he could get were some pants. He thanked the consul for his help, they exchanged numbers, and Jesper returned to the airport hotel. He called Gitte again.

"I'm safe," he said, crying.

The plan was for Jesper to fly to Europe with the Lufthansa crew, but it turned out to be complicated.

"You can't leave if your passport doesn't have a stamp showing you arrived," said the immigration officers at the airport. Jesper tried a story about being the boyfriend of the stewardess Desiree, but the officers didn't buy it.

"You'll have to return to your hotel and wait," came their reply. It apparently meant nothing to them that the hotel was on fire.

A close friend of one of the Lufthansa crew members was apparently dead, after having jumped out of a window during the attack. The immigration officers were of no help here, either:

"Where is your passport? Can you remember your passport number?" they asked the distraught woman, who had fled after the attack.

Jesper tried calling the Danish consul, but his cell phone's battery finally died. Then he tried using one of the immigration officers' phones, and when he succeeded reaching the consulate handed the handset to an officer. Jesper heard him say, "Yes, sir," about ten times to the consul. With that, Jesper was allowed through the security checkpoint.

On the flight to Europe, they all talked about what had happened that evening. What they had seen, what they had thought. A smoking section was created in the back of the plane, where they drank some alcohol and tried to sleep. It was no use. Nor when Jesper made it back home to Denmark was he able to distance himself from the events. The newspaper *Ekstra Bladet* had seen the story on *Asia Times Online* about the Dane who was caught up in the Mumbai terrorist attack, and now it announced on its front page: DANE FACE TO FACE WITH TERRORISTS: JESPER CHEATED DEATH.

Jesper was shaken and completely wiped out. But he didn't want his children to see him like that. He took a strong sleeping pill and shut himself in for the first few days.

Nobody called Nariman House, either from the Israeli embassy in New Delhi or from the government of Israel, in order to negotiate directly with the hostage takers. It was Thursday evening. Twenty-four hours had gone by, and the hostage takers, Akasha and Umar, spent the time shooting at random out the windows.

"All citizens are to stay indoors," came the warning from the Indian authorities.

Telephone recordings reveal that the terrorist leaders in Pakistan were uncertain as to their next steps in Nariman House.

"Do you want them to keep the hostages or kill them?" asked Sajid Mir of an unknown man in the background in the control room.

Sajid then turned back to the terrorists in India.

"Listen," he said. "Just shoot them now. Get rid of them. Because you could come under fire at any time, and you'll only end up leaving them behind."

"Inshallah . . . Everything's quiet here for now," said Akasha, hesitating. It was clear that he didn't care for the situation.

"Shoot them in the back of the head."

"Sure. Just as soon as we come under fire."

"No. Don't wait any longer. You never know when you might come under attack. Just make sure you don't get hit by a ricochet when you do it."

"*Inshallah.*"

"I'll stay on the line."

There was silence for fifteen seconds. Not a single gunshot to be heard.

"Do it. Do it. I'm listening. Do it!"

"What, shoot them?"

"Yes, do it. Sit them up and shoot them in the back of the head."

"The thing is, Umer is asleep. He hasn't been feeling too well."

A short pause.

"I'll call you back in half an hour. You can do it then."

A short time later, the two spoke again. Sajid Mir was angry and spoke harshly. He wanted the hostages killed immediately.

"Stand the women up in a doorway so that when the bullet goes through their heads it then goes outside, instead of ricocheting back into your room."

"Okay."

"Do one of them now, in the name of God. You've tied them up, right?"

"Yeah, I'll untie their feet."

"Just stand them up. If they're tied up, leave them tied up."

Akasha complained again. He didn't particularly want to kill the two women in the same room he and Umer were in.

"It'll only take two shots. Do it in the room where you are now."

"All right, yes," Akasha replied, reluctantly.

"Do it. Shoot them and shove them over to one side of the room."

From the recordings, it's apparent that Akasha moved something around. For seven minutes, it was almost completely silent. Sajid Mir called out several times for Akasha without a response. The call was then disconnected.

Ten minutes later, they were connected again.

"Have you done the job yet or not?"

"We were just waiting for you to call back, so we could do it while you're on the phone."

"Do it, in God's name," said Sajid impatiently.

"Just a sec . . . hold the line . . ."

"In God's name."

The roar of a machine gun could be heard from Nariman House. There were no screams.

"Hello?"

"That was one of them, right?"

"Both," said Akasha softly.

On the eighteenth floor of the Oberoi-Trident, late on Thursday, the special forces assault reached Fahadullah and Rahman. At this point, the two had killed at least thirty-five at the hotel. The sprinklers were going full blast.

"How are you, my brother, Fahadullah?" asked Sajid Mir by telephone from Karachi.

"Praise God. Brother Abdul Rahman has passed away."

"Really? Is he near you?"

"Yeah, he's near me."

"May God accept his martyrdom."

"The room is on fire, it's being shown on the TV. I'm sitting in the bathroom."

In the background, there was a large explosion. The connection was lost as the special forces approached. Sajid Mir called back a little bit later. Fahadullah was still in the bathroom.

"Don't let them arrest you. Don't let them knock you out with a stun grenade. That would be very damaging. Fire one of your magazines, then grab the other one and move out. The success of your mission depends on your getting shot. God awaits you in heaven."

"Yes, I know."

"God is waiting for you. Stay on the line and keep the phone in your pocket. We like to know what's going on."

Several shots and the sound of an alarm could be heard on the crackling connection.

"Fahadullah? Fahadullah?"

There was no reply.

The mission was nearing its end.

The leaders in Karachi had decided this. Several hundred civilians, according to the media, had already been killed; images of the burning buildings were broadcast for the third straight day on international TV, and the captured terrorist Kasab couldn't be rescued.

Now it was all about making sure that neither of the two remaining terrorists was captured alive. Both of them had to die.

"Okay, so the thing is, Brother Akasha . . . you've run out of water and you're tired. They know this too. They're hoping to arrest you once you're weak from hunger and thirst," came the message from Karachi to one of the two terrorists in Nariman House, shortly after midnight on Friday night. "It's Friday today, so it's a good day to finish it."

It wasn't long before his wish was fulfilled.

Indian special forces stormed Nariman House while TV stations broadcast live images of the helicopter that flew over the building, dropped five soldiers, and disappeared, all in under ninety seconds. It was 7:15 a.m. on Friday when Akasha spoke with Sajid Mir once again.

"Yes, I think there's a helicopter on the roof. Shoot, shoot! They've opened fire. They've opened fire. Umer, take cover! Take cover! They're firing into our room, into our room!" said the voice on the line.

Later, the men spoke with each other, most likely for the last time.

"I've been shot. I've been shot. Pray for me."

"Oh God. Where have you been hit?"

"My arm. And one in my leg."

"May God protect you. Did you hit any of them?"

"Yeah, we shot a commando. Pray that God will accept my martyrdom."

"Praise God, praise God. God will protect you."

The attack in Mumbai was one of the bloodiest terrorist attacks in recent history, surpassed only by the attacks in New York and Washington, DC, on September 11, 2001, and the attack in Madrid in 2004.

The 166 dead in Mumbai were primarily Indians, but there were also victims from the United States, Germany, Australia, Canada, Israel, France, Italy, the Netherlands, Cyprus, Japan, Jordan, Malaysia, Mauritania, Mexico, Singapore, and Thailand.

Throughout the world, memorial services and ceremonies were held, and state and government leaders took part in funerals in many countries. In Israel, the couple Gavriel and Rivka Holtzberg from the Jewish center in Mumbai were remembered in Jerusalem, where President Shimon Peres, Defense Minister Ehud Barak, and Likud leader Benjamin Netanyahu were among the more than 15,000 who turned out.

"I vow that we will avenge the deaths of Gabi and Rivki. But not with AK-47s, not with grenades and tanks. We will take revenge in a different way. We will add light. We will add good deeds," said Rabbi Moshe Kotlarsky.

During the funeral, the couple's two-year-old son could be heard again and again, screaming, "*Ima! Ima! Ima!*"—Hebrew for "mother."

In many ways, the Mumbai attack was unusual: no specific person was targeted. No single building had to be set aflame, and the five targets—two luxury hotels, a café known for its Western guests, the city's central railway station, and the Jewish center—had but one thing in common: they were all places where it would be easy to kill a lot of Western tourists, Indian locals, and people in general.

The goal was not a military one but a strategic one: to humiliate India, to make it fearful.

At some point during the attack, twenty-five-year-old Akasha received a call at the Jewish center. From the control room in Pakistan, Lashkar leaders urged the young man to contact the Indian authorities or a TV station by phone.

"Give the government an ultimatum. Tell them that this is just the trailer. Just wait till you see the rest of the movie. It's a small example. A preview," came the message from Karachi.

"And the rest of the movie is coming. Should I write that?"

"Tell them this is a small dose. Let them sit and watch what we do next."

5

BURN DENMARK DOWN

Lahore, Pakistan
Early December 2008

Sajid Mir appeared tired.

There had been some rough days, and he had barely slept at all in the sixty hours of the attack in Mumbai.

He embraced Headley. It was really a success. The two men had done it together.

It was difficult to grasp, despite the evidence being everywhere. If Sajid or Headley were to open a newspaper, turn on the radio or TV, or go online, or if they were to go out on the street in Lahore and strike up a conversation with the first man they saw, they'd hear that it was true. Everyone was talking about the attack in Mumbai. How much India deserved it—or didn't deserve it. How masterfully it had been executed. How arbitrary the killings had been.

Government leaders and intelligence services in the Western world had suddenly met a new enemy in the last few days, and Lashkar had proven that attacks of such a magnitude were absolutely possible. In just a few hours, Lashkar-e-Taiba had gone from being an almost unheard-of regional terrorist group to having the entire world's attention and being the object of its fear.

In the West, the attack was described as barbaric. Outgoing president George W. Bush called the Mumbai killings "an assault on human dignity." This served only to prove to the men that what they had done was right.

Sajid Mir sat himself down on a chair in Headley's house in Lahore and spoke of the days and nights in Karachi when he had coordinated the operation from the control room filled with cell phones, TV screens, and laptops. He told about the powerful bombs the ten young men had hidden in random taxis. This had caused the Indian special forces to believe that the attack was much more widespread than it actually turned out to be, and their response was therefore further weakened and chaotic.

He recounted how two of the terrorists had fooled the authorities into thinking that they numbered at least seven by rushing around one of the hotels and shooting out of various windows.

It had only been a week since the attack, and some details had yet to be revealed. The precise death toll, for example, was still uncertain, though official numbers were around 170. Sajid Mir was convinced that the numbers were at least twice that. Maybe 400, maybe 500.

Sajid Mir mistakenly believed that Ismail and not Kasab had survived and been captured. But regardless of who it was, that was the only error—that one of the men did not end up a martyr and could now reveal far too many details about Lashkar and the plans.

Both Headley and Sajid Mir were convinced that the Indians would torture the survivor until he had spilled his entire life story, from his birth to Mumbai, several times.

Pakistan continued to disavow them. No, the ten men couldn't possibly have come from Pakistan, said the official explanation, which denounced the Indians' statements of blame as "madness." And no, there hadn't been any control room in Karachi or in any other location in Pakistan.

None of the men behind the scenes was arrested.

That was fantastic, Headley and Sajid Mir agreed.

Headley's house in Lahore was hidden behind a high wall. Which, in many ways, was very convenient.

It had been his father's home originally, and Headley had slowly taken it over, with all its furnishings and the servant and handyman, who lived in a small extension and kept the house's nine or ten bedrooms and five bathrooms in working order.

This wasn't the first time Sajid Mir had been in the house.

Some months earlier, in October 2008, the men of Lashkar had begun to think about what would happen after Mumbai. Once hell had been visited on India, it would be taken to a new country, a new target.

At that time, a small, tight-knit circle met in safety behind the walls: Headley, Sajid Mir, and Iqbal. Together, they would comprise the new team. The nearly invisible planner, the terrorist leader of Lashkar, and the man from the Pakistani intelligence agency.

Lashkar had a number of big plans, but slowly an agreement was reached on a target in Europe. For Lashkar, involving itself in global jihad in this way was not without risk. But with Mumbai, they had opened a door, and there was no reason to close it again.

London, Madrid, and several other large European cities had experienced the bombs and blood of Islamic terrorism in the past year, but one country had miraculously managed to escape, and that was both incomprehensible and unforgivable. None of the men could understand why the country hadn't been struck by a terrorist attack. Especially because it seemed like such a perfect target.

It was Sajid Mir who named it.

"Denmark," he said.

The men were in agreement.

The idea for the cartoons of the prophet Muhammad came about almost by accident. But it wasn't random.

In November 2004, the controversial Dutch director Theo van Gogh was shot while biking to work early one Tuesday morning. He had tried to go to the other side of the road, but the shooter—a young Islamist of Moroccan background—followed him.

"Have mercy, have mercy! Can't we talk about this?" Theo van Gogh had said before the man stabbed him several times with a knife and attempted to decapitate him. The young Moroccan left a manifesto attached to van Gogh's body, which contained threats against the West, Jews, and Ayaan Hirsi Ali, with whom van Gogh had made *Submission*, a film critical of Islam. The man then fled the scene. He was later arrested, tried, and convicted.

In Denmark, comedian Frank Hvam said in an interview in the newspaper *Information*, on September 7, 2005, that the murder of Theo van Gogh had inspired him to reflect on how he made fun of taboos on the TV comedy series *Clown*: "After the murder of Dutch director Theo van Gogh, it hit me one night that I honestly didn't dare to piss on the Qur'an on camera. That made me incredibly angry. I can't imagine what sort of scene that would be a part of, but the thought that I didn't dare to do it got me worked up a little," said Frank Hvam toward the end of the one-hour interview.

He added that he certainly would dare to "piss" on the Bible, but "there's not really any challenge in that, since the fundamentalist Christians are already on the ropes. It's much more of a challenge to go for the fundamentalist Muslims, because some of the more extreme elements are so rabid and aggressive. There's a certain indignation in not being able to say what you want that gets to me. I kind of want to goad them a bit. It's the prankster in me coming out. You've got to respect other people's beliefs, but that's also why you have to really question the way they live."

On September 16, author Kåre Bluitgen told the Danish national news agency Ritzay that he couldn't get an illustrator to draw and sign a series of drawings of Muhammad for his children's book about the Qur'an and the life of the prophet Muhammad and instead had to use the work of an anonymous artist in order to publish the book. The refusals came on the grounds of the van Gogh murder and another incident that had occurred not long before that one: on October 5, 2004, a professor at the Carsten Niebuhr Institute in Copenhagen was attacked and beaten by three young Arab-looking men. The apparent crime of the internationally-known professor was having read aloud from the Qur'an to non-Muslims during a lecture at the institute. The attack received wide press coverage.

These events and the public debate about the tension between fear, freedom of expression, and the demands of religious groups that their beliefs be protected against attack led to an idea at an editorial meeting at the Danish newspaper *Jyllands-Posten* in September 2005.

"What'll happen if we write to all the members of Danske Bladtegnere* and ask them to create a drawing of Muhammad?" asked a journalist. The idea was rejected at first but later given a new lease on life.

In his years as a correspondent in Russia, culture editor Flemming Rose had seen with his own eyes what happened when freedom of expression was restricted or bent for various reasons, religious or otherwise. He sat down and wrote letters to forty Danish illustrators, inviting all of them to draw Muhammad in whatever way they saw him.

"We are writing to you after this past week's public debate about the depiction of the prophet Muhammad and freedom of expression in connection with a children's book by Kåre Bluitgen, for which several illustrators apparently declined to draw Muhammad, fearing the possible consequences. The morning paper *Jyllands-Posten* stands on the side of freedom of expression. We would therefore like to invite you to draw Muhammad as you see him. The result will be published in the newspaper this coming weekend," wrote Rose in the letter.

Rose addressed the envelopes himself and biked past a post box on the way home from work. It was also Rose who penned the words that accompanied the drawings in *Jyllands-Posten* when they were printed on page three in the weekend section, on Friday, September 30, 2005.

---

* An association of illustrators in Denmark.

Under the headline MUHAMMAD'S FACE, Rose spoke about both the incident with Bluitgen's drawings and Frank Hvam's worries. He also wrote that an art museum had removed a work, fearing Muslims' reaction to it, and named other examples of what Rose saw as self-censorship.

"The examples cited are reason for concern, regardless of whether or not the fear they experienced arose on false grounds," wrote Rose, who felt that the artists, authors, illustrators, translators, and actors and directors were giving a "wide berth" to the meeting of cultures between Islam and the West.

"Modern, secular society is rejected by some Muslims. They are demanding special status when they insist that their own religious feelings be taken into particular consideration. This is unreconcilable with secular democracy and freedom of expression, where one must be prepared to be the subject of mockery and scorn. It's certainly not always nice to see, and it doesn't mean that religious sentiments must be made fun of at any expense, but it is secondary in this context," wrote Flemming Rose in the text.

There were twelve very different drawings. *Jyllands-Posten* published every one they received. Even despite the fact that some of them made fun of the whole idea of the cartoons.

One of the drawings depicted a fictional young man by the name of Muhammed in seventh grade at a local school in Denmark. He was drawn with a soccer jersey from Frem Soccer Club with the word *Fremtiden*, the Danish word for "the future," written on it. In his right hand, he was holding a stick pointing at a board in the background, on which was written, "*Jyllands-Posten*'s editors are a bunch of reactionary provocateurs" in Persian.

Jyllands-Posten didn't have the text translated before the drawings were printed.

Another drawing showed Kåre Bluitgen with "PR-stunt" written on his forehead.

Even though it wasn't the cartoon printed on the front page of the paper that day, it was Kurt Westergaard's drawing of a full-bearded, bulging-eyed Muhammad with a bomb in his turban that received the most attention.

Westergaard has since explained that the drawing could be interpreted as the terrorists' unreasonable taking of Islam and the prophet Muhammad hostage, but the illustration was understood that way neither in Pakistan nor in the rest of the Muslim world.

The context, too, was likely a key factor. Thirteen days earlier, September 17, *Information* had replaced their front page with an illustration of Muhammad riding a white camel, reprinted from Kåre Bluitgen's book. Nobody had protested it. But now, several Muslim organizations in Denmark were demanding that *Jyllands-Posten* repudiate the illustrations and apologize.

Chief editor Carsten Juste said that he "wouldn't dream of" doing such a thing. Instead, the paper hired security guards, while the artists and Flemming Rose received death threats. Several of them decided to lay low for a while.

The illustrations and criticism took on a life of their own. A group of Danish imams traveled to the Middle East and attempted to convince Arab leaders to put more pressure on Denmark. This served only to fan the flames. Several of the imams later regretted the trip, but it was too late. The damage was already done.

Before long, the Danish embassies in Syria, Lebanon, and Iran were set on fire, and several people were killed during protests against *Jyllands-Posten*, Denmark, and other countries in which some newspapers had published one or more of the controversial illustrations.

Osama bin Laden demanded that the artists be extradited to face "prosecution and sentencing" by al-Qaeda. The Danish government rejected these demands.

In February 2008, plans to murder Kurt Westergaard were discovered, and the following day, seventeen Danish papers—among them *Politiken, Ekstra Bladet, Berlingske, BT, Information,* and *Jyllands-Posten*—published the controversial drawings again.

In a five-minute audio recording, released one month later, Osama bin Laden threatened all of Europe with "a response" after various European newspapers also reprinted the drawings in a sort of show of solidarity.

"This talk of mine is addressed to you and concerns the insulting drawings and your negligence in spite of the opportunity given you to take the necessary measures to prevent their being republished.

"To begin with, I tell you: hostility between human beings is very old, but the intelligent ones among nations in all eras have been keen to observe the etiquettes of dispute and the rules of fighting.

"This is best for them, as conflict is ever changing and war has its vicissitudes.

"However, you, in your conflict with us, have in practice abandoned many of the rules of fighting, even if you hold aloft their slogans in theory.

"How it saddens us that you target our villages with your bombing: those modest mud villages that have collapsed onto our women and children.

"You do that intentionally, and I am witness to that.

"Although our tragedy when you killed of our women and children was very great, it paled when you passed all bounds in your unbelief and freed yourselves of the etiquettes of dispute and fighting, and went so far as to publish these insulting drawings. This is the greater and more serious tragedy, and the reckoning for it will be more severe," said bin Laden.

The terrorist leader claimed that the world's 1.5 billion Muslims would never even imagine drawing Jesus in such a derogatory manner. All prophets were promised the same protection, and the manmade rules of freedom of expression were "null and void, aren't sacred, and don't matter to us," if they contradicted the rules God had given men, with instructions that they be followed to the letter.

"In closing, I tell you: if there is no check on the freedom of your words, then let your hearts be open to the freedom of our actions. And it is amazing that you talk about tolerance and peace at a time when your soldiers perpetrate murder against even the weak and oppressed in our countries. Then came your publication of these drawings, which happened in the context of a new Crusade in which the Pope of the Vatican has played a large, extensive role.

"And all of that is confirmation on your part of the continuation of the way as well as a testing of the Muslims in their religion: is the Messenger—peace and blessings of Allah be upon him—more beloved to them than themselves and their wealth? The answer is what you see, not what you hear, and may our mothers be bereaved of us if we fail to help the Messenger of Allah—peace and blessings of Allah be upon him. And peace be upon he who follows the guidance."

In Pakistan, thousands of protesters took to the streets.

"*Allahu akbar,*" they yelled, in protest of the Muhammad drawings. They burned Danish flags and made signs encouraging people to boycott Danish products like milk and butter.

Headley agreed completely. The drawings were a disgrace. In an email to a friend, Headley wrote that some things ought to remain inviolate until the end of time.

"Everything is not a joke," wrote Headley, and added that Islam wasn't some sort of American entertainment program.

"Making fun of Islam is making fun of Rasoolallah, SAW* who delivered it to us. And call me old fashioned, but I feel disposed toward violence for the offending parties, be they Cartoonists from Denmark or Sherry Jones or Irshad Manji," wrote Headley.†

---

* A somewhat mistranscribed version of the Arabic phrase meaning "the messenger of Allah." SAW stands for *salla Allah alaihi wa sallam,* which means, "may Allah's peace and blessings be upon him."

† Sherry Jones wrote *The Jewel of Medina,* which is about Aisha, one of Muhammad's wives. Irshad Manji, who wrote *The Trouble with Islam,* is openly lesbian and was called "Osama bin Laden's worst nightmare" by the *New York Times.*

Headley made fun of his friend for even taking the Danish artists seriously.

"Would you invite these folks for tea and have a little discussion while you are roasting marshmallows?"

The great Muslim men of times gone by would have reacted differently, said Headley.

"They never started debates with folks who slandered our Prophet. They took violent action," wrote Headley.

That was what you ought to do, Headley suggested. And even if God might not want to give Headley the chance to "give us the opportunity to bring our intentions to fruition," come Judgment Day, he would be rewarded for at least having had the thought and the will, wrote Headley.

In the beginning of November 2008, a few weeks before the Mumbai attack, Headley traveled to Karachi and checked into the local Marriott Hotel. The city was full of young protesters yelling "Death to the Muhammad illustrators."

At a McDonald's in Karachi, he met with Sajid Mir.

Mir gave Headley a USB drive filled with information about Denmark, gathered from various sites on the Internet. There was basic data about the country—like the Danish GDP and a map of Copenhagen. There were news articles about the Muhammad drawings. And there were photographs of cartoonist Kurt Westergaard and the editor Flemming Rose, whom he treated as the men behind the grand plot against Muslims.

Rose was likely Jewish, explained Sajid Mir. That was just one more reason to attack him.

Sajid Mir gave Headley the responsibility for the mission.

Take these three thousand euros, travel to Denmark, have a look around, use your eyes, find targets, find a way into the building, said Sajid.

Sajid Mir gave Headley the freedom to improvise—including if he saw another possible target besides the newspaper or had some other idea that would cause significant damage in Denmark.

They discussed the possibility of reusing his cover story from India: he would go to Denmark, and if there was a need for it, he could tell people that he was a lawyer or consultant and was working on plans to open a branch of an immigration business that helped Indians come to Denmark and get jobs.

It would scarcely be possible to send the terrorists to Denmark by boat as they had done in Mumbai, and likely it would also be very difficult to put a team of young Pakistani men trained to commit terrorist acts on a flight to Copenhagen without attracting a certain amount of attention.

But initially, the men weren't Headley's problem. Others could take care of that, Sajid Mir explained. Lashkar hadn't ever carried out a mission of this sort in a Western country like Denmark, but they could certainly solve that.

Headley suggested at one point that they could publish some humiliating drawings of Jesus to level the playing field. If you do that, we'll have to kill you, Mir explained, as he reminded Headley that "all Muslims also love and believe in Jesus."

Headley had another plan, too. His very own plan. He would personally pay a visit to Flemming Rose and Kurt Westergaard and shoot them. That would be more manageable than planning a comprehensive attack in a country like Denmark, where weapons were difficult to come by, and where the authorities would be expected to discover their plans more easily than in India.

At their third meeting concerning *Jyllands-Posten*—in Headley's Lahore house, shortly after the Mumbai attack—he suggested to Sajid Mir that such an operation could reasonably be carried out. Less dramatic, sure, but also more manageable and simple.

Sajid Mir may have been considerably younger than Headley, but when it came to terrorism planning, his experience was greater. And after the bang made by the operation in India, which was big and loud, he certainly wouldn't be satisfied with a puny double murder in Europe.

He wanted *Jyllands-Posten's* headquarters in Aarhus and the paper's office in Copenhagen bombed and the employees shot. He wanted to see death and destruction in Denmark, and it could only be a good thing if some civilians were killed in the process.

"All Danes are responsible," said Sajid Mir, who explained to Headley that he dreamed of "burning Denmark down."

Headley sent an email to his Indian friends, Rahul Bhatt and Vilas Varak.

"Hey guys, so sorry to see what has happened in Mumbai. We should go over there and kick their ass. I should be coming there in a couple of months. . . . Stay safe, Dave."

He sent the email from his "ranger1david" Hotmail account. That kept his cover story alive, should he later need to return to India and search for new targets.

In Pakistan, he tried to keep a low profile, but it was difficult. Headley had a burning desire to scream to the world that he was the brains behind the Mumbai attack. That was his work. As the days passed, with Headley still a free man, he simply couldn't stop talking about Mumbai. The urge was too great.

He told some friends that the actual death toll was more than double the two hundred or so stated in the press. At no time did he directly reveal that he had participated in the planning of the attack, but nonetheless he couldn't keep himself from showing off knowledge that only few had access to.

"Yes, they were only ten kids, guaranteed. I hear three of the kids were *hafiz** and two were married, each with a daughter under three years old," Headley told a group of old friends in Pakistan.

It was less than two weeks after the attack, and the personal details Headley knew about the men behind the Mumbai attack hadn't

---

* The Arabic term for a Muslim who has memorized the Qur'an.

appeared yet in the press. Nobody took notice of Headley's privileged knowledge, though.

In an email to a friend, Headley wrote that he "suspected" that the ten young men had been "brainwashed" after, among other things, having seen the violent video clips from 1992, when the Babri mosque in northern India was smashed by about 150,000 angry Indians, who attacked it with nothing but their fists. About 2,000 were killed in the subsequent battles between Muslims and Hindus in several large cities. Those were some violent videos.

The men had probably also seen the video clips of the right-wing Indian nationalist Babu Bajrangi, who bragged that he "has cut open pregnant Muslim girls and on at least one occasion sewn their stomachs shut with a puppy inside. So I think the motive might have been something like this," wrote Headley.

Again, he was unusually well-informed—he himself had seen these two video clips barely a year earlier at a meeting with the Lashkar leaders in Muzaffarabad. And it's very likely that some of the ten young men took part in the same meeting. It was also in Muzaffarabad, Headley had been told, that the many murders in the coming attack were the "price" for the nearly seven-ton Daisy Cutter bombs that had been dropped time and time again over Afghanistan and killed more than 70,000 people in Kashmir in the last twenty years.

But even among the Pakistanis who thought the attack in India was reasonable, there was a certain worry about the many civilian killings. Soldiers and foreigners might be legitimate targets in the fight for freedom for Kashmir province but hardly small children.

Headley explained to his friend that Mumbai, technically, was a "retaliatory attack." Regardless of whether or not war had been officially declared, it was raging all-out between the Muslim and Western worlds. And the attack in India could, therefore, easily be compared to the American atomic bombs dropped over Hiroshima and Nagasaki. Sure, it was brutal, he admitted. But it was necessary to stop the shedding of more Muslim blood.

"No matter how many civilians died in Mumbai, they are far less than Hiroshima. And if you condemn Hiroshima but can 'live' with it, then live with this too," was Headley's argument.

He was most angry, though, with the Indian special forces, who had previously also operated in Kashmir. He called them "Black pussy cat commandos" because of how they put an end to the attack in Mumbai, when they lowered themselves from a helicopter and shot the two men in Nariman House.

The special forces soldiers were also responsible for at least one hundred of the dead civilians, claimed Headley, as he praised the ten young men in Mumbai: "As you can see that more than 500 commandos had a hard time containing 10 kids. These pieces of shit have no stomach for a fight. All their valor is reserved for the girls in Kashmir."

When he really got himself worked up, his hatred for Indians was unstoppable. It also encompassed the so-called Gurkha soldiers from Nepal, who helped defeat the terrorists in Mumbai. Some years before, Headley had seen a BBC documentary about some Gurkhas in a military training camp in Kashmir, who had hesitated when they were asked to twist the neck of a chicken. They ended up having to draw lots.

Headley concluded: "There will always be a huge difference in the morale and esprit de corps between a man fighting for a paycheck and a man fighting to achieve everlasting life in the company of the Prophets and Martyrs in Paradise. Of course the biggest reward—more than the rivers of milk and honey and wine and more than the Eternal Virgins—is the Good Pleasure of the Almighty. May we all achieve this. *Ameen.*"

When Pakistan decided to detain some suspects for a few days, it was reported in the Indian media that several Pakistanis from Lashkar had revealed that they were behind the attack. Here, too, Headley was able to threat his friends to his insider analysis:

"Nobody has 'confessed' to anything. I suspect the Indians orchestrated the whole thing. But if they didn't and it was Pakistan, you can safely assume that this event was known to all agencies, all the way to the top," wrote Headley, presumably making a hidden reference to his friends in the intelligence service, ISI.

He rejected wholeheartedly the notion that any captured Lashkar men would talk—or 'sing,' as Headley called it—about the men behind the attack.

"There is no need to 'sing' as the song (both lyrics and composition) would already be known to the relevant agency. So my prediction is that Pakistan will never turn over anyone to India, and the US—looking at the 'larger picture'—will not put too much pressure either. This thing will slowly just go away, till of course Bharat mata is embarrassed again," wrote Headley.

The terrorism plans against Denmark were initially dubbed the "Mickey Mouse project."

Sajid Mir didn't really care for the name and the oblique reference to the cartoons, so he insisted on calling it the "northern project." Headley accepted this but continued to use "Mickey Mouse project" or simply "MMP" in his own notes and emails and when he, in complete confidence, discussed the project with other Lashkar leaders.

Nine days after the attack in Mumbai, Headley packed a bag in Pakistan to travel to the United States. From there, he planned to continue on to Denmark.

A few hours before his departure, he compiled a to-do list of sorts based on the notes from his conversations with Sajid Mir. He didn't dare travel with the list, either on paper or in electronic form, so instead he chose to write an email to himself without sending it, instead saving it as a draft with the title "Mickey Mouse":

Route Design (train, bus, air)
Cross (Cover Authenticator)

Trade? Immigration?
Ad? (Lost Luggage)(Business)(Entry?)
Kings Square (French Embassy)
YMCA
Car Trip + Train Option (Nufoozur Rehman)(weekend?)
Residence for clients
Complete Area Coverage (P.S. e.t.c.)
Counter surveillance (magic eye)
NDC option
Lunch + Coffee spots
Security (armed)?
Foreman residence
Zoom
Entry and exit method in the house
Feasible plan
On return, procurement of machinery
Uniform
Mixed Fruit Dish
Cell phone and camera
Border Crossing
City Guide Map
Alternate Investment
Got Papers? (Clients)
Make Visiting Cards

In and of themselves, most of these items are innocuous, but together in the list they provide rare insight into the first steps of a terrorist attack like the one that struck Mumbai.

Many were either written in code or with abbreviations that were meaningful only to Headley. The "Mixed Fruit Dish" might initially sound like the dried fruits the men from Mumbai carried in their bags. But in Headley's notes, the words were code for an attack with both handguns and explosives like hand grenades.

Headley's "Alternative Investments" was code for exploring Aarhus in Denmark as an alternative target instead of Copenhagen. "Foreman's residence" was code for Flemming Rose's private residence, which Headley wanted to try to find. "P.S." was short for "police station," and with "Zoom" Headley was reminding himself to look out for rooftops and other places in Copenhagen where the police's antiterrorism unit would be likely to place snipers during a terrorist attack.

"NDC option" was a notion to attack *Jyllands-Posten* in the same way Headley had previously discussed attacking the National Defence College in India. Namely, with a truck filled with explosives.

"YMCA" was code for Headley's search for a cheap place to stay the night, where a group of foreign men wouldn't draw attention.

Headley also weighed the possibility of having the would-be perpetrators carry Christian crosses. In the Siddhivinayak Temple in Mumbai, he had bought *kalava* string bracelets so the ten men would look like local Indians—and anything but Muslim men on their way to a suicide attack.

"Nufoozur" was apparently Arabic for "infiltration"; Headley added the surname "Rehman" just to muddy things up in the event the document was discovered.

As Headley prepared himself for the big trip, he thought about who he really was. And what he really represented. He took to the keyboard and wrote that "the Mujahideen will NEVER surrender," and instead, they would "lie in ambush" to kill "by the bushel."

He was good with words, and he got an absolute high as he wrote page after page of praise for the jihad movement and its holy right to smash all it saw as evil. A Middle Eastern proverb says that the fruits of patience are sweeter. Headley agreed.

"This is an enemy that won't go away, isn't impressed by superior forces or technology, always believes in Allah's promise of Final Victory and the righteousness of his Cause. The Angels do descend to assist them in battle and spread their wings under their feet when they walk. Those who oppose them are destined for Hell and will never even smell the fragrance of Paradise, let alone enter it," he wrote.

Was the battle between good and evil something that could be called terrorism? No, thought Headley. This was not terrorism, but a necessity on the way to achieving "holy justice," both in heaven and on earth.

"A world wide mechanism needs to be developed in which Justice can be given to all. It is not a privilege but a right of every human being. The way an individual is accustomed to it through the court system in the USA and Europe. If not, then this nightmare is not ending. Death and mayhem will hurt American and European Broilers more than the already destitute and disenfranchised Muslims," he wrote, echoing the threat that the Lashkar operative in the Pakistani control room had issued in the final hours of the Mumbai attack:

"The worst is yet to come. . . . This fight has just begun."

6

THE PRINCE

Cadet College Hasan Abdal, just outside Pakistan's capital, Islamabad
1974

The cadets gathered around him and listened to his many imprecations. He thundered on in Punjabi. The words just kept coming and coming. They sat in his chest and wanted out.

He could become very angry, and once he began to vent his frustrations, it was difficult for him to shut down again. It was far from the first time this had happened.

Everyone knew that if there was a fuss being made it was certain that Daood Gilani—as David Headley was called at that time—was nearby.

Many things caused Headley stand out as a fourteen-year-old. First, he was a full head taller than many of his friends. He was white. And he had those eyes. One blue, one dark brown. Some thought they looked freakish, others that they were cool. At any rate, all the cadets paid attention to him.

The flock surrounding Headley's rage was composed of sons of the country's elite: the best doctors, officers, high-ranking officials, and others with solid incomes and family trees they were all too happy to show off. A Pakistani air force chief, a defense minister, and several of the country's richest businesspeople were among the school's past students. Nothing less was expected of Headley's friends.

The school was founded as Pakistan's first military academy in 1954, and the strict, heavily-regimented routines in place at the school were designed to develop the cadets to their "full potential"—while wearing khaki military uniforms with black berets and polished shoes. They were to develop "punctuality, self-discipline, and true leadership," so that they, too, might bring honor to Pakistan one day.

There wasn't much group work or circle time to be had at Cadet College Hasan Abdal. Instead, there were clear, absolute rules. Sons were allowed visits from their parents only on Sundays, and only within a certain time period. The parents were at no time allowed to see the cadets' quarters. All mail was liable to be inspected at any time. Apart from the few annual holidays, free time away from the school was only granted in the case of full siblings' weddings.

The school had its own enormous mosque, which woke the students each morning with the call to the first prayer of the day. The day began with a Qur'an verse and then interpretation of the verse. It was expected that all students read the Qur'an regularly if they hadn't already memorized it. In history class, the cadets studied the Battle of Karbala, which took place in present-day Iraq in the year 680, and they analyzed step by step how Hussein ibn Ali—grandson of the prophet Muhammad—defended against 30,000 soldiers with just 100 of his own.

If anybody had doubts about the military character of the academy, they had only to take a walk around the large green space closed off to the public behind a redbrick wall and a large black iron grid. Not far from the mosque but still in the academy area, there was a tank on display with a long gun barrel, a gift from the Pakistani military, while a real F-86 Sabre fighter plane was also exhibited, rising toward the heavens, not far from a large anti-aircraft gun from the Pakistani navy.

War? It was everywhere. If a young man, or perhaps his parents on his behalf, dreamed of a career in the Pakistani military, Cadet College

Hasan Abdal was the obvious choice. Young women, naturally, were not admitted.

Among the cadets taking in Headley's outburst was Tahawwur Hussein Rana. He had never heard so many Punjabi curse words pour out of a white man's mouth. That was impressive, thought Rana.

Rana was born in the province of Punjab between the metropolises of Lahore and Multan, in the somewhat smaller city of Chichawatni, mostly known for being the home of Pakistan's largest cattle market. He was as Pakistani as the day was long, with short dark hair and a calm, disappearingly quiet, careful voice.

The two young men were about the same age and lived in the military academy's yellow wing—Liaqat Wing, it was called—but until that day, they hadn't had much to do with each other.

Headley calmed down again, exhaled, and the flock surrounding him dispersed. The reasons for Headley's anger that day aren't clear, but the result was that Rana began to speak to him.

From that point on, the two sat next to each other during prayers in the mosque. They chatted and laughed openly. They drank evening tea in the mess. They ran laps in the yard, practiced cricket together—in white V-neck T-shirts with short, white shorts. Headley was one of the best bowlers at the academy, though he was pretty wild when it came to basketball—a rather curious sport to be good at in Pakistan in the mid-seventies.

As so often happens, it was a pairing of opposites: Rana was ambitious, disciplined, and received the highest grades at the academy. It wasn't a walk in the park, either: he worked for it, which made him one of the strongest candidates among the applicants to the school in his year.

Headley, on the other hand, was a disappointment at school. He was uninterested, never opened his books of his own free will, and was one of the very last of the ninety-six to be admitted to his year; he took his place as the one with the lowest or almost-lowest grades throughout the years. Headley's time at Hasan Abdal taught him, above all else, how to smoke on the sly and how to perform forty push-ups at lightning speed—the typical punishment for breaking the school's rules.

One day, Headley woke all the cadets early in the morning and yelled that they were to gather in full dress in the yard. The groggy cadets ran about confused, pulling down clothes from the shelves, stepping into their boots, and finding their way out to the yard in their school uniforms.

In the morning sun, there were no officers or instructors waiting. The cadets looked around at each other in confusion.

For his part, Headley had crawled back under his comforter, where he lay smiling. Soon enough they'd discover that he was the one who tricked them, but that didn't mean anything. It was still funny.

Headley's father was something of a celebrity.

As an employee of Radio Pakistan, the national public service radio station, Syed Saleem Gilani took part in the search for musicians to give voice to Pakistan's clamorings for a real national identity after becoming independent from British India in 1947.

A young Muslim nation needed storytellers, thought Syed Saleem Gilani.

Saleem Gilani asked the songwriters to make their messages more obvious. Their songs couldn't just sound good; they needed first and foremost to tell a story and shape a nation.

He was a man of his times, always wearing a suit, and he quickly understood that Pakistan was about to open itself to the rest of the world. In the late 1950s, he was stationed in America, where he worked as a diplomat at the Pakistani embassy in Washington, DC, and for the radio station Voice of America.

Alice Serrill Headley was a strong-willed woman with black hair and snow-white skin. Her women friends often compared her to Rosalind Russell, an attractive American actress who was known for her record number of Golden Globe awards and for playing proud women who didn't take "no" as an answer to anything. That was Serrill.

Serrill was born on her father's farm in a Catholic family in the state of Maryland and grew up around Main Line, home to the nicer citizenry of neighboring Pennsylvania. As a fifteen-year-old, she had more or less left home to come out and see the world, and as a nineteen-year-old that adventurousness took her to Washington, DC, where she had a job as a secretary at the Pakistani embassy.

Serrill dreamed of seeing the world on the other side of the Atlantic, a place her coworker Saleem Gilani, ten years her senior, was no stranger to. A nice, charming man from a mystical land.

Naturally, the two got married.

And in June of 1960, Serrill gave birth to a son in a hospital in Washington, DC. He was named Daood Syed Gilani. The name he would change many years later to David Coleman Headley.

From birth, Headley was both Pakistani and American. Both Daood and David.

Saleem Gilani's tour at the embassy ended, and when Headley was just a few months old, the family traveled from the United States to England and soon thereafter to Lahore in the Punjab province of what was then West Pakistan, where Saleem himself had grown up.

In Lahore, Headley was joined in short order by a little sister, and the children received a traditional Muslim upbringing in a large house filled with domestic servants.

Serrill loved wild Pakistan. The many crooked streets and houses, quirky people in colorful clothes, and certainly not least the exotic spiced food, which had yet to make its way to America, a place that now seemed so far away.

But the adventure wasn't over yet. Serrill had a hard time with all the traditions and prohibitions in everyday Pakistan, and she felt that she could be doing more than taking care of the family. She wanted to be where things were happening. Not just sitting somewhere nearby, talking about children and food.

After some years, she and Saleem were divorced—an extremely untraditional choice in Pakistan in the mid-1960s. And Serrill was separated from her two children, whom she was allowed to visit only once a month, and always under the supervision of Saleem or other men in the family.

"In Pakistan, men own the children. There are no rights for women," as Serrill later explained.

Serrill Headley initially stayed in Pakistan to be close to her children, and she wrote home to family and friends in the US that she had married an "Afghan prince." Shahzada Muslehuddin was his name, and in reality, he was an insurance agent more than anything else. But for Serrill, that was yet another part of her adventure.

When her Afghan man was shot and killed—perhaps the victim of his first wife's jealousy—Serrill married the film director Akhtar J. Kardar, thirteen years her senior, who was known as "AJ." Things became stormy almost immediately, and already a few months later the marriage was over.

In tears, Serrill left her daughter, son, and Pakistan behind, and traveled back to America.

Headley grew up with his father in a relatively strict religious environment. His father made it abundantly clear that Allah had created the world as it was. And that it was not the job of men to doubt.

This conviction was supported by Headley's first school year in one of Pakistan's best boarding schools, Habib Public School in the large city of Karachi. Here, the students began studying the Qur'an in third grade, and by seventh grade at the latest they had finished reading the whole thing. Those who showed promise then started all over again, memorizing the most important parts.

When Headley was eleven years old, Pakistan attacked eleven air force bases in India in an attempt to stop a potential Indian invasion. The attack, which took place on the evening of December 3, 1971, was well coordinated, and the mission, in which a total of fifty fighter planes took part, was kept secret until the very last moment. Pakistan was proud of the surprise attack, and the media spoke excitedly of the nation's impending victory over the wretched Indians.

The pleasure was short-lived.

The then-prime minister of India, Indira Gandhi, replied in a direct speech to the nation with a declaration of war on Pakistan, and before midnight that night the first Indian planes were already in the process of bombing targets in Pakistan.

These events marked the beginning of the Indo-Pakistani War, considered one of the shortest wars in world history between two sovereign nations. At least 8,000 Pakistani soldiers lost their lives in the thirteen-day war, many thousands were badly wounded, and more than 90,000 were taken captive by the Indians, who easily crushed the Pakistani military's tanks, planes, and ships. With the signing of the peace treaty, Pakistan lost populous East Pakistan, which became Bangladesh. All at once, Pakistan's population was cut in half, and West Pakistan became the entire Pakistan. The country was devastated by the loss.

At one point during the intense conflict, two Indian missiles were fired toward Karachi. They struck Headley's school, where one person was killed by shrapnel and several others were wounded. One of the school's buildings was so badly damaged that it had to be torn down.

The attack on the school had been in error, said the Indians, but Pakistan's defeat and the explosion at the school made lifelong impressions on Headley. He wasn't even a teenager yet, but he no longer had any doubt who his enemy was.

He learned to spit on the street when he saw an Indian.

As Pakistan attempted to stand back up with Zulfikar Ali Bhutto as its new president, Saleem Gilani made sure that his son went to Hasan Abdal Cadet College. And while Headley and Rana were cadets on course toward a career in the Pakistani military, spending their hours in school studying the great battles of history, Pakistan made a serious entry into the nuclear arms race with India. Bhutto had made this promise many years earlier with the words: "If India builds the bomb, we will eat grass or leaves, even go hungry, but we will get one of our own. We have no other choice."

Bhutto won the March 1977 election but was accused of having cheated his way to victory. Under the code name Operation Fair Play, General Muhammad Zia-ul-Haq took over in a military coup d'état in the summer of the same year.

Times in Pakistan were not peaceful, and when Headley was home from boarding school with his family in Lahore, he fell out with his father's new wife repeatedly. Serrill had a suggestion: she would travel to Pakistan and bring Headley to America, his birth country but also a land he hadn't seen since he was a baby. He would be safe there, and he could always return to Pakistan when peace returned, Serrill explained.

Headley accepted.

In the summer of 1977, he landed in America.

Headley's mother had paid for his ticket, and she also offered to fly Rana with him, so Headley wouldn't be alone. There was a future in the United States for anyone who had the right skills or the right passport. Rana had the former, but Headley was lucky enough to have the latter. Serrill also offered to pay for Rana's high school.

Rana's family said no thank-you, and the two friends said good-bye to each other.

For more than one hundred years, there's been a bar at 56 South 2nd Street in Philadelphia. Even during Prohibition, it was filled with cheap bootleg alcohol, men, and women who sometimes went home with each other when the bar ran out of alcohol, or when the police shut the party down. In 1977, not much had changed.

The regulars showed up faithfully to the dimly lit hole sometime around breakfast and didn't leave until late at night, when they had forgotten their worries.

Behind the bar stood Headley's mother. And she was the bar's biggest attraction.

Serrill had bought the place a few years back and renamed it to the Khyber Pass Pub—after the mountain range that separates Pakistan and Afghanistan. The American burgers disappeared from the menu, and instead Serrill served light Afghan food and arranged Pakistani weddings in the bar. The regulars would stay and watch in awe as their meeting place became a decidedly alcohol-fueled version of entertainment in the Arabian Nights.

Everything was new to the young Pakistani. Here, there was free-flowing beer and TV screens with sports and other shows. In Pakistan he'd never been alone with a girl at any time, apart from his sister and sometimes the maids that worked for his family. Outside of his family, he had never seen women without veils. He'd never had a girlfriend.

Now, Headley lived above a noisy bar in the Christians' land, spending his evenings watching the TV series *Happy Days* and, as a server, pouring wine at Miss Headley's Wine Bar, which Serrill had opened on the second floor, above the first floor's more beer-centric establishment.

It's difficult to determine what thoughts went through the young man's head in those first weeks after his arrival in America, but it's a fact that after just a few weeks, he was having a glass, too, when his mom served her regulars. It also appears that it wasn't long before Headley experimented with drugs, and from there began the young Muslim's fall from grace with the women from Serrill's bar, whom he learned to entice with stories from Pakistan, a place that most people in Philadelphia at the time likely knew only by name but couldn't locate on a map.

The women in the bar called him "the Prince."

The following year, Rana visited Headley in Philadelphia briefly while on vacation and witnessed his new life. He returned to Pakistan shaken. Without having tried alcohol, drugs, or girls.

A few years later, Headley returned to Pakistan.

He'd gotten a fantastic idea for a trip, he told Rana, and asked his old friend to visit northwestern Pakistan with him.

The two had kept in touch by mail and the occasional phone call, but they hadn't seen each other in the intervening years. Rana had naturally done what one would expect of a cadet at a military academy, and he was now about to study to become a military doctor, while Headley in America tried in vain to find a middle road between his Pakistani and American DNA. No part of this went right for him. For a short time, he attended the Valley Forge Military Academy just outside Philadelphia, but he was soon expelled for using drugs. He also tried to get an accounting degree at a university in Philadelphia, but he never finished the program.

His father in Pakistan ought to have been severely disappointed: Headley had stopped praying, he drank, he took drugs, and he was with women even though he didn't marry any of them. He had lost all contact with Islam.

From the early 1980s, he more or less took over the Khyber Pass Bar from his mother, while he himself took more and more heroin and made questionable friends. And then he got the idea for the trip up north in his other home country. Together with Rana.

They were all too happy to see each other. Together with a mutual friend from their time at Hasan Abdal and one of Headley's other friends, they drove off, first on a multilane highway and then on small, winding mountain roads up north.

The men, all in their mid-twenties, enjoyed the freedom and the adventure. As they approached their destination in the tribal areas near the border with Afghanistan, Headley disappeared for a short time, but he returned without anybody really thinking much about the fact that he had been absent.

But this short detour was the entire purpose of the trip and had been since the beginning. Now Headley had a bag filled with heroin that he hid in the car. None of the many border guards in the unrest-filled area would search a car with a combat medic on board, Headley guessed. They'd be too busy and have too much respect.

At any rate, he was nervous when they later drove south and the car was stopped again at the border, where they had to show their identity documents. If Headley was wrong, the four men would instantly end up in a Pakistani prison, and they wouldn't be getting out quite as quickly. But Headley was not wrong, the car was never searched, and Rana never suspected that he had been exploited.

Several days later, Headley was arrested in Lahore for possession of heroin. For unknown reasons, he managed to escape a conviction.

One Tuesday in the summer of 1988, Headley stopped over in Frankfurt in West Germany. He was tired after the long flight from Pakistan and looked forward to coming back to America after a vacation. He would drive from the airport in Philadelphia and head down South 2nd Street in the historic part of town. He'd say hello to his mother and friends and maybe grab a bite to eat.

And then he'd empty the books and clothes from his suitcase, remove the false bottom, and pull out the nearly five pounds of pure heroin and hide it in the apartment. The bags would be worth a whopping five million dollars on the street.

He was twenty-seven years old and soon on his way to becoming a millionaire. He already had the suit and the lifestyle. Now he just needed to fill up his bank account.

But in customs in Frankfurt, Headley was asked to follow the officers to an area off to the side. His suitcase was slowly emptied, book after book, one piece of clothing after another. In the end, they found the heroin in the bottom of his luggage.

The narcotics authorities gave Headley a simple choice: a comprehensive police investigation that would most likely end with new discoveries of his criminal activities, and subsequently, imprisonment. Or, alternatively: Headley would turn in his friends and help the authorities to catch more.

That day, Headley could look back on a life in America that was a car wreck from the very beginning. In 1985, he married an American woman he had met in his mother's bar. But the marriage was a short-lived idyll, and the two were divorced two years later. New Year's Eve that same year, the bar closed. The local paper wrote in its obituary that the Khyber Pass Pub, with its 180 different beers, had revolutionized the city's nightlife. It had also been a place where unknown artists could come and perform, but that made little difference for its bottom line.

Officially, Serrill claimed that the failure was the result of a tax debt and her bad health. In reality, there was another very important element: Headley had run the bar into the ground.

After a full day in Frankfurt, Headley had admitted everything, turned over the names of most of his drug contacts, and was sent on a plane back to Philadelphia with agents from the Drug Enforcement Administration—the DEA.

Two days later, he showed up at an apartment on 4th Street near the intersection with New Street, where thirty-nine-year-old Darryl H. Scoggins and thirty-four-year-old Gary Roundtree were waiting for the goods from Pakistan. The apartment had been equipped in advance by the DEA with hidden microphones and video cameras.

"Is this all ours?" asked Scoggins in surprise when he saw all the heroin laid out on the table.

He gave Headley two thumbs up.

And then, all three were arrested as the police broke in through the doors.

Headley's unconditional cooperation with the authorities and an otherwise clean criminal record meant that he got away with four years in prison, while the two others got ten and eight years, respectively. At the conclusion of the trial, Judge James McGirr Kelly gave Headley a stern look and said that it was now up to him what he would do with the rest of his life.

"You are still a young man," said the judge.

While Headley was in prison, the Middle East was in a state that would give new direction to international jihad.

Under the cover of darkness, at 2:00 a.m. on August 2, 1990, Iraqi special forces and the broader army attacked the oil-rich but poorly protected neighboring country of Kuwait by land, by sea, and from the air. More than six hundred oil fields were set alight during the battles. Iraq's 5,700 tanks rolled steadily forward.

No country was more worried about the attack than Saudi Arabia. The Iraqi army was one of the world's largest, and while the Saudi royal family had spent their oil money partying at European night-clubs, Saudi Arabia was easily vulnerable to being overrun by the Iraqi military. The generals closest to Saddam Hussein had the will and daring.

The Americans immediately offered help. All the necessary planes, soldiers, and materiel—everything could be ready in just a few days if Saudi Arabia were to request it officially, said Washington, DC, while the rest of the Western world denounced Saddam's attacks and his con-quest of Kuwait's vast oil resources.

Behind the scenes, the relatively unknown Osama bin Laden—who up until that point had primarily been involved in the jihad in Afghanistan—urgently asked the Saudi royal family to tell the Americans no thank you.

"You don't need any other non-Muslim troops. We will be enough," was his contention.

Bin Laden told prince Sultan, the Saudi defense minister, that he could assemble 100,000 men and have them "battle-ready" without a problem in three months. But the prince shook his head at bin Laden. The tall, slender resistance leader's experience from Afghanistan was mainly of battles from cave to cave. A war against Iraq on open plains and sand, on the other hand, would require something completely different. And what if Saddam Hussein used his feared chemical and biological weapons against bin Laden's men?

"We'll fight him with faith," bin Laden replied. And he believed it.

Four days after the invasion of Kuwait, American defense minister Dick Cheney arrived in the large Saudi Arabian city of Jeddah with his entourage. The Iraqi army is twenty times as big as yours, and you'll be destroyed if you don't accept our assistance, said Cheney in his presentation. That offer wasn't good enough, though. Only when the Americans agreed to leave Saudi Arabia immediately after an Iraqi defeat in Kuwait—or if Saudi Arabia requested it—did King Fahd's attitude thaw, and he began to deliberate with his advisors in Arabic.

A short time later, King Fahd turned to Cheney.

"Come with all you can bring. Come as fast as you can."

Cheney called President George H. W. Bush, and soon forty-eight F-15 planes were on their way to the Middle East to protect Saudi Arabia. After that came an even larger force.

The defensive mission quickly became an offensive one against Iraq, with the participation of a number of countries under the UN flag and the famous name of Operation Desert Storm. In Iraq, the humiliated soldiers waved white flags in the air, and the Western forces sent them packing back to Baghdad.

After the war, most of the American forces remained in Saudi Arabia. The royal family didn't dare to protest. Officially, the mission was to protect the country's northern border against new attacks from its aggressive neighbor. But for many Muslims, the mere presence of American soldiers near Islam's holy places—the cities of Mecca and Medina—was a disgrace. And even if the Americans kept away from the large Saudi city centers, the damage was done. The West had arrived in the Middle East. They felt occupied.

Behind bars, Headley followed the war in Iraq on CNN, and he realized that two worlds were about to collide. The Americans were increasingly engaged in the Muslim world. And the Muslims increasingly distanced themselves from the West's worldview. Headley had to choose a side.

In prison, Headley met a number of semi-militant African-American Muslims, who were in for crimes considerably more serious than Headley's petty smuggling. They could hardly even believe he called himself a Muslim. He had stopped praying, he had taken drugs, he had wallowed in women, and neither in practice nor in theory did he behave like a good, orthodox Muslim. Not even close.

When Headley left prison, he felt a desire to start over. Of course, it also helped that everyone in Philadelphia knew that he had ratted on his friends. So Headley decided that New York might provide the clarity he was missing in his life.

In New York, Headley met again with Rana, who gave his friend the big sales pitch: he had to give up drugs, alcohol, and the random women and start living his life as a real Muslim. It was in his blood.

"I won't allow you to see my children or my family so long as you're like that," said Rana.

Headley's father, who meanwhile had become the general director of Radio Pakistan, also visited his son in New York and didn't mince words either. Headley told both of them that he would consider a new path.

For the next few years, he lived at a series of different addresses in Manhattan, and from the mid-1990s—with about $100,000 from his father and another $75,000 from selling heroin—he opened a chain of video stores that specialized in delivering videos with pizzas. Among them was Flik's Video to Go at 175 West 72nd Street, from which highly dubious copies of popular films were rented, and where the customers were pressured to buy expensive "platinum" memberships with advance payment plans.

Headley enjoyed his video store in Manhattan. He loved movies, the whole world surrounding film production, and all the explosions, car chases, and grand dramas.

But other temptations were too great in the noisy American metropolis. According to police records from February 6, 1997, Headley paid $3,000 in a hotel room in New York—perhaps just a down payment—for a suitcase containing a kilogram of heroin. And then the police put him in cuffs. The seller was an undercover DEA agent.

When one is arrested, rule number one in the offender's handbook is very simple: deny everything. No, you suddenly can't remember your contacts or your friends, you can't remember where you were a few minutes before it happened—and certainly not where you were going to go after.

No, that exact photo? You don't recognize it. And no, that telephone number doesn't ring any bells either. Only vaguely can you remember your own name.

Headley chose the exact opposite strategy. The one kilogram of heroin was but a drop in the ocean. He had actually participated in the distribution of about fifteen kilograms of heroin in the past few years, and he had no problem remembering where it came from. And where it ended up, he said.

The strategy was the same as when he was detained at the airport in Frankfurt, and he was excited to see that he could once again turn his defeat into a sort of victory. He became an important man with tons of connections that the agents from the American narcotics authorities would love to know more about.

In February 1998, Headley traveled to Pakistan, where he helped the Americans discover a series of Pakistani mid-level suppliers who planned to smuggle heroin into the USA. He made over one hundred phone calls, all of which the narcotics authorities listened to and recorded.

With "information, assistance, and testimony," Headley had "provided substantial assistance to the government in the investigation and prosecution of others," wrote the prosecutor in a letter to the court in September 1998. He explained that the agents who had worked with Headley had found him "reliable and forthcoming. The arrests and seizure of 2.5 kilograms of heroin would not have taken place without his assistance."

This was the beginning of a long-term job as an agent for the American narcotics authorities.

Headley got off with a sentence of fifteen months in prison, and then five years of so-called supervised probation, a sort of parole that required him to request permission to travel abroad and to provide urine samples from time to time that would be checked for traces of drugs. He also had to get used to a life with several unannounced visits from the government, whose agents had the right to search through his closets, drawers, and clothing without warning for illegal substances.

Monday, November 6, 1998, Headley walked through the door of Fort Dix prison in New Jersey to do his time.

The following summer, Headley was allowed to travel to Pakistan for a month, where he married Shazia, a Pakistani woman from Lahore. Shazia initially remained in Pakistan while Headley returned to the US to do the rest of his time. During that period, Headley continued to help the American authorities, which resulted in the seizure of another kilogram of heroin.

They had good reason to trust him.

"Send money for the jihad against India."

Headley read the words on the sign a few times.

It was winter in the year 2000, and Headley was out of prison once again. If he was to follow the rules of his parole, he would have requested permission to leave the US and travel to Pakistan. He didn't waste time on that. The authorities hadn't confiscated his passport, so he simply bought a ticket and left.

Now he sat in the al-Qadsia mosque in Lahore, one of the city's largest, with room for 15,000 praying men. He tried one more time to give his life some meaning.

He looked at the sign again. There was a phone number at the bottom, which he made a note of as he weighed his next move.

Headley hadn't ever actually been particularly religious. His life hadn't been filled with limitations, and the various demands of Islam to refrain from worldly pleasures didn't fit his lifestyle.

Yes, he had read the Qur'an, and yes, he'd had some periods where he read books about Muhammad's achievements. But only now did he seriously start to want more from it. He had recently turned forty, and to put it nicely, the first forty years of his life had been a mess.

He needed change. Needed to believe that there was a place in the world that was right for him. At the same time, he had a hard time seeing himself living without excitement and without opportunities to put to use everything his life had taught him. His pulse had been quick his entire life, and he wanted it to stay that way. But if there was a spot for him in the fast lane somewhere out there, he'd take it.

The prophet Muhammad had also experienced a lot in his life. All of it had made him stronger.

At home, Headley called the number on the sign and spoke for the first time with a Lashkar-e-Taiba representative. We'll come by, they said, and the same day, some people from the mosque came to visit his house and tell him about their organization, about their charitable work and the holy war against all that is unclean and unjust.

The men presented themselves as members of Jamaat-ud-Dawah, a religious movement that had started an armed branch in the 1990s, Markaz-ud-Dawa-wal-Irshad, which later came to be known as Lashkar-e-Taiba. When the religious fellowship ended and the militant part began is notoriously unclear—which is why the UN today considers Jamaat-ud-Dawah a terrorist organization.

Headley gave the men 50,000 Indian rupees the same day, about $800, and as thanks, they invited him to a private lecture that same evening at the home of a Pakistani businessman in the neighborhood, in the affluent district of Model Town.

Things suddenly got serious. If faith could move mountains, then cash could move whole mountain ranges.

The main speaker at the lecture was a man by the name of Hafiz Saeed, whom Headley quickly recognized by his henna-colored red beard. They called him "the Professor." The charismatic leader of Lashkar was a man with close connections to pretty much everything of any importance in Pakistan. An untouchable man.

At the meeting, which had about two hundred participants, Saeed quoted a holy text that explained that "one instant spent on jihad" pleased God more than millions of prayers. Action meant more than nice words.

Saeed had no problem speaking confidently about war. He especially wanted to throw India out of the Kashmir province and to "swallow" the rest of India. The Professor was also ready to plant "the flag of Islam" in the front yards of Washington, DC, Tel Aviv, and New Delhi.

"Democracy is among the menaces we inherited from an alien government. It is part of the system we are fighting against. Many of our brothers feel that they can establish an Islamic society by working within the system. They are mistaken. It is not possible to work within a democracy and establish an Islamic system. You just dirty your hands by dealing with it. If God gives us a chance, we will try to establish the pure concept of an Islamic Caliphate," he said.

Jihad, for Saaed, had two clear goals: independence for Kashmir province. And physical revenge on the Indians for the civilians they killed there. Jihad wasn't a choice; it was a must, the Professor explained.

At this juncture, Headley was still officially working as an informant for the American authorities. But he kept his experience in Model Town to himself.

After the event, he got a handshake and a brief conversation with Hafiz Saeed, and he could hardly wait to get home and look everything up in the holy texts.

Was it really true, what Saeed had said about jihad? Headley flipped through his books in the house in Lahore, and that same evening, he was convinced. It all made sense.

On his next trip to the United States, Headley landed with a feeling that he had found an unknown path, and a reason to follow it. And in the spring of 2001, he promised himself that if he could find a way out of his unsuccessful stints as a middleman in the drug business or a DEA informant and get back on his feet, he would devote his life to Islam. Unconditionally.

He reread the Qur'an, he began praying again, and when the sun stood high over Manhattan in May of the same year, he put out his last cigarette.

He had decided: his life belonged to jihad. He would enlist and go to the training camps. He wanted to make everything right again.

A few months later, the world became a little bit more complex.

While passenger planes traveling at about five hundred miles per hour went hurtling toward their targets on the East Coast of the United States on September 11, 2001, Headley's position between two worlds was starker than ever before.

United Airlines Flight 175 and American Airlines Flight 11 struck Tower 1 and Tower 2 of the World Trade Center in Manhattan, not far from Headley's own apartment in the city. The Pentagon was in flames in his birth town of Washington, DC. In Pennsylvania, where he had lived for much of the time he spent growing up with his mother, the wreckage of United Airlines Flight 93 lay in flames in a field near Shanksville.

If Headley had an America, it was the America that was attacked that Tuesday.

At the same time, he experienced both an inner and outer Muslim awakening. Words became truths. Suddenly, so much made sense.

Headley himself had a number of reactions to the attack and the killing of roughly 3,000 civilians on September 11, 2001. He was outraged, angry, and hungry for vengeance when he spoke with his American friends. Yes, he was Muslim, but more than anything else, he was an American citizen, and that was what was deepest in his heart, he explained.

It wasn't quite that simple.

Already the day after the attack—while the dry dust from the collapsed towers still hung in the air over Manhattan—Headley received a call from his DEA contact. Everyone was summoned into work, and the American authorities were searching for any sort of clues as to the men behind the attack, or details about additional possible attacks.

The clues those days were pointing to Afghanistan, Pakistan, and many other Middle Eastern countries. All contacts with those countries were checked out. And at this point, Headley's name and dossier came to light.

Even though he had already devoted himself to the global fight for jihad and had made his first contacts with Lashkar in Pakistan, Headley said nothing. Instead, he became angry over the fact that the authorities could somehow entertain the idea that he was involved in, or had the slightest knowledge of, the attack; or that he, in some way, sympathized with the men on board those four planes.

He felt the authorities suspected him of working against his own country. He would never do that, he explained. Why should he? He was born here, after all.

The FBI confronted him with statements that friends had heard about his potential engagement in the "fight for freedom" in Kashmir.

That was all just a cover, Headley explained. He had said those sorts of things in order to maintain his credibility while he infiltrated Muslim circles that were dealing in heroin.

In the period that followed, Headley supplied the authorities with information about religious extremists in Pakistan. He also worked undercover at a mosque in Queens, New York, on behalf of the authorities.

His very closest friends, though, saw a different Headley. He was excited by the attack and said that the US had simply gotten what it deserved. They had tasted their own medicine, and it wasn't the worst that could happen, either.

After the attacks of September 11, the American intelligence agencies had but one goal: it must never happen again. Never again could attacks of this sort be planned against the United States and executed, with so many thousands killed. No matter the price. From the White House, methods of torture that had previously been banned were approved for interrogations in gloomy prisons, and in Cuba the prison at Guantánamo was constructed shortly after the counterattack against the Taliban in Afghanistan.

Technically, Headley was still on parole in the United States, and until 2003 he was supposed to meet regularly with his supervising officer, Luis Caso. The prosecution had fought hard to secure that, based on Headley's intense clinch with heroin.

But then, something unexpected happened.

A few moments before a hastily called meeting on Friday, November 16, 2001, in the district court's offices in Brooklyn, Headley's lawyer, Howard Leader, received a crucial letter. Who its sender was remained a secret.

"Your honor, I would like to hand up a copy of a fairly brief letter that might be of some assistance to the Court in this matter," said Howard Leader.

"I don't know. . . . Have you given me a recommendation on this?" replied Carol B. Amon, the judge.

"No, your honor, pardon my appearance. I wasn't expecting a hearing today. I was informed at the last minute. I just received the documents this morning."

Michael Bays, the attorney for the prosecutor's office, interrupted for a helpful word: for two and a half years now, Headley had been on parole, and he had two and a half years left. But the prosecution was prepared to excuse Headley from the associated obligations.

It was never said aloud in the court, but the reasons behind this were clear enough: Headley needed the freedom to travel to Pakistan or other countries to help the American authorities gather information about militant Islamists, without having to request permission to travel each and every time. He looked unmistakably American but had intimate knowledge of Pakistani conditions and was fluent in Urdu, Arabic, Punjabi, Hindi, and English—in other words, the dream of any intelligence service and a country that was on its way to war against an unknown enemy.

"He's been an outstanding supervisee. No complaints," said Michael Beys—not knowing that Headley actually had traveled to and from Pakistan without the knowledge of the authorities, and had devoted his life to Lashkar-e-Taiba in the process.

Headley himself said nothing to the court.

"What is the letter that you have, Mr. Leader?" asked the judge of Headley's lawyer.

"Your honor, yes, I would like to hand up a copy of a letter that I was given about twenty minutes ago."

"From who?"

"It speaks for itself, your honor," said Leader, avoiding the question. He knew that every word spoken would be recorded and transcribed. And it was no ordinary letter.

It became quiet in the courtroom.

After having read the letter, the judge was instantly prepared to set Headley free. But she didn't know offhand which section of the law would allow her to release a person who still had several years left on his parole.

After bending the relevant paragraphs of the law a little, the attorneys came to the conclusion that Headley could "certainly" be set free, referring to a rule that concerned assisting the authorities, as he had.

The public has never had a chance to see the letter that decided Headley's case. Initially, the authorities revealed that it was kept in a locked safe deposit box in Brooklyn. Then that it had gone missing. And then that it was found again but still could not be made public.

But regardless of the contents and the sender, the letter had the desired effect: on December 18, 2001, Judge Amon signed off on the formal papers and gave Headley his freedom back, without restrictions.

It was also around this time that Headley entered into a controversial agreement with the authorities. He would travel to Pakistan and promised to pass along any useful information if he came into contact with terrorism, drug trafficking, or other suspicious activities. The agreement with the American authorities was set to last for one year, and according to Headley's interpretation, it would automatically expire in September 2002.

"I want to do something important in my life. I want to do something for my country," said Headley, who told his friends that the authorities had asked him to infiltrate Lashkar.

Headley's actions, however, don't support that interpretation.

Shortly after the court's decision, he was at JFK airport in New York with a plane ticket to Pakistan, by all accounts without any plans to ever help the Americans again. He burned all bridges and never worked for the United States again, at least never officially.

The terrorist attack on September 11, 2001 had, paradoxically, freed him of all his ties to the United States. And Headley took advantage of his freedom to devote himself to jihad.

A few months later, he visited his first training camp.

7

A Dream about the Prophet

The gray town house sat quiet and undisturbed.

On North Francisco Avenue, nobody cared too much to speak with their neighbors, so if you wanted privacy in the metropolis that is Chicago, this quiet street in the northern part of the city was a good place to be.

According to the lease and the buzzer downstairs, the two-thousand-square-foot apartment on the third floor in the three-story town house was occupied by Adeem Kunwar Aziz, an older Pakistani businessman who had lived in Chicago for several years. He kept to himself most of the time.

In fact, his neighbors hadn't seen him at all lately. But that was for a different reason entirely: Aziz had died of a heart attack and been buried, and his wife and children had been sent back to Pakistan.

Instead, Headley had secretly taken over the apartment, using it as his base when he was staying in America. He had taken his cell phone and even used the name Aziz when he needed an extra identity.

A few months before the Mumbai attack, he had moved his wife, Shazia, his two daughters, Haider and Sumya, and his two sons, Hafsa and Osama, to Chicago. Now the whole family lived in the town house with the little green lawn.

If the mission were to fail, if someone was caught, or if he was killed, his family would at least be safer in the United States than in Pakistan, Headley had concluded.

Shazia was Headley's confidante. She knew the double game he was playing and supported her husband.

"Congrats on your graduation . . . Graduation ceremony is really great. Watched the movie the whole day," she wrote in an email to him sent from Chicago while she watched the Mumbai attack on the television.

A few weeks after the attack, Headley traveled to Chicago to be with his family.

While in Pakistan, their sons had seen their father practice shooting targets behind the wall in their big backyard, and in Chicago he continued to inculcate military discipline in them. He hoped one day to see his sons become members of the Pakistani special forces, the Special Services Group. He told them this often.

In fact, the military training in the family was so intense that at soccer practice five-year-old Osama didn't kick the ball when the coach yelled, "Shoot!" from the sidelines. Instead, Osama flung himself down, took a rolling fall, and made as if he was holding a handgun. He'd seen his father do this when he heard the word "shoot" before.

Headley thought this was a fantastic story. He was proud of his children. And yes, he had indeed named his son after Osama bin Laden. Naturally.

That part of Chicago was a good fit for Headley. When he walked out the front door and took a right down the street, he came to West Devon Avenue, in the heart of the Pakistani and Indian neighborhood. A large group of Pakistanis had settled there, and Chicago had one of the largest Muslim populations of any American city. The location of the apartment was also perfect for other reasons. Often he walked the not quite quarter mile from his apartment to 2809 West Devon Avenue, where he could he could visit his childhood friend Rana at his business and give him a good hug.

Rana was actually the reason that Headley had chosen to settle in Chicago.

"Uncle!" Rana's children would exclaim excitedly whenever their father's close friend from Pakistan would come to visit him at home.

Their friendship was stronger than ever.

For the now full-bearded Rana, the journey to Chicago had been a long one.

While Headley was in an American prison for smuggling heroin, Rana had finished his training as a combat medic and was sent to Saudi Arabia to help the Americans with their military operation against Iraq during the attack on Kuwait.

He had distinguished himself during that operation and was later awarded a medal for his efforts, but Rana had been injured too and spent the end of the war recovering in a hospital in Germany.

Later, he was sent to the Siachen glacier along the border between Pakistan and India. Soldiers from both sides contested the border demarcation in almost inhuman conditions: it could easily get as cold as minus 60°F, and every winter, about thirty feet of snow fell. The glacier is around two to three miles high, and for that reason the border has been called the world's highest combat zone. Some soldiers lost their lives to the brutal conditions rather than to the battles themselves.

During his posting in the mountains Rana endured chronic altitude sickness. He tried to have himself reassigned, but the Pakistani military told him that wasn't possible.

During a trip outside the country, Rana decided that he wouldn't return. He deserted from the army, and like many other deserters, moved to Canada to begin a new life with his wife, Samraz. They settled in Ottawa, where they bought a house—which Rana had to mortgage soon after in order to post Headley's bail following his arrest for dealing in heroin in New York.

After a few years in Canada, Rana moved more or less permanently to the United States, though neither he nor Samraz actually received residence permits. In the summer of 1995, Rana bought a modest, tree-sheltered redbrick house at 6018 North Campbell Avenue—less than a mile from Headley's clandestine apartment.

On the roof, Rana installed what was without a doubt the largest satellite dish in the neighborhood, ensuring that he could watch the news from Pakistan every day. The Rana family did not watch American TV. They kept entirely to themselves. Though Rana always greeted his neighbors cordially, none of them was ever invited in.

The house had cost Rana $147,500, and to swing this amount he had borrowed a large sum from Headley. Or, rather: since it is against the Qur'an to charge interest, there was no talk of a loan in the ordinary sense. Instead, Headley "deposited" the large sum with Rana, which Rana—without interest or fees—would hold for him. When Headley needed money, a plane ticket, or something else, Rana covered it, and the amount was tallied on a statement that Headley would send Rana regularly.

It was also by means of Samraz's private credit card that the secret mobile phone—still in the deceased Adeem Azis's name—was paid for. The charge too was deducted from Headley's "deposit." In this manner, Headley avoided having an account at an American bank, and Rana acquired a large sum of money with which to start his new life in America.

Rana abandoned the medical profession and devoted himself to running an immigration business by the name of First World Immigration Services, which helped Pakistanis and others to receive temporary or permanent residence permits in the US and Canada. The company had offices in various countries around the world, among them one on the 53rd floor in the Empire State Building in New York and another in Toronto, Canada. But it was on West Devon Avenue in Chicago that he had his headquarters under the name Immigrant Law Center, with three coworkers and a lawyer who took care of papers. Rana himself worked in the headquarters sometimes.

Apart from the immigration business, which had clients from many Middle Eastern countries, Rana was involved in several smaller businesses: a convenience store in Chicago and some other, rather shady operations. In the city of Kinsman, a few hours' drive from Chicago, he ran an agricultural business where lambs and goats were slaughtered according to halal principles for Muslim customers.

Rana was creative—with finances, too. He cheated his way out of more than one hundred thousand dollars in taxes, according to the authorities.

He found several methods of falsifying documents so Pakistani friends or clients could more easily acquire American visas. For example, he wrote fictional employment contracts backdated to 1983. The contracts showed that their holders had worked faithfully as a cook for a number of years but had chosen to resign from the job to look for newer and better jobs.

"Cook" was always a big hit with the Americans, Rana knew. He was careful about the small details: laser printers hadn't been invented in 1983, so the fake contract would be typed up on a typewriter.

Rana was very good at keeping secrets.

There was a story Headley told Rana often.

One hundred men are standing on a dock when they see ten men far out in the ocean, flailing with their arms, about to drown. From the dock, three men jump in the water, and they're not able to rescue more than one each out of the ten men. The other seven drown in the waves.

The hundred men on the dock were there by chance. They hadn't asked to be put in that situation. Maybe they were running late for work. Maybe they weren't particularly good at swimming. Maybe they simply didn't want to get their clothes wet. But for whatever reason, those ninety-seven committed a sin by choosing not to jump in the water and help. They all bore a portion of the blame for the seven dead men.

Muslims all over the world were in this same situation, Headley explained.

In the province of Kashmir, in Afghanistan, in Palestine, and in many other places, Muslims were about to drown, and far too many other Muslims stood on the dock and watched. They let it happen.

Headley was convinced that an angel sat on his right shoulder counting his good deeds, while another angel sat on his left, noting all his errors and shortcomings. The one on the left was a tad too busy in his younger years, so now it was time for him to make the effort to restore the balance. He couldn't be one of the men on the dock any longer.

Headley cited the story to argue that Lashkar and other terrorist groups were justified in using bombs and suicide bombers. After all, it was in reality self-defense against a greater power. It was defensive jihad, not offensive jihad, he said.

And civilian deaths were permitted, too, Headley thought. Sure, the Qur'an says that one shouldn't kill civilians. But exceptions could be made, provided they were defensible.

"If the enemy is doing that, then in response, it would be allowed," he said.

Rana disagreed. He thought Headley was interpreting the Qur'an too loosely, in contrast to the more literal reading Headley would always invoke in other matters.

As a *deobandi*—a member of a certain branch of Sunni Islam—Rana was of the opinion that militant jihad was legitimate but that it must be declared by a state leader in the form of a fatwa. If that hadn't happened, nothing could be done.

Like all the other members of Lashkar, Headley was a Salafist and believed that Islam was perfect in the time of the prophet Muhammad. Nothing should be added, nothing removed.

He had previously succeeded in making Salafists of all of his in-laws, who were now followers of this orthodox version of Islam, and he naturally tried to do the same with Rana. Lashkar had given him advice on how to win Rana over. In the summer of 2006, Headley told him that he had begun training with Lashkar in the mountains in Pakistan.

He provided Rana with a succession of books about terrorism, among them an encyclopedia of the rules of Islamic jihad and a book entitled *The Judeo-Christian Mischief and the International Jihad Movement*, which featured the cover illustration of a cross and a star-of-David in flames. He also gave him *The Religion of Ibrahim*, a book contending that unbelievers should be punished.

Though Rana would listen as Headley sought to persuade him, often at length, that a stricter interpretation of Islam was the only correct one, he wasn't convinced. Nor did they agree on whether twenty or eight prayers were required for Eid al-Fitr, the holiday that marks the end of Ramadan.

But, despite these difference, Headley and Rana shared a world they tried to keep hidden from most others. In Rana's living room they watched movies with footage from terrorist attacks in Afghanistan while their families were busy with other activities. They discussed such things as the right revenge for the cartoons that depicted the Prophet Muhammad.

Headley felt that the men responsible should be hanged or killed in some other way. He would grow extremely angry when he talked about it.

Rana had never seen the drawings himself, but that didn't stop him from having strong views about them and the people who were responsible for their dissemination. The artist behind the drawing with the bomb was just one man, sure, but why didn't anybody stop the newspaper? Why hadn't a responsible editor and a responsible country done something to stop the illustrations from being published? And why was nobody held responsible afterwards?

It didn't make sense.

The men went to the mosque every Friday, they watched cricket together, and they often sat in Headley's secret apartment or in Rana's house late into the evening, discussing politics, Islam, and terrorism—which were often one and the same to them. Or the subject could be the rumor that the young senator Barack Obama was Muslim. Obama lived just half an hour away by car, farther south in Chicago, and had just won the presidential election. Neither Headley nor Rana trusted him. Muslim or not.

Headley never shared any actual plans for the attack in Mumbai with Rana, but he did ask if he could open a branch of First World Immigration Services in the city. He explained that he was doing this at the behest of Pakistani authorities, though it's not clear whether he named the ISI as having given him the assignment.

For Rana, there were real advantages to the prospect: he'd fulfill his dream of opening an office in India, and he wouldn't have to pay for it. Headley wouldn't even draw a salary.

Rana was sometimes a slightly chaotic man, so busy he would answer his mobile phone in the middle of a conversation and try to carry on both conversations at the same time. He managed his finances in a similar fashion: he often had to buy lambs for his slaughterhouse but then would put off payment for months, paying only when the lamb had been sold in the shop. There was no way he'd be in any shape to pay back Headley's "deposit" if Headley asked for it. So the offer of a new office with new clients was fantastic.

Headley also let Rana know that his informal cooperation with the Pakistani authorities might make it possible for him to return someday to Pakistan, where a prison sentence for desertion still awaited him.

Of course, he said yes.

Rana was so unaware of the plans for the terrorist attack that he took his family to Mumbai on a combined vacation and business trip in November 2008 on short notice. He didn't know that the attack was going to take place that month. On their way home to the United States, the Rana family had layovers in Dubai and China, and it was during one of these stops that he discovered on a TV screen that an attack had begun. They had gotten out just in time.

Samraz watched Rana weep when he learned of the many deaths in Mumbai, but he later told Headley that he felt that the nine perpetrators who were killed deserved Pakistan's highest military honors, Nishan-e-Haider.

After the attack, Headley apologized to him for having used the office when he was planning it. That wasn't right. He knew very well that he already owed Rana some favors, and now he owed him one more.

"And we will surely test you with something of fear and hunger and a loss of wealth and lives and fruits, but give good tidings to the patient, who, when disaster strikes them, say, 'Indeed we belong to Allah, and indeed to Him we will return.' Those are the ones upon whom are blessings from their Lord and mercy. And it is those who are the rightly guided."*

Headley read the three verses from the Qur'an in his apartment in Chicago right after Christmas Eve 2008.

Your father is dead, the message from Pakistan had said. Now Headley was reading the many condolences sent by friends and family. It hurt.

He had always been close to his father—even after having left Pakistan in the 1970s to live with his mother in the States. But heroin and prison didn't suit Syed Saleem Gliani, and he had asked his eldest son's half-siblings to stay far away from their brother.

Yet he himself spoke often with Headley. And while it may be that Saleem Gilani thought his son had "gone completely insane" when it came to Islam, there was great respect between the two men.

Saleem Gilani had lived to be eighty years old, and he was slated to receive the prestigious Hilal-i-Imtiaz, Pakistan's second-highest honor, given for a "praiseworthy effort" for Pakistan's "national interests, world peace, or culture." The prize was to be awarded by the president of Pakistan.

---

* Verses 2:155–157 from the Qur'an.

"I hope it won't be posthumous," Saleem Gilani had joked in one of the last conversations Headley had had with him.

After Syed Saleem Gilani's death, the Pakistani prime minister, Syed Yousuf Raza Gilani, came to the family's house in Lahore to pay his respects. Despite their first and last names, Headley's father and the prime minister weren't related, though Headley's half-brother on his father's side, Danyal Gilani, did happen to work as a spokesman for the prime minister at that time.

The prime minister offered the family his condolences and praise for Saleem Gilani's work for Radio Pakistan for more than forty years.

"He prayed to Allah Almighty to rest the departed soul in eternal peace and grant courage to the bereaved family to bear this irreparable loss with fortitude," the local media wrote of the visit.

The Lashkar leader Hafiz Saeed also sent a man to show his respect for Headley's father.

As is the Muslim tradition, Saleem Gilani was buried on the same day he died in the Shah Jamal cemetery in Lahore. The ceremony took place on in the evening of December 25, right after the fourth of the five daily prayers. Because of this constraint, Headley wasn't able to fly home in time for the burial. He remained in Chicago, where he was preparing to review the final details before the trip to Denmark.

"So that's it. I can never make up for this loss. I hope and pray Allah admits him into Paradise and request all you brothers to pray for the same," Headley wrote to his friends in Pakistan.

"I am very upset about dad passing away. Our fathers, mothers, children and ourselves, everything must become Fana [pass away] one day no matter what we do. I spoke to him only a day before. The things I learnt from him nobody can tell me anymore. He was like an encyclopedia of information."

In addition to his good friends Sajid Mir and Iqbal, Headley was also increasingly in contact with Abdur Rehman Hashim Syed, a

Pakistani best known by the nickname "Pasha." He was a hard-core jihadist fighter who for religious reasons had refused to fight the Taliban when, in 2001, they'd fled the cave battles in the Tora Bora mountains in Afghanistan and crossed the border into Pakistan. Because of that refusal, he was thrown out of the Pakistani army.

Headley had a lot of respect for him because of it.

Pasha reserved his love for Lashkar, and Headley had received weapons training from him, when he was at a training camp in the mountains in northwestern Pakistan. Some years later, Pasha decided to leave Lashkar, but he kept in touch with Headley, whom he affectionately called Dave Salafi.

Pasha warned Headley to be careful: Lashkar was known for abandoning projects. They often developed enthusiasms for good ideas that never materialized. If that occurred, all Headley had to do was to let him know. Pasha had a contact who could make miracles happen.

He didn't give a name. But he made it known that his contact had direct access to al-Qaeda. Pasha had previously met Osama bin Laden in a number of apartments. There weren't many who could boast of that.

"Yes, I am ready for Mickey Mouse project, but I think it will be better to go after new year as everything is shut down from Christmas to new year," Headley wrote in an email to Pasha in Pakistan.

"I will spend a week or so the first time to get a feel of the property. If you have any other helpful info on this project, send it to me. If God wants, I will return by middle of next month to you," wrote Headley.

He asked Pasha to push hard to get the Mickey Mouse project quickly "approved" and financed, for the "situation is desperate," as he wrote in an email.

The "situation" was a thirst for revenge, not Headley's own situation. He was ready to leave.

"Pray that I make a lot of money on the project," he wrote, in reference to the honors he would receive when the offices in Denmark were in flames. And then, he added an unusual request: if the attack in

Denmark was approved by Allah and Headley were to receive honors for it, he would like those honors to be awarded to his now deceased father.

"Is this possible?" Headley wrote to Pasha.

"Your every good doing is definitely returned towards your deceased parents, if they had true faith," came the answer from Pakistan.

Headley's mother had been a Christian her entire life, and despite Headley's best efforts, he never got her to convert to Islam. Their disagreement on religion led to long periods during which they didn't speak to each other. She died barely a year before Headley's father, at sixty-eight, and was buried in a cemetery next to the Anglican church in Beltsville, Maryland.

Several friends from Pakistan wrote long emails to Headley containing excerpts from the Qur'an and assuring him that he would meet his father again in Paradise.

"The ayat [verses from the Qur'an] quoted by you are really appropriate and give me strength," wrote Headley, who in the same email used his father's death to allow his thoughts and words to wander into the subject of jihad.

"This life is only temporary. Look at the slaughter of over 200 Palestinian civilians today by the Israelis without the world batting an eye. Their blood means nothing to the UN or EU. You can bet some Mu'min [faithful Muslim] somewhere, is planning retaliation today, not caring about whether the targets are civilian or military. The doors of Justice are firmly closed for Muslims, which is why they have taken matters in their own hands. They intend to bring death to the doorstep of the Pharaohs of today, even as they suffer themselves."

Headley was speaking about himself. He was ready for Denmark.

In Chicago, Headley fell asleep. In a dream he found himself in Saudi Arabia at the Holy Prophet Mohammad's tomb within the old Prophet's Mosque in Medina.

A man was standing by the Prophet's tomb, and when Headley asked who the empty one alongside it was for, the man answered:

"When you die, you will be buried here."

Osama bin Laden, too, had dreams before large operations and assigned great importance to them.

Headley woke on a crystal-clear morning that Sunday, January 11, 2009. In his mind there was no doubt. The dream was blessed. And the tomb would be his reward, should the mission in Denmark succeed.

PART 2

COPENHAGEN

8

IN DENMARK

Copenhagen
Sunday, January 18, 2009

The Eagles were behind for most of the game, which looked like it would end in a loss. In the third quarter, though, Philadelphia fought its way to 25–24, so there was still hope. But then the Arizona Cardinals' Tim Hightower made a touchdown with less than three minutes to go, and it was all over for the Eagles. They lost 25–32.

Headley was watching the game in a bar in Copenhagen. Though he really was more of a basketball guy, he rarely missed a game when the Eagles were playing—not even when he was, on a rather unusual trip.

It was after midnight by the time Headley returned to his room in the Mission Hotel Nebo, a few feet from Copenhagen's Central Station.

He was in Denmark for the first time. From the outside, it seemed like a wonderful country, with friendly people and beautiful women, yet they clearly felt some need to walk all over Islam and Muhammad. He had no trouble reminding himself why he was here.

To cover his tracks, Headley had flown from Chicago to Philadelphia, New York, and Dubai before finally touching down at the airport in Frankfurt on Friday, January 16. This was where he had been caught with heroin-filled luggage nearly twenty years before. But he had no problems getting through customs and received a stamp on page 48 of his extended passport. He didn't even need a visa to enter Europe.

In Frankfurt, Headley rented a car and drove to Copenhagen. Almost immediately upon his arrival, he began to check out the city.

The game between the Eagles and the Cardinals had caused him to miss a phone call from Rana, but he sent an email soon after and the two remained in touch throughout his stay in Denmark. Normally, they spoke Punjabi together, but to avoid attracting unnecessary attention, they used English now during their phone calls and in emails. Headley wrote Rana:

"I checked out business opportunities here. They seem quite promising. I am going right now to see if I can put an ad for our company and also check the feasibility to open up an office here. Sun comes out at 8:30 am here. . . . I am 7 hours ahead of you. . . . Bye for now. Dave."

In Kongens Nytorv, or King's New Square, in central Copenhagen, some young people were ice skating. Their blades danced sharply on the ice as they squealed with joy. Overnight, temperatures had reached nearly freezing; now it was a few degrees warmer but still cold. January sales had been under way for a few weeks, but the big department store Magasin, located in the center of the square near the skating rink, was doing a brisk business.

Headley walked past them on his way to an unusual building. He was tense but in control.

Eight Kongens Nytorv had been the headquarters of A. P. Møller's shipping company, A. P. Møller-Mærsk, for more than sixty years. The owner's son, Mærsk Mc-Kinney, had worked his first day at his father's company in this very building at the age of nineteen. That was back in 1933. After A. P. Møller moved headquarters to the Esplanade in 1979, the building in Kongens Nytorv was leased to a series of businesses, until, in 1997, the *Jyllands-Posten* took over all five floors with its staff of two hundred, making the building its Copenhagen office.

On the ground floor, five large plate glass windows faced the street, while all four upper floors had five high windows with a view of the square, the skating rink, Hotel d'Angleterre, and the Royal Theatre. On the roof, the newspaper's name was spelled out in big yellow letters, with the six-pointed star in the middle: MORGENAVISEN JYLLANDS-POSTEN. There was no mistaking it.

Headley pressed the button for the intercom.

From the other side of the security doors came a high-pitched tone, and the female receptionist looked up.

Outside in the cold stood a tall, middle-aged man in a suit and tie, with a friendly smile—probably another American or British tourist on the way from the popular Nyhavn by the harbor, thought Gitte Johansen, the receptionist.

"No, we don't sell stamps, unfortunately," was something the people on the ground floor of *Jyllands-Posten* were used to saying with a patronizing smile to those who mistakenly thought that *Jyllands-Posten* must be a post office, because of the "Posten" part.

Gitte pressed the button. The first glass door opened, Headley stepped in, the door behind him closed, and a few seconds later door number two was opened.

He walked calmly up to Gitte at the front desk.

Headley had hoped that by coming unannounced he might make it farther into the offices and have a look around. But after walking past the building several times, he sensed it wouldn't be quite that easy. Security had been tightened considerably since the cartoons were published.

Instead, he chose another solution that he had also prepared. The trick was to make it seem natural, almost a little casual.

"I'd like to run an advertisement," he said in measured English as he pulled a stack of typed papers from a folder. Pointing to some text, he began asking questions.

A short while later, the phone rang in the fifth-floor office of a young advertising salesman, whom the receptionist had seen head upstairs not long ago.

"He's at the front desk? Okay, I'm on my way right now," he answered before rushing down the stairs. It wasn't every day that a potential client just showed up on his own without an appointment, but late on a Tuesday morning was just fine for this advertising salesman.

The two men shook hands and sat down at a round glass table near the front desk. From their gray chairs, they could gaze out on King's New Square where pedestrians went by in heavy jackets.

"I represent a company in Chicago," the American said, explaining his plans to expand the company and establish a brand-new office in Copenhagen. It would be an immigration office, helping traveling American and Pakistani engineers with work permits, visas, and housing in Denmark, among other things. The first of what would hopefully be many offices in Europe.

Such a business would naturally need some locations in Copenhagen—maybe near *Jyllands-Posten*, he'd have to look into that later—and advertising in the country's largest newspaper. What would that cost?

The salesman gave the price of a small front-page advertisement—a popular solution—and discussed the paper's readership and business clientele as well as the advantages of choosing *Jyllands-Posten* over a competitor.

Headley listened attentively, took notes, and asked questions to clarify. He sounded engaged. But, of course, the cost of advertising wasn't the reason he had traveled from Chicago more than 3,000 miles to sit in this very chair. Far from it.

While seated there, Headley could look about casually and gather impressions that might help him later on. He cast his eyes over the carpets, the large world map with small gold stars representing the paper's correspondents, the receptionist's high steel desk, and the big Fujitsu TV on the wall, showing the day's news along with small snippets of text and announcing that Barack Obama would be inaugurated as the next president of the United States in just a few hours.

Not to mention the double doors to keep unauthorized people out and the large plate glass windows with shatter-resistant film designed to prevent glass shrapnel in the event of an explosion—either from the street or from within the building. And the security system that first locked people in the main entrance and then locked off the stairs to the offices on the higher floors where the next day's paper was taking shape and the writers for the Internet news desk crafted news stories around the clock.

Headley pictured the front desk becoming the site of a battle so impressive the whole world would remember it. They wouldn't forget the date either. It would be on the cover of every European newspaper the next day, in big letters. Like September 11, 2001, in New York and Washington, DC, March 11, 2004, in Madrid, July 7, 2005, in London, and November 26, 2008, in Mumbai.

Upstairs, the editorial rooms filled with reporters and photographers would be shrouded in smoke and death. Explosions and the pistol shots would be felt and heard in the French embassy next door and busy adjacent streets.

And soon after that, the entire world would follow the drama on live TV, as young well-trained Muslim men killed everyone in their path. Even those who just happened to be in the building by pure chance. Allah would be on the murderers' side. Jihad, the holy and eternally just war.

Fifty-five days had passed since the onset of the Mumbai attack. And now he was sitting here.

Headley left his business card, which presented him as a lawyer and immigration consultant. They had talked for a good while, about twenty minutes. But with his Western appearance and his mild, innocuous American sentences, it wasn't impossible that the salesman might quickly forget him. That is, were it not for Headley's blue and brown eyes.

The meeting with the salesman ended with a handshake, a "Thank you," and "We'll talk later, send me an email." And the American businessman disappeared through the security doors.

That evening back in his hotel, Headley sat down at his keyboard.

"Everything is fine here. I went to a newspaper to find out about advertising our company. I gave him my card so they might call any of the three offices to verify. Ask New York and Toronto offices to remember me," Headley wrote in an email to Rana, which had "Copenhagen" as the subject line. He carefully avoided naming *Jyllands-Posten* explicitly. Keeping up his cover story, he went to grouse about the advertising rates.

"The rates are pretty steep, like 3000 dollars for the front page, for one time," he wrote. He had persuaded the salesman to send him more pricing information.

"I gave our business email, so keep alert for his mail. Forward this e-mail to me so we can invite him for a visit to Chicago and make friends with him to get better rates."

Headley didn't actually intend to invite the salesman to the United States but wanted to keep his options open. A friend in Copenhagen might be useful later on—the way Rahul Bhatt and Vilas Varak had been in Mumbai. If it gave him access to sensitive information about the paper's security system, a friendship with a *Jyllands-Posten* employee could be worth its weight in gold.

Later, he returned to 8 Kongens Nytorv to make a series of video recordings. He paid attention to the building's entrances and exits and imagined how the workers might try to escape in the event of an attack. He couldn't leave that sort of thing to chance.

In Copenhagen, Headley also met with an attractive young Danish woman whose email address he had obtained. She was a student and lived in the Nørrebro district, northwest of the city center. Headley hadn't yet decided what he would do with the woman, but he might be able to use her as a secretary at the fictional immigration office he planned to open as part of his preparations for the attack.

When the woman said she had plans to go on vacation in the States that summer, Headley promised he would find a place in New York where she could stay for two weeks in June. He asked Rana if she could stay with a mutual acquaintance or perhaps with Rana's brother in Newark, close to New York. Nothing ever became of the trip, though.

The woman had no idea that Headley was in the process of planning a terrorist attack.

Headley told Rana that Denmark was full of attractive women.

"The girls are hot. You and I should come here without our girlfriends and have a good time," he wrote one evening.

While he was in Copenhagen, Headley shot several videos from Copenhagen Central Station and explored the city. He also worked to track down Flemming Rose, among other things trying to discover Rose's home address, but was unsuccessful.

He couldn't know that the two of them had already been just feet away from one another. While Headley had been speaking with the advertising salesman close to the front desk, Rose was sitting just a few floors up in the same building, being interviewed by a German journalist about the backstory for the Muhammad cartoons.

They could easily have crossed paths in the doorway.

In an email to Rana, Headley attempted to make his next move appear random.

"I will leave this hotel Thursday morning and go to another city in this country for my vacation. I haven't decided which one, maybe Aarhus."

The trip to Aarhus was anything but random. Just outside the city, at the top of a small hill in the Viby district, is *Jyllands-Posten*'s headquarters. When Headley arrived, he explored the area: out onto Skanderborg Street, right onto Ravnsbjerg Street, and then to the main

entrance on Grøndals Street. He thought the building looked like connected train cars, almost like a labyrinth.

On at least eight occasions throughout the day, Headley walked
around the perimeter of the building with his video camera, research-
ing conditions of access, parking, and the vulnerabilities for an attack.

Late Friday morning, Kurt Westergaard sat in the headquarters as
usual, working on a drawing. The threats hadn't stopped him from
coming to work.

Headley went to the main entrance. Here, too, he introduced himself as a lawyer. He explained that he was interested in running an ad
but would like to get some pricing first.

Headley was brought to the front desk, where an advertising sales-
woman responded to his questions. He listened to the different options and
thanked her for her help. Nobody in the advertising department would
have noticed that the same man had shown up with the same questions
in the same week at two different offices within 150 miles of each other.

That evening, Headley wrote to Rana again:

"Ok Doc . . . I checked for our office ad in Aarhus as well. You
might be receiving price quotes in your other email address. Did the
Copenhagen guy send you any mail yet? I think our company has a
really bright future here. We will become rich or should I say richer?"

By rich, Headley meant rich in a religious sense—not a stack of
money. There was great glory and a place in Paradise waiting for the
two men if the mission could be carried out successfully, he thought.
He was satisfied with his trip.

After his visit, Headley concluded that the building in Aarhus
wasn't "suited" to a terrorist attack. It was too long, too flat, and had
far too many exits, which would offer journalists and others in the
building the means to escape.

Copenhagen was another story entirely. The building on Kongens
Nytorv was easy to attack. And the Danish police suspected nothing of
Headley's activities in Denmark.

Everything was going according to plan.

* * *

The next day, Headley drove to Frankfurt. Saturday evening, he got on a plane to the United Arab Emirates, and from there, on to Pakistan.

Not realizing that she had fallen into the trap, one of the employees at *Jyllands-Posten*'s office in Viby wrote to the email address for First World Immigration.

She began her email, "Dear David C. Headley. Thank you for your visit at *Jyllands-Posten* Friday last week concerning advertising in our newspaper." The consultant offered Headley a 20 percent discount on an advertisement for 6,670 Danish kroner before VAT, if he bought a run of four weeks.

In Chicago, Rana wrote back, pretending to be Headley.

"Thank you for your reply. I will be in touch soon. I am trying to coordinate with a local attorney in Denmark for taking care of our clients locally. I intend to visit you in the coming spring. Sincerely, Dave."

Neither Headley nor First World Immigration ever ran an advertisement in *Jyllands-Posten* or any other Danish newspaper.

Headley had brought a little present to his friends in Pakistan: a stack of funny hats with the word "Copenhagen" on them.

Sajid Mir and Pasha got the point.

Headley had decided: the attack would take place in Copenhagen, and Sajid Mir would soon know if the *Jyllands-Posten* offices were arranged in such a way that, as in Mumbai, they were suitable for an assault in which the perpetrators fought to the death and took numerous lives with them.

Headley thought it was certainly possible. He showed his videos from Denmark, and they quickly started getting new ideas. Headley had made a recording of the Royal Life Guards in Copenhagen, and Sajid Mir suggested that the young men throw grenades at the soldiers and steal their weapons. They discussed the attack for several days.

During this time Headley saw, among other things, the draft of a plan for the attack that Sajid Mir had developed.

For his efforts, Headley received a DVD of one of the potent propaganda films targeting Denmark that had been produced by al-Qaeda's press division, known as As-Sahab Media.

The DVD, *The Word Is the Word of the Swords,* contained recordings from the assault on the Danish embassy in Islamabad barely one year earlier. That attack came in June 2008 as revenge for the reprinting of the Muhammad cartoons by several Danish newspapers.

A car bomb—hidden in a white Toyota Corolla—was driven up in front of the Danish embassy. First, there was a loud bang. Then, flames, and then a cloud of smoke that could be seen over most of the city. The windows of all the nearby cars were blown out by the shock wave, glass shards and bricks flew like projectiles through the air, and about twenty-four people were injured in a split second by the bomb.

That was especially true for local guards, who were knocked down. Six people were killed. Among them were a Danish citizen, a child, and several local employees.

The car containing the bomb shot up about a hundred feet in the air and landed in a neighboring yard. The car's motor was found even farther away.

"We've been afraid of this since the printing of the caricatures. But when you think about what they did to your religion, they deserve it," said an anonymous neighbor in the embassy district to journalists who gathered after the explosion.

The foreign ministry issued a warning with immediate effect against any and all travel to Pakistan, while the attack was condemned by Ban Ki-moon, the UN Secretary-General, as well as American president George W. Bush.

"We condemn the terrorist attack; there is no justification for it. The president has been briefed. He offers his condolences to the victims of violence and their families," said Bush's spokeswoman, Dana Perino.

"I consider the bombing an attack on both Denmark and Pakistan, and condemn the operation in the strongest terms. At the same time, I want to express my deepest sympathy for the victims and their families. We don't yet know who was behind the attack, as nobody has taken responsibility for it. It's important to show calm and levelheadedness in the current situation," said Danish foreign minister Per Stig Møller.

The Pakistani president, Pervez Musharraf, wrote personally to Queen Margrethe and promised to find the perpetrators: "We strongly condemn this terrorist act, which has affected our whole nation deeply."

The As-Sahab film ran for fifty-four minutes and, besides shots of the burning building, also contained a tribute to a man named Kamaal Saleem Atiyyah al-Fudli al-Hadhli. He was in the white Toyota for the suicide attack.

Al-Qaeda leader Mustafa Abu al-Yazid intoned: "What you have seen and experienced in the Danish embassy and prior operation is but the beginning, God willing, if you don't end your errant ways and aggression."

Fifty-four-year-old al-Yazid was a veteran of jihad and was considered number three in al-Qaeda at this time. He had earlier been imprisoned for assisting in the murder of Egyptian president Anwar Sadat in 1981 and was responsible for the group's operations in Afghanistan.

"We have warned previously—and we warn once more—the Crusader states which insult, mock and defame our Prophet and Quran in their media and occupy our lands, steal our treasure and kill our brothers that we will exact revenge at the appropriate time and place," said al-Yazid.

In the recordings, he encouraged every young Muslim in Europe to take an active role in the fight. "There is no excuse for your remaining among the unbelievers unless you join the caravan of jihad and discharge your duty to Islam and Muslims by fighting and killing the enemies of Allah and His Messenger (peace and blessings of Allah be upon him). It's time to stand up for your religion and kill the blasphemers and mockers of your Prophet (peace and blessings of Allah be upon him)."

In the summer of 2008, the rumor spread that Mustafa Abu al-Yazid had been killed in a firefight with the Pakistani military on the border with Afghanistan, and everyone considered him dead.

Later, he reappeared, and it wasn't until nearly two years later, May 21, 2010, that American authorities could confirm that al-Yazid, his wife, and his three daughters as well as a grandchild had died in a drone attack carried out in Pakistani territory.

On the DVD, you could also see the suicide bomber al-Hadhli in the process of packing the white Toyota with explosives. A voice said that he "screamed with joy" and "threw himself on the ground" when he learned that he had been chosen for the suicide mission against the Danish embassy.

"My final message to the worshippers of the cross in Denmark is that, God permitting, this is not the first nor the last act of revenge," said al-Hadhli.

"Sheik Osama bin Laden won't abandon you, nor will the mujahideen abandon you. Allah willing, we will wipe you from the face of the earth," said the man, who was originally from Saudi Arabia.

Finally, al-Hadhli was filmed by the car. Surrounded by dancing red flames that had been added to the image later on, he told his mother good-bye.

"I dedicate this song to my precious mother, who will—Allah willing—be the first one I intercede for on the Day of Resurrection, if Allah accepts me as a martyr," he said, singing:

"Mother, I can't let this humiliation go on. And I can't let a cursed infidel disgrace my sister. I don't want the women of this world. I want the women of Paradise."

With that, Kamaal al-Hadhli calmly got into the car, which was idling with its hazard lights flashing.

"*Salaam alaikum*," said a voice from behind the camera. Peace be with you.

Next a short sequence showed the attack in a simple but violent 3-D animation. Then, some pictures from the destroyed embassy, before the camera finally zoomed in on a sign that read Kongelig Dansk Ambassade.[*]

Headley was excited to see the film, and when he later returned to the United States, he made sure Rana got a copy too. The DVD captured what he'd felt with his entire being after his first visit: it was time for the Danes to feel pain.

---

* Royal Danish Embassy.

9

THE WOMEN

United States
2001

Osama bin Laden's father, Mohammed bin Laden, had at least fif-ty-four children with twenty-two different wives. So while Osama was attending college, he and a friend decided they would each also take several wives and have large families. For many of his peers, though, polygamy had acquired a bad rep because it had gotten so out of hand with their parents' generation.

Osama bin Laden later developed a theory on the advantages of having several women in one's life. Four was the optimal number, pre-scribed by the prophet Muhammad himself.

"One is okay, like walking. Two is like riding a bicycle: it's fast but a little unstable. Three is a tricycle, stable but slow. And when we come to four, ah! This is the ideal. Now you can pass everyone!"

Headley was, as usual, very excited about Osama bin Laden's thoughts, including those on women.

Headley himself loved women. And he had many of them.

He bragged to a group of friends that he had been with more black women than his entire class at the military academy combined. That was about one hundred students.

But he found Pakistani women to be cumbersome. They'd all seen too many Bollywood movies with big, dramatic romance scenes, and they didn't want to live their lives as the third or fourth wife in a complicated marriage.

"Arab women are much more understanding and open to it. They only ask that you be fair," Headley wrote to his friends.

Headley's many women were also his Achilles heel.

He could manage the American narcotics authorities; connections to the drug trade; heroin smugglers in Pakistan; Major Iqbal from the intelligence service; and Pasha, Sajid Mir, and the others in Lashkar, and he could juggle all his roles and opportunities at once—without everything coming crashing down to the ground.

But when it came to women—wives, girlfriends, friends, and his own mother—everything went wrong. He revealed too much. And there was always one who talked.

In the period after September 11, 2001, Americans were encouraged to report strangers, friends, or family members if they showed even the slightest signs of connections to radical groups. The war on terror had to also be fought on American soil, so the authorities asked citizens for help.

IF YOU SEE SOMETHING, SAY SOMETHING signs in the New York subway read just days after the terrorist attack.

The message was directed particularly at unattended bags and suspicious behavior, but it was clear: if you know something, yell loudly.

In New York, one of Headley's female acquaintances—a bartender—confided to a colleague that she had heard Headley talking about being ready to fight in Pakistan and about how the United States had hurt Pakistan's interests. He openly supported some suspicious groups in Pakistan, and she wondered whether they might be terrorists. The colleague called the FBI.

This led to a conversation between Headley and the authorities on October 4, 2001. Two agents from the Department of Defense and

Headley's DEA contact questioned him about his connections in Pakistan, but he plainly denied that he was connected in any way to, or interested in, Islamist terrorism. He was an American deep at heart, he said.

Three people in all were questioned in connection with the report, among them Headley's mother, Serrill. And then the FBI closed the case. They bought Headley's story.

A few months later, in 2002, the FBI's tip hotline was ringing in Philadelphia. On the other end was Phyllis Keith, the owner of the Morning Glories café, often visited by Headley's mother.

In a confidential conversation, Serrill Headley had described her son as "an increasingly fanatical extremist," and, according to Phyllis Keith, Serrill said that Headley had taken part in military training with sixteen-year-old boys who were later killed in armed conflicts.

Phyllis Keith had also met Headley himself at least once, and she felt that he definitely seemed suspicious. That was why she had decided to contact the FBI.

The conversation lasted five minutes. The FBI apparently checked up on Headley because of the call, but after they didn't find anything immediately suspicious, they closed the case again.

The reports were dismissed as the kind that come from jilted lovers and crazy neighbors.

Since the mid-1990s, Headley had been in a steady relationship with a Canadian woman living in New York. He proposed to her with a diamond ring, and they got married in Jamaica near the end of 2002. Headley said nothing about having already been married to Shazia in Pakistan, having several children, and being deeply involved with Lashkar. He maintained the lie without any problems for a few years, and he frequently stayed with wife number two in New York.

But the threads of his double life couldn't hold together in the long run. At one point in 2005, Headley hadn't been in touch with

The Taj Hotel burned for days during the attack in Mumbai. In total, 166 people were killed during the attack. (AP)

The beach where the terrorists made landfall in Mumbai. (FBI)

Kasab, seen here on his killing spree at the Victoria Terminus. He was the sole surviving perpetrator from the Mumbai attack.

David Headley's class at the military academy in Pakistan. Headley is the tall student second from the right at the back. Tahawwur Rana is all the way to the left. The two would stay friends through most of their lives.

The former classmates Headley and Rana met at a reunion in Pakistan in December 2004. By that time, Headley had long been a member of the terrorist organization Lashkar-e-Taiba. He kept that information to himself.

A05 805887   Mar 06, 09   Mar 04, 09   20:13

5532   543:124   3   59   0

FIRST JUDICIAL DISTRICT OF PENNSYLVANIA
COURT OF COMMON PLEAS OF PHILADELPHIA COUNTY
TRIAL DIVISION—CIVIL
NOVEMBER 2005

IN THE MATTER OF   :   TERM, _____
PETITION FOR CHANGE OF   :
NAME OF   :

DAOOD GILANI   :   003377
_____   :   NO. _____

DECREE FOR CHANGE OF NAME

AND NOW this _15TH_ day of _February_, 200_6_, on

hearing of the within Petition, and on motion of Petitioner, and on presentation of proof

of publication of notice as required by law together with proof that there are no

judgments or decrees of record or any other matter of like effect against the petitioner,

and it appearing that there is no legal objection to the granting of the prayer of the

petition,

IT IS HEREBY ORDERED and DECREED that the name of the Petitioner be

and is hereby changed to ___DAVID COLEMAN HEADLEY___

BY THE COURT:

_____ J.

COPIES SENT
PURSUANT TO Pa. R.C.P. 236(b)

FEB 15 2006

First Judicial District of Pa.
User I.D.: _bJ 6_

DOCKETED

FEB 15 2006

D. BRENNAN
DISCOVERY

CERTIFIED FROM THE RECORD ON   FEB 2 8 2006
JOSEPH H. EVERS
PROTHONOTARY OF PHILADELPHIA COUNTY

BY: _Joseph C. Mangin_

Born Daood Gilani in Washington, DC, Headley changed his name in 2006 to David Coleman Headley, taking the surname of his American mother's family. (FBI)

Headley was always a complex person. He enjoyed Hollywood action movies, TV host Jay Leno, and the books of former president Jimmy Carter. Privately, he wore traditional Pakistani clothing and used his evenings to write inflammatory emails about the United States.

Three important people in David Headley's life: his childhood friend Tahawwur Rana (above left), from an interview he did with a local TV station years before his arrest; Pasha (above) and the only know photo of Sajid Mir (left), Headley's main terror contacts. (FBI)

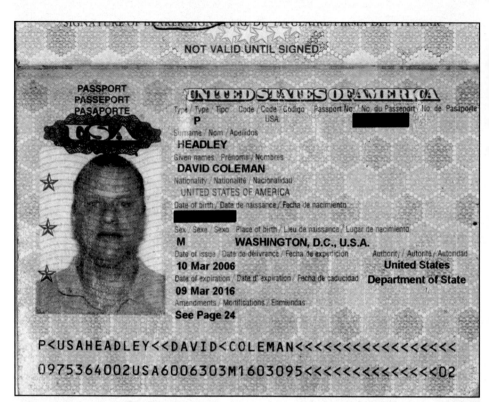

Headley was a frequent traveler. Toward the end of 2009, his three-year-old passport had an impressive eighty-nine stamps, for an average of one flight every twelve days. The bottom image shows the stamp from Headley's only flight out of Copenhagen Airport on August 5, 2009. He would usually use other airports when he traveled to Europe in order to protect his cover. (FBI)

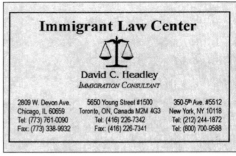

The Immigrant Law Center on West Devon Avenue in Chicago was owned by Rana. Headley used to come here and borrow the computers.

Headley's business card as he presented to the Danish newspaper *Jyllands-Posten*, which published the Muhammed cartoons. The address in New York is that of the Empire State Building. (FBI)

Tahawwur Rana's white BMW was bugged by the authorities, and the FBI recorded several conversations between Rana and Headley.

Rana's house had one of the largest satellite dishes on the street and was like a second home for Headley.

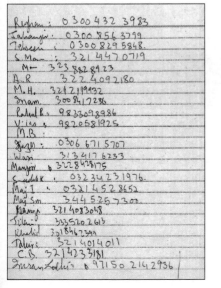

A handwritten list of phone numbers taken from Headley's private notebook. Notice his friends Rahul Bhatt and Vilas Varak from the fitness center in Mumbai. The terrorist Sajid Mir is also here, listed under one of his main cover names, Wasi. (FBI)

Posing as a tourist, Headley used his cell phone to make a number of seemingly innocent videos of locations in Copenhagen: the main train station; Kongens Nytorv, or King's New Square, in central Copenhagen; and, of course, the offices of the newspaper *Jyllands-Posten*. The pictures shown here are stills from those videos.

the Canadian wife for months, and she contacted Headley's father in Lahore. Suddenly, she knew everything.

She quickly declared that she wanted a divorce, which led to an altercation in front of Headley's video store in Manhattan on August 25, 2005. According to the police report following the incident, the Canadian woman claimed that Headley struck her several times in the head.

The day after, she called the Joint Terrorism Task Force, JTTF, in New York and told them everything she knew:

When Headley was "at home" in New York, he bought unusual things—rope, sturdy hiking boots, and books about war and conflict—which he took with him when he traveled to the Middle East. He had also researched the prices of infrared goggles. And that wasn't all.

Throughout the course of three meetings in total with the JTTF agents, Headley's Canadian wife said she was convinced he was a member of Lashkar and was active in raising money for the organization. She showed the agents some cassette tapes with speeches and other ideological material from the group. She also explained that Headley often received emails and telephone calls from suspicious people in Pakistan. She even offered to retrieve some of Headley's private emails for them, which the agents presumably declined.

The information was entered into the FBI's enormous Guardian Threat Tracking System, which at the time was tracking more than 40,000 tips in connection with allegedly suspicious persons and activities.

"No connection to terrorism" was the conclusion after a cursory investigation. With that, the FBI closed the case on David Headley for the third time.

On August 31, 2005, Headley was arrested and jailed by the local police in New York for the attack on his wife a week earlier. He quickly got out, though, and charges were never pressed.

A few years later, another woman came close to costing Headley everything.

Her name was Faiza Outalha. She was originally from Morocco, but she was studying medicine at the university in Lahore, and it's not difficult to see why Headley fell for her. Faiza had large, beautiful eyes and long, dark hair, and she was full of the same restless energy as Headley himself. The twenty-four-year-old woman didn't put up with anything, complained loudly about unreasonable taxi fares, and always made sure she got her way.

And when she met Headley, nearly twice her age, while visiting a mutual acquaintance, neither of them had any doubts. In late February 2007, the two got married in Pakistan.

Faiza was warned in advance that Headley was already married and had children, but she accepted that as long as the other wife didn't come to know about her.

And Shazia didn't. At least, not in the beginning. Headley kept the marriage with Faiza a secret from his first wife. All he did was contact Shazia's uncle Saulat to get his appraisal of whether it was permitted within Islam to take an additional wife while keeping it a secret. The uncle apparently approved of this.

Faiza's temperament quickly caused problems for Headley in their hidden marriage. She insisted, for example, on going with him to Mumbai, where she had learned that her new husband worked at an immigration office.

Headley hadn't informed Faiza that his purpose in going to Mumbai was actually to plan a terrorist attack—nor did he intend to do so.

To get out of this pinch, Headley arranged the next trip to Mumbai so that it would be the couple's official honeymoon. The two had beautiful views of the sea while staying at the Taj Hotel and Oberoi-Trident, where Headley took plenty of notes for his plans for the attack. Both locations ended up on the list of targets, and their vacation photos from Mumbai were later used for further terrorism plans. Faiza's face was covered with a black bar in several of the photos, according to proper Salafist tradition.

But it all became a mess for Headley.

In Pakistan, he had pressured the otherwise very Western-minded Faiza to wear a hijab. But on their honeymoon in India, he did everything he could to hide his Muslim background. And when the couple met some of his acquaintances, he explained that Faiza was one of his clients who wanted a work permit.

Headley and Faiza had several violent clashes during their honeymoon. It got to the point where Headley tried to put his new wife on a flight home to Pakistan, but she refused.

The new, secret marriage also resulted in a number of awkward situations in which Headley had to travel the world to get his cover stories to mesh.

A simple example: On July 23, 2007, he flew from Lahore to New York with a layover in Europe. In New York he spent a day with a cousin. He then flew to Morocco and was with Faiza for a good week or so before flying Emirates Airlines on August 3 from Casablanca back to Lahore to be with Shazia and the children. He told Shazia that he had been on a business trip.

In these circumstances, Headley had to be very focused not to slip up. He would send his emails to Shazia in Pakistan to haidergilani1@hotmail.com, while emails for Faiza went to faizagilani@ymail.com.

Near the end of 2007, less than a year after they got married, his relationship with Faiza was on the verge of collapse. Headley had tried to break up with her in a letter. The two fought about the secrecy with Shazia, which led to regular fistfights in front of Headley's house in Lahore in December 2007.

Headley was arrested and put behind bars at the Race Course police station for eight days, until Shazia's father bailed him out. It also helped that Major Iqbal pulled a few strings here and there. Headley got away once again without being charged for domestic violence.

But Headley's anguish only worsened. That same month, Faiza talked her way into the American embassy in Pakistan. She was angry and loudly let the agents from the Department of State's security agency know that her husband, an American citizen, was a terrorist. He had stayed in Lashkar-e-Taiba training camps and sometimes spoke about suicide missions, she said. And he might be involved in some activities in Mumbai.

Faiza also claimed that Headley was in the process of planning "jihad against the USA" and was involved with some "very important people."

Later, Faiza returned with new information, in the hopes that the Americans would arrest her husband and fly him to Guantánamo. She told them that Headley had received a "special mission," apparently fabricating a story wherein he had been involved in a bombing attack on a train in India the previous year.

"He is either a terrorist or he's working for you," Faiza apparently told the American authorities.

It was clear, though, that Faiza was mixing facts with pure fiction, and the embassy staff didn't find her particularly trustworthy. Even though it seems she showed the agents a picture of herself with Headley in front of the Taj Hotel.

There was no proof of anything at all.

The information about Headley and a possible attack in Mumbai was never passed on from the American embassy to Indian authorities. Later, the Americans did give India a weak warning about a possibly approaching attack, but it didn't include the name David Headley.

A few months before the Mumbai attack, Faiza went directly to Lashkar leader Hafiz Saeed—the Professor—and asked for help in saving their troubled marriage. Hafiz Saeed then paid a visit to Headley, who downplayed the matter and explained that he had been busy with his Lashkar duties and hadn't had much time to take care of wife number two.

It's uncertain whether Hafiz Saeed's involvement was the deciding factor. What is certain is that Faiza and Headley got back together again, and that they watched the terrorist attack in Mumbai together on Headley's TV in their house in Lahore.

But there's no evidence Headley ever revealed his role to her, either.

* * *

The many TV images from the attack in Mumbai in late November 2008 got another of Serrill Headley's friends wondering.

She had previously heard Serrill talking about her son having fought in Pakistan for five or six years to free Kashmir, and now she put two and two together. On December 1, 2008, she called the local FBI office, which sent the tip on to Washington, DC.

The FBI visited one of Headley's cousins in Philadelphia on December 21, 2008. The cousin was the only family member they could immediately locate in the country, and he told them that Headley had lived in Pakistan for the last five years. The FBI would have to contact Headley there if they wanted anything from him.

The FBI agents told the cousin that if he ever saw Headley, to ask him to stop by the American embassy. But Headley never contacted the American embassy in Islamabad, and without further investigation, the authorities filed the case away due to a lack of evidence.

Meanwhile, Headley was in Chicago, planning his first trip to Denmark.

It's still something of a mystery exactly how David Headley managed to complete his terrorism training in the farthest reaches of Pakistan while flying in and out of the United States, Denmark, and other Western countries for years—all without being discovered. It's particularly strange given his background as a known smuggler of narcotics and his having previously been convicted.

Some of Headley's old friends are convinced he was born under a lucky star, so to speak—the kind of person who would walks away from a bad traffic accident uninjured or leaves a party two minutes before the police shut it down. The kind of person who ought to play the lottery.

Islam doesn't allow room for such theories, though. In Islam, one's destiny is said to be predetermined by Allah.

There are also other possible answers to the mystery.

Perhaps it was a question of pure coincidences—of incompetence in intelligence circles and database entries that weren't put together correctly.

Or perhaps the American authorities let Headley off time and time again because he convinced them that he was only gathering information for his old employer—the American narcotics authorities. Maybe the DEA believed above all else that he was still an agent for them. Or at least a friend they could trust. He was an American citizen, after all.

Or perhaps the answer was Headley himself. He had a way of talking himself out of everything.

10

Why This Talk of Death?

Pakistan
January 2009

Headley had once met a Jewish man in Philadelphia who was about to eat a ham sandwich. Headley remarked that the meat in his sandwich came from a pig, so the sandwich couldn't be kosher.

"That commandment came at a time when there was no refrigeration, in an area with really high temperatures, so pork spoiled very quickly," replied the Jewish man. "Pigs were given filth to eat, but now these swine are corn-fed with living quarters cleaner than most third-world country folk's homes—not to mention the highest standards of sanitation and refrigeration. Now it is completely healthy and fit for consumption."

The man continued munching on his sandwich.

That encounter made a lasting impact on Headley, and he repeated it, as he remembered it, in a series of emails to a select group of former classmates from Pakistan.

Were such religious requirements really something that would disappear with time? Would there one day be a situation where a computer or mobile phone could perform the five daily prayers, so performing them oneself wouldn't be necessary? If a majority of the population one day suddenly decided to accept adultery, would it suddenly become acceptable from a religious standpoint? If politicians accepted homosexuals as being partners, would that be marriage in God's eyes, too?

Was everything really up for grabs?

Headley wouldn't accept that. That sort of watering down of the meaning of the religion led to the collapse of everything. For the same reason, Headley fought against any kind of contemporary interpretation of Islam.

Headley considered himself a Salafist. He tried to live life as the prophet Muhammad and the two generations succeeding him did. These first generations were particularly pious, and their long beards, their clothes, and their ideals became Headley's. When he wasn't in India, the United States, or Denmark, he let his beard grow.

He explained his beliefs as follows:

"Rasulullah SAW is the messenger of God and everything coming from him is directly from the Almighty. After I accept that, I must accept, as the Quran says, 'Take whatever he (Muhammad SAW) gives you and refrain from what he prohibits' or 'he who does not judge by what has been revealed to us is amongst the losers' and so on and so forth. This 'opinion' makes me a Muslim."

Lashkar-e-Taiba was built upon precisely that idea when a group of men gathered in Pakistan in the mid-1980s. Some of them had fought the Russians in Afghanistan, some were religious scholars from Palestine, and others were disillusioned Pakistani engineers. One of them was Abdullah Azzam, one of Osama bin Laden's ideological mentors. Another was "professor" Hafiz Saeed.

The founders agreed that modern innovations in Islamic practice were a corruption. Islam had already answered everything, so rightly-led Muslims were obligated to say "No, thank you" to capitalism, communism, democracy, reforms, and all religions besides Islam. There was but one God, and he had already given man his set of rules in the form of the laws of Sharia.

For Headley, religion was a question of bookkeeping. The books had to be balanced. Nobody could add and subtract as they pleased. Word for word meant word for word. No exceptions.

That also meant that Headley had to distance himself from Islamic reformists, Islamic feminists, Islamic homosexuals, and Islamic democrats. All of that was irreconcilable with true Islam.

"I must reject anything that contradicts the Holy Book," Headley wrote. "Science can never prove the Qur'an or Hadith wrong. . . . Since I cannot accept the Creator as being the Author of confusion, I accept everything exactly as it is stated in the Book. . . . So anything that clashes with this Book must be rejected and not pursued further. This, as far as I know, has been the way the Qur'an and Islam have been understood by the people taught by the Prophet Saw and those closer to him in time."

The debates Headley had with his Pakistani friends sometimes lasted several days, involving men all over the globe in different time zones, and they resulted in numerous long emails with both religious and secular arguments for and against one idea or claim or another.

In 2008 alone, the former classmates wrote more than four thousand emails to each other.

Headley quickly wrote himself into a state of heated anger, calling his friends "godless," "traitors," and outright "cowards." Though his emails often ended with the word "peace" or "God's peace," the sentences in them were filled with harsh words.

"I have had enough. Good bye," wrote one friend after yet another debate that lasted several days and had prompted a strong dose of unfriendly words from Headley.

Headley quickly replied.

"What's the matter, man? I wasn't trying to disrespect you. Please do not feel offended. Why are you taking this stuff personally?" And he apologized for the provocation in the previous post, concluding, "So please, no 'good byes.' Ok?"

Headley promised to hold back the harsh words in exchange for a "free debate," and on several occasions he explained that he was open to being corrected and learning from his mistakes. But he always required a direct reference to a holy text if he was to be put in his place; personal opinions were irrelevant. And despite the promise of an open mind, there are no examples of instances where he allowed himself to be convinced of a more moderate viewpoint. Quite the opposite.

If anybody asserted that, "Islam is ever changing and evolving," Headley would also require a reference to the Qur'an for that claim. He wrote of his Pakistani friends who had moved to the United States that their evolving views of Islam might make it easier to live in a country where the FBI could come knocking on their door at any time. "Holding and promoting their 'New Islamic beliefs' will get them much further in the countries they have made Hijrat* to and raise their families."

Headley rejected the whole idea that Islam needed a "reform," despite discussions of issues brought up by Muslim scholars in the West, imams in Pakistan, and other learned people. The entire concept was a "well-funded and well-coordinated attack of our enemies," Headley declared.

He could easily see the genius in the strategy: if the "Crusaders" succeeded in destroying Islam from within, they wouldn't have to bomb Afghanistan, Iraq, and Pakistan to bits. That was well thought out.

The Muhammad cartoons were a part of that cunning strategy, he thought. They were designed to break down the idea of Islam as being pure, instead putting it on par with all the other religions. For the enemies in the West, it was about trampling all over Islam and watering down their faith into nothingness.

---

* Hegira, a journey, i.e., countries they have traveled to. Also *hijrat*.

"They want to mainstream Islam to make it palatable and acceptable. They are now working harder on reforming Islam than on fighting Muslims," Headley wrote.

But as an Islamic soldier, he had to maintain that this "crusade" to reform Islam was doomed to fail. The reform would "never become anything."

"Islam will remain Pure and unadulterated till the Last Day. No new and 'hidden' meanings will be 'discovered' as the Prophet did that job very well," Headley wrote.

Few things could make him angrier than the idea of female imams in congregations with men. That was for Headley an example of the total debasement of Islam in the modern world's interpretation. He wrote numerous emails to his friends on the subject, in harsher and harsher tones. Headley suggested that Amina Wadud—a fifty-three-year-old woman and expert on Islam who had led Muslim prayer in the United States in 2005—should be immediately beheaded. He called her a "ho" and replied in a condescending, sarcastic tone when others asked him to rein in his language.

She had five children with different partners. That wasn't normal. Not even in America, Headley wrote. He shouldn't have to be distracted by a "10"—a very attractive woman—while at Friday prayers, and it was for good reason that the Qur'an prescribed that women sit behind the men.

"It's an attempt to put 20th century Western values into Islamic clothing. I can just see people very soon talking about Gay Rights in Islam or justifying Abortion. If we constantly look to change or adjust our religion to the values of the day can you imagine what our religion will look like 200 years from now?" For Headley, the religion revealed by Allah was perfect from the start and intended to endure unchanged to the end of time. It wasn't for petty humans to suggest refinements. "If it weren't perfect and amendment-free then it wouldn't be divine," Headley argued.

145

* * *

Headley also found in the Qur'an his arguments for jihad, understood as armed struggle against oppressors.

Suicide attacks, car bombs, and attacks against, say, train stations, airports, and police stations were all completely legitimate if they served a higher purpose.

He wasn't concerned about the labels "terrorism" or "terrorist." They indicated that one was doing something wrong. But what he did wasn't wrong. For Headley, there could be no definition of terrorism because any definition would be an indictment of the West.

"The Crusaders and their Murtadd [apostate] allies know that the day they come up with a definition the same second we will point out to them a hundred instances of terrorism committed by them for every one of which we are accused. Terrorism and torture is their specialty, they have been doing it for a millennium and our Security officials go there to learn it from them. Yes, Inshallah, it is beautiful and full of Blessing to terrorize the Terrorist," Headley wrote.

Yet when one of his friends used the word "terrorism," Headley broadsided him, asserting that he never used that term to describe actions by Israel or NATO that resulted in civilian casualties, no matter how many.

"On the other hand you judge actions by Muslim fighters very harshly. You are prolific in using words like 'Islamists,' which were coined by Jews very recently, in your statements, just like we use words like Crusaders and Zionists. You feel 'terrorists' are 'brain washed' by viewing videos of atrocities against Muslims without realizing that you yourself have been hoodwinked into believing Western causes as your own by watching FOX news or CNN. . . . Your views have been conditioned by your life in the USA," Headley wrote to a friend who had moved from Pakistan.

* * *

For Headley, jihad was a way to become clean.

A large portion of Headley's past—his drug smuggling, his drinking, his womanizing—was one great Muslim sin, one that he could remedy through jihad.

Jihad was "the most selfless act" a true Muslim could devote himself to, and Allah promised jihadists a place in Paradise.

A friend wrote that he wished the worst on those who took part in jihad.

Another classmate replied that the friend understood nothing about the world.

"Jihad in the way of Allah (SWT)* will continue till the entire earth comes under the fold of Islam. This is the verdict of Allah (SWT), not mine," wrote one.

This classmate had been known as a partying sort of guy among his American friends, and he had "amply seen and mostly enjoyed" everything the Western world had to offer. But he had come to see it as a "hollow as well as stinking filth under the deceptive glitter of a superficial veneer."

His best days were in the beginning of 1992, when, by "Allah's grace," he participated in the mujahideen's battle in Afghanistan against the Soviet-backed regime and was there when Kabul was captured.

"Those were my happiest and most contented days, despite the fact our diet was minimally austere and sometimes we didn't even know if and when we got the next meal," he wrote, describing how the mujahideen were shelled all day long and bombarded from the air with cluster bombs and napalm, and how they sometimes had to sleep in shifts on the open plains in the nighttime frost in order to secure the front line against the communists.

---

* The honorific *Subhanahu wa ta'ala* in Arabic, which means, "May He be glorified and exalted."

"Allah (SWT) gave us sakeenah [serenity] and peace in otherwise most frightful conditions. The feeling of fear was totally absent from us. All we desired first and foremost was shahadat [martyrdom] in the way of Allah (SWT). Some got it then and there. Others later and in other places like Kashmir. And some unlucky ones like me are still around," he wrote, saying he found that Allah fulfilled his wishes without him even needing to pray for them.

"Whenever we got up from our sleep, we found our hearts to be amazingly delighted as if we had been to or seen something most wonderful in our dreams."

Headley read the email as he prepared his plans for the attack on Denmark.

"Mash'allah . . . I am proud to know you and have you as my brother. And I wish extinction for every Kafir who despises Islam and our Prophet SAW, and all of their supporters and tax payers and financers, all their stooges, all those who cooperate and assist them, all of those who sympathize with them, all those who emulate them and aim to make their kids brown versions of them, all those impressed by them, all those dying for their acceptability, all those who embrace their values, all those who feel inaad [hatred] for Islam and hold Keena [vengeance] in their hearts for its teachings, all those who seek to change or modify it, all those who resent Mu'mineen [believers], all those who speak against them and wish evil on them, all those attempting to make innovations in the perfect deen [faith].* I pray for their unhappiness in this world and the next. I pray to see them collected in Jahannam [hell] with their leaders," Headley wrote.

"Please write more about your visits to Afghanistan . . . it strengthens my faith."

---

* *Deen* is a central concept of Islam having to do with the believer's relationship with Allah.

* * *

As a rule, Headley did not shun any weapon in the war against injustices. The West—not least of all the United States and Israel—had written off their chances for a fair fight.

"For a Muslim the correct aqidah [creed] is that he present himself in the battlefield in the face of Zulm [tyranny] with whatever means are available to him and not wait for the 'right time,'" Headley wrote, explaining that he followed the Medina Convention, instead of the Geneva Convention.

Everything was allowed. Even killing civilians, cheating, and lying.

Headley referred to a hadith about an incident near Medina in the year 627, where a Muslim who had secretly converted from Judaism asked permission from Muhammad to mix with the Jews in order to gather information for his new master.

"War is deceit," the Prophet had replied, and gave him permission to spy. That was how Headley presented that hadith, anyway, and he remarked that Sun Tzu had reached the same conclusion in *The Art of War* many years earlier.

And when American or Pakistani imams or Islamic parties wouldn't officially approve that tactic, it made no difference to Headley.

"Even if the whole world opposes it, the Hadith will still be true," he wrote.

Several of his friends considered jihad a cowardly act. But Headley wouldn't accept that.

"You may call it barbaric or immoral or cruel, but never cowardly. . . . You will never find a European Broiler soldier [i.e. a big chicken, a coward] lying next to a bomb. This courage is, by and large, exclusive to the Muslim Nation. For these NATO criminal vermin, courage is dropping a 22000 lbs bomb on unsuspecting and unarmed Afghan villagers or napalming southeast asian farmers or nuking large (innocent) civilian populations," wrote Headley.

149

In many of the emails, there was no doubt that his own birth country, the United States, was his main enemy, even if Israel and many of the Western countries were "born from the womb of Satan."

He suspected the American government of being in the process of developing new, mini atomic bombs specialized for "our brothers in Afghanistan," and he called it an "undeniable fact" that the US is "the most vicious and barbaric power the world has ever seen."

He cited as evidence, as he had many times before, the atomic bombings of Hiroshima and Nagasaki during World War II, which he went on to contrast with the attacks on September 11, 2001.

"Do you also then agree that an entity that kills 2900 civilians at the World Trade Center would be a 'lesser' terrorist than an entity that obliterates 250,000 civilians in Hiroshima? If so, then should we not all join forces to combat the greater evil?" Headley wrote in a heated debate, adding that all major powers in the world embraced the principle of the right to retaliate for the killing of civilians, and it was hypocrisy to deny that right to Muslim fighters.

But there was no reason to fear the Americans.

"But don't worry, Inshallah their head is now in the meat-grinder, and our brothers have got a hold of the handle," Headley wrote.

A victory over the United States and Europe wouldn't be necessary, though, much less achievable in the first place.

"Not to mention the Glory awaiting the Believers in the Hereafter, that of course, will be the real Victory, the Supreme Triumph and the day of ignominy for those who opposed the Holy and Pure Shariah of the Almighty," Headley wrote.

One of Headley's friends—a professor from Islamabad who is now responsible for a large part of the state-run educational system in Pakistan—wrote that jihad wasn't only about fighting.

"Let us become good muslims first. A good muslim is educated, looks after his neighbor and would therefore work on providing clean drinking water, basic health, justice, employment and security. Should a Jihadi organization not work first to improve the conditions of the people? What stops them from building e.g. a sewage system so that water and sewage is not mixed?" he wrote, declaring that one's faith is measured only by one's willingness to give his or her life to Islam.

"When you are dead, it is over and there is nothing more you can do. Why not live and achieve something? Is it easier to take a bullet or work hard everyday for fifty years so that your fellow people benefit and improve their standard of living?

"Why this talk of death? Any moron or brainwashed idiot can strap a bomb and blow himself up. It will take much more to build a great, just Islamic Society. This new world order can not be built on the ruins of a terrorized Pakistan."

Headley replied that there quite simply wasn't a choice.

"We will not be working on providing basic health and employment when our lands are being occupied, our mosques are being demolished, our blood is being spilt mercilessly. We will, in this instance, bring death and destruction on Allah's enemies as they have done to us," Headley wrote.

That was how it would be in any correct interpretation of Islam, and that was how it had always been, he claimed.

Another former classmate—who today is a professor at a university in the United States—wrote to Headley that, after having written at such length, he had given up trying to persuade him through reason.

A literal interpretation of the Qur'an would require one to accept slavery, even in our times, the professor wrote.

"If this is the 'Islam' you want, please count me out. I labor under the delusions that mercy is better than retribution and that slavery is evil. What was or was not done 1400 years ago was in the context of those times. We live in the 21st century even if some people want to take us back to the 7th. As for mass murder by Western powers, I don't disagree with you that acts such as Dresden, Hiroshima and Nagasaki were crimes against humanity, as were the actions taken by Germany and

Japan. Man's inhumanity to man has been amply demonstrated throughout history; we don't need to add to the count in the name of Islam.

"However, I am encouraged by the extreme nature of your point
of view, which guarantees that it will never succeed with the public at
large. Such rigid fringe movements have erupted in that part of the
world several times before, and have never amounted to much in the
end, though they may enjoy some success for a while. Your heroes too
will end up in the trash heap of history," he wrote.

Headley wrote that his friend from the States was "reciting poems"
rather than presenting arguments, that the burden was on him to prove
that anything in the Prophet's example was not Islamic. "The 'delusions
that you do labor under' regarding Mercy, Retribution or Slavery cannot be used as an argument against our religion and are of absolutely
no consequence. All these issues have been explained verbally and practically shown by the most merciful man SAW who ever lived. If his
SAW sunnah is the Islam you want to be 'counted out of' then what
ever you do follow is a creation of your own mind."

He also disagreed with the statement that his heroes would end up
on the rubbish heap of world history.

"My ONLY hero is Muhammad Mustafa SAW and whatever he
gave us will prevail and every thing else that stands against it is doomed
to be decimated and end up in the trash heap of history, as you put it."

Despite the violent disagreement, Headley was still very determined to keep his friend in the debate.

"I hope you don't get angry even when you totally disagree with me
and do still and always consider me as your friend as I consider you,"
Headley wrote to him.

"No, I am not angry at what you say—just sorry that this is what
you have come to think," the professor wrote back, and went on:

"There is no point in my providing 'evidence' for my viewpoint,
since we disagree on the basic premise here. Evidence requires that
the parties agree on the terms of what constitutes evidence. You are
operating from the viewpoint that 'true Islam' requires a literal reading

of the Qur'an and exact emulation of the Prophet's (SAW) actions. I don't think that literal reading of a text across centuries is even possible, let alone desirable. And I think that religions, like everything else, have to change with time, retaining only their abstract spirit, not their outer forms. Nor do I think that religion should be the basis of the state. So what you call 'evidence' and 'precedent,' I just call history— to be noted with interest and to be learned from, but not to be copied. Just because something was done a certain way at a certain time does not, to me, mean that it must be done that way forever. Just because the Prophet (SAW) allowed slaves does not mean that we must allow slavery today; or just because he had a beard does not mean all Muslims must quit shaving. I don't regard such literalist, mindless following as Islam, but as a caricature of it. You regard it as the True Path. Therefore we have nothing to discuss [or] to argue. Of course, I do hope that your interpretation does not succeed, because I regard it as atavistic, violent and destructive."

The professor added that he would rather see an Islam where the focus was on the Prophet's goodness, attitude, perseverance, and his care for the weakest among his followers.

"If your only hero is the Prophet (SAW), then you don't need to worry since history's verdict about him is already pretty clear. However, I don't think that is what history has in store for the Zawahiris and Mulla Omars of this world. They will end up where they belong," the professor wrote about Osama bin Laden's right-hand man and the leader of the Taliban in Afghanistan.

Another former classmate joined the discussion and said that the professor from Ohio was practicing a "very liberal" interpretation of the Qur'an, for which he had a hard time finding any support in Muslim scriptures. The professor replied:

"I do not disagree with you that this a very liberal interpretation of Islam. I am a very liberal person. The point is that I don't seek to impose my interpretation of Islam on anyone else, to call them 'kafir', or to try and hurt them for that reason. That is all I ask of others. I don't care if they personally believe that shaving is haram or that the Earth is flat. Just don't kill me for believing otherwise. Thank you."

Headley wrote back coolly.

"Nobody will argue that you don't have the right to believe what you want, but the problem arises when you want to pass off your whims as Islam. Nobody has that right, not Rumi not Baba Farid and definitely not you or me," Headley wrote, repeating that the prophet Muhammad's laws and rules applied word for word, "even if the world survives another 10,000 years.

"But I do agree with your words that the Zawahiris or Mulla Omars will end up 'where they belong.' As will you."

11

BRIGADE 313

**Waziristan, Pakistan, near the border with Afghanistan
February 2009**

The small house in front of him was empty. The man apparently hadn't arrived yet.

Headley was staying in North Waziristan, an out-of-the-way but inhabited little corner of northwestern Pakistan, not far from the border with Afghanistan.

He was happy to wait if it meant a chance to meet the man in the house. The man was someone Headley might be able to use in his terrorism plans in Denmark. A man with some powerful contacts.

The house was near Miranshah, the capital of the province, and likely a bit south of the city of Razmak, which had previously been home to a large terrorist training camp controlled by the man Headley had come to visit: Ilyas Kashmiri.

Kashmiri's deeds have been recounted over and over by Muslim jihadists in the last twenty years, to the point where it's difficult to discern what is true and what exaggeration. Even Interpol had gleaned only a few details about him—including both that he had black eyes and that he had brown. He had apparently been born in the Samhani Valley of Kashmir in the mid-1960s. Kashmiri himself gave the date of

February 10, 1964, though intelligence circles have pointed to at least three other possible birth dates for him.

What's certain, though, is that Kashmiri pursued media studies at Allama Iqbal Open University in Pakistan but abandoned his studies when he became a mujahid and devoted his life to armed struggle.

In the most widespread stories, the young Ilyas Kashmiri then received his physical training in the Pakistani military's special forces, the Special Services Group. Here, he quickly rose through the ranks and impressed everybody with his brutality. Kashmiri himself denies that he ever received so much as a day of training in the military.

It's clear, however, that Kashmiri lost one eye and an index finger while fighting Soviet forces during the war in Afghanistan in the 1980s. After that, he seems to have dedicated himself to the fight against the superior Indian forces. In the 1990s, he was imprisoned for two years in India, and when he escaped—likely with some help from friends—he became a hero and continued fighting.

One day in 1994, a milkman knocked on a door in a small town just outside of New Delhi. He delivered the milk but noticed that the house's owners had a suspiciously large number of weapons, so he contacted the police. The authorities broke in and found one American and three British hostages. Ilyas Kashmiri had—so the story goes—left the house to run an errand just before the police stormed in. His good friend Omar Sheikh was arrested during the operation.

On Christmas Eve, 1999, a group of terrorists took the 178 passengers of Indian Airlines Flight 814 from Nepal hostage in a complicated operation in which they flew to India, Pakistan, and Dubai before landing in Kandahar in Afghanistan and demanding the release of Omar Sheikh and two other convicted terrorists in exchange for the passengers. They were successful. Here, too, Kashmiri played a part.

Omar Sheikh was later behind the murder of the Israeli-American journalist Daniel Pearl from the *Wall Street Journal*. Pearl was kidnapped and eventually beheaded in 2002, and a video in which his throat is cut open before he is decapitated was popular in fundamentalist circles. Pearl's body was found cut into ten pieces.

In late February 2000, Ilyas Kashmiri personally beheaded a young Indian soldier by the name of Bhausaheb Maruti Talekar during a guerrilla attack on the India-Pakistan border. This was in revenge for an Indian assault on Pakistan the day before, in which three Pakistani girls were reportedly raped and subsequently decapitated.

Seven others were killed during Kashmiri's revenge attack near the border post. The soldier's severed head was displayed in several Pakistani newspapers, and according to one part of the story that hasn't been verified, Kashmiri drove around with the head somehow mounted on his car before delivering it to the chief of the army, Pervez Musharraf, and receiving a large cash reward for killing an Indian officer.

Later, Kashmiri was arrested and tortured for attempting to murder none other than Pervez Musharraf with a car bomb. By that time Musharraf had become the president of Pakistan.

Kashmiri escaped with his life from that incident, too.

Headley had never heard of a more worthy fighter.

Kashmiri had been his own man for a long time.

Sure, he had connections to several terrorist groups and organizations, but he always seemed to fall afoul of them. Since 2005, he was the so-called operational leader of the feared terrorist group Harkat-ul-Jihad-al-Islami—commonly known as HuJI—which was behind acts of terrorism in Pakistan, Kashmir, Bangladesh, India, and Afghanistan. Kashmiri promoted himself at the same time as the leader of a faction known as Brigade 313, named after the 313 men who fought for the prophet Muhammad in the city of Badr, routing Abu Sufyan and his thousand men in a violent clash in the year 624. It's considered one of the most important battles in the Muslim narrative about Muhammad.

Brigade 313 was a sort of umbrella organization for a long series of different terrorist groups, consisting of Taliban supporters from

Pakistan and several Lashkar-e-Taiba members, in addition to members of HuJI.

In the only interview Kashmiri gave in later years, he wouldn't directly say just how big Brigade 313 was.

"I cannot tell you," Kashmiri told the *Asian Times* journalist. "Except war is all tactics and this is all Brigade 313 is about: reading the enemy's mind and reacting accordingly. The world thought that Prophet Mohammad only left women behind. They forgot there were real men also who did not know what defeat was all about. The world is only familiar with those so-called Muslims who only follow the direction of the air and who don't have their own will. They do not have their own minds or dimensions of their own. The world has yet to see real Muslims. They have so far only seen Osama and Mullah Omar, while there are thousands of others. Wolves only respect a lion's iron slap; lions do not impress with the logic of a sheep."

"Can we expect more attacks in the same fashion as the one in Mumbai?" the journalist asked. Before the interview he had been taken to Kashmiri blindfolded and moved from place to place for several days, to make sure he wasn't being followed.

"That was nothing compared to what has already been planned for the future," Kashmiri answered coolly.

"Even against Israel and the USA?"

"I am not a traditional jihadi cleric who is involved in sloganeering. As a military commander, I would say every target has a specific time and reasons, and the responses will be forthcoming accordingly."

Kashmiri stepped into the room and gave Headley a very strong handshake.

Heavily armed guards protected Kashmiri around the clock, but even so, he was rarely seen without an AK-47 on his shoulders. Always prepared for the unexpected.

Kashmiri's face was more worn than his forty-five years justified. But he was in good shape, strong and fit.

In the only known photo of him, Kashmiri is wearing classic American Ray-Ban aviator sunglasses, which he rarely took off and which half hid his missing eye behind red-tinted lens. He had colored his long beard with henna so that it had a reddish glow—perhaps as the prophet Muhammad did, according to some accounts, when he was en route to war.

Kashmiri was always at war—with everyone and anyone who wronged his Muslim brothers and sisters, or denied or offended Islam in its strictest, most literal form.

"The entire Muslim community is one body and we will take revenge for all injustices and tyranny," he said.

Headley and Kashmiri spoke of the injustices committed in Denmark and of the cartoons of Muhammad, which Kashmiri found both "humiliating" and "degrading."

Headley also told Kashmiri about his trip to Copenhagen and Aarhus earlier in the year, and of his increasingly detailed dreams of an attack that would balance an account that had sat in Denmark's favor for too long.

Kashmiri quickly declared that he would help punish Denmark.

Jyllands-Posten was chosen as the target. The time was "soon." The reason was the Muhammad cartoons. And the response would be deadly.

Headley was brought to Kashmiri by Pasha, who feared that Lashkar was losing its courage and might give up the plans for an attack on Denmark. Pasha and Headley had taken two others, Nawaz and Ijaz, with them to visit the one-eyed legend.

Nawaz was a close friend of Pasha's, and Ijaz was one of Headley's old classmates from the military academy. Ijaz had resigned from Pakistan's air force, and it just so happened that Ilyas Kashmiri knew his brother, who likely worked for the Pakistani intelligence agency, ISI.

It was a small world. Especially in these circles.

Kashmiri and Headley spoke of the international jihad for several hours.

Headley couldn't help but laugh to himself when the terrorist leader said "shistem" instead of "system." His pronunciation was strange. But Headley listened attentively to each and every word.

There are many ways to look at al-Qaeda.

The terrorist organization was born out of the cooperative effort of several men with different backgrounds and in different countries who were all seeking to pull the fundamentalist Muslim battle for freedom in different directions. Through a series of coincidences, the men were gathered in "the Base"—the literal Arabic translation of "al-Qaeda"—in the late 1980s by the charismatic Osama bin Laden and the ideologically fervent Ayman al-Zawahiri, with the stated goal of throwing the Americans and other infidels out of the Arabian Peninsula and ultimately gathering the Muslim countries under one leader in one caliphate.

There is still disagreement as to how centrally run al-Qaeda really was and is. The group has put out numerous videos, speeches, magazines, audio recordings, and manifestos, but often it has confirmed its connections with known militant Islamists only after they've died. In other cases, not at all. It's more or less impossible to draw a precise diagram of the organization.

Al-Qaeda was behind the double bombings of the American embassies in Dar es Salaam in Tanzania and Nairobi, Kenya, on August 7, 1998, in which 223 were killed and several thousand injured. The group also took responsibility for the attack on the American destroyer USS *Cole* two years later.

The attack on the United States on September 11, 2001, though, was unquestionably the group's greatest "achievement." Despite the earlier attacks, very few people had ever heard of Osama bin Laden before the Twin Towers came crashing down. The day after, bin Laden's name was probably the most widely spoken one on the planet.

Behind the attack lay a broader philosophy. For one, as bin Laden emphasized several times in his speech after the attack, the United States of course needed to be punished for its role in the many conflicts of the Middle East. But more importantly, bin Laden personally saw the United States as a weak nation on the brink of collapse. It just needed a little push.

Bin Laden often used Vietnam as his favorite example. Sure, over fifty thousand Americans had been shipped home in body bags, but it wasn't until after a series of grim pictures showed the realities of the war that opinions changed and people demanded the end of the war.

It was the same with the two Black Hawk helicopters shot down in Somalia in October of 1993, when the American soldiers' bodies were dragged through the streets of Mogadishu. That, too, made the American people give up their desire for war, and the United States soon pulled out of the conflict.

The Americans were weak, easily scared people who lacked the courage for a long, hard battle. They were people without faith in a real religion that could keep morale up.

That was their weakest link. That was how they would conquer the country, bin Laden concluded.

The terrorist attack on September 11 also had the goal of dragging the United States into Afghanistan—a country that notoriously had never been conquered. The United States could probably overpower the Taliban and kill a few thousand jihadists, but in the process the country would also become worn out, economically—the wars in Afghanistan and Iraq have cost the United States at least $1.5 trillion—as well as in human terms with the loss of many soldiers' lives and increased resistance against the foreign policy activism in the Middle East.

Bin Laden figured it like this: if America could first be wounded on her own soil, she could then be crushed when her soldiers landed for close-quarters combat in Afghanistan.

Bin Laden and al-Qaeda saw the economic crisis in 2008 as further proof of their theory: the US was grasping at straws, and before long the states would secede one by one; and one by one, the stars would disappear from the Stars and Stripes.

Maybe president Bush's home state of Texas—the Lone Star State—would be the first.

By some accounts, Ilyas Kashmiri was directly connected to al-Qaeda even before the September 11 attacks. However, he was mostly engaged in the fight against India in the occupied portion of Kashmir until sometime around the year 2005, and then in the large spring offensive in Afghanistan in 2006, when he began to see the world in a new light. Peace would not come to Kashmir, Palestine, Afghanistan, or any other place until the United States had been brought to its knees. The struggle for jihad must be global. Ambitions needed to be greater than to simply cause minor damage to the Indians.

"We are sick and tired of the great Satan's global intrigues, and we aim for its demise to make this world a place of peace and justice," Kashmiri stated.

He also judged that, if they could choose freely, the citizens of Muslim countries would choose either Osama bin Laden or Mullah Omar as their leaders. He had to accept the consequences of that conclusion and allow himself and Brigade 313 to be absorbed into al-Qaeda—which happened through a connection to Mustafa Abu al-Yazid.

From al-Qaeda's side, reward came in the form of bringing Kashmiri into the inner circle. The terrorist group was otherwise led by Arabs, but they made an exception for Kashmiri. In letters from his secret hiding place in Abbottabad in Pakistan, bin Laden wrote to "brother Ilyas" and asked him to prepare a missile attack against Air Force One, should President Obama visit to Pakistan or Afghanistan. Killing Barack Obama would make Vice President Joe Biden the president, which—according to bin Laden—would throw the United States into even deeper water.

Kashmiri was considered a proper leading member of al-Qaeda by many, and he was entrusted with the task of organizing attacks in the West. Later, he was named as a possible successor to Osama bin laden.

Kashmiri hadn't given up India as a terrorism target, but he now saw a real war between Pakistan and India as a way of making the Pakistanis give up their struggle against the Islamists and al-Qaeda in Waziristan—and of drawing India's attention away from the Kashmir region. A war between the two countries would, in a roundabout way, make life easier for Ilyas Kashmiri and his people.

One theory says that it was Kashmiri who, while he was in hiding, pulled the strings and got Lashkar to make their Mumbai attack so violent. There is much that points to Kashmiri and Headley having indirectly worked together in the past. Headley simply didn't know it.

In the house in Waziristan, Kashmiri praised Headley for his planning and surveillance in Mumbai.

"Well done. Good!" he said.

Kashmiri had several good contacts in the West aside from Headley. Among others, he had a loyal Pakistani taxi driver in Chicago whom he had known for fifteen years and who was willing to donate money for a possible terrorist attack on American soil. He might even help with the attack.

Kashmiri also knew people in Europe who had all given their word that they considered him their leader. All he had to do was call.

Headley was impressed by Kashmiri's approach to their plans for terror. It was brutal but based on logic, with a clear line drawn between what was just and what was unjust, Headley thought.

In Kashmiri's mind, there were no limits, only opportunities for bringing about the goal of a unified Islamic nation with Sharia as its law. It would be costly in blood, for sure. But it was necessary.

Kashmiri knew that killing civilians was forbidden by the Qur'an. If anyone slew a person—unless it be in retaliation for murder or for

spreading mischief in the land—it would be as if he slew all mankind.*
To kill a Muslim would be even worse.

But there were ways around such laws. In the Qur'an, Kashmiri
could also find support for the death penalty for apostate Muslims.
So, if a government leader didn't introduce sharia, or—maybe even
worse—if he entered into shady agreements with the American
infidels, then he was not a true Muslim, which in Kashmiri's uni-
verse was the same as apostasy. Thus it was perfectly fine to kill
him.

Kashmiri took it upon himself to decide whether or not Muslims
were on the true path. For example, he judged that Pakistan was certainly not. Pakistan had failed Afghanistan when it had really needed a
helping hand, and now Pakistan was courting America. That was also
why he—unlike Lashkar-e-Taiba—had no problems with attacking
deep in the heart of the county if it was necessary.

Anybody who would not submit to a fundamentalist belief in Islam
could, in reality, be punished by death. Everything could be attacked.

Headley declared that he now considered Kashmiri his new *pir
Sahib*—his master.

He swore an oath of eternal fidelity and loyalty.

Kashmiri was happy to help Headley. In the course of their discussion,
he announced that he had already seen the first "broadcast" of video
recordings of potential targets in Denmark, and he fully trusted Headley to make the plans.

It would be magnificent.

Kashmiri envisioned an attack on *Jyllands-Posten* that would create
the maximum number of casualties, and he immediately proposed a
plan that was far more concrete:

---

* Sura 5, verse 32.

Fill a truck with explosives and drive it either right up to *Jyllands-Posten*'s offices in Copenhagen or directly into the building at full speed. And then push the button.

Kashmiri made it very clear that Headley needn't to wait for his friends from Lashkar if they didn't have the manpower for an attack on Denmark. Kashmiri would provide the necessary men, funds, and weapons, if Headley would just deliver a fully prepared plan.

The attack on Denmark was a mission for Brigade 313. A mission for al-Qaeda.

12

THE WILL

The men opened fire without warning.

First they shot at the wheels of the large bus carrying Sri Lankan cricket players. Then, directly at the police escort. They fired an anti-tank rocket at the bus but, despite the short distance, it flew right over its target and instead struck a utility pole.

It was 8:49 a.m., and in the following seven minutes, all was chaos near the Liberty Market Roundabout in Lahore.

The bus's windows were blasted to pieces, and glass shards flew through the air and lodged themselves in the athletes' shoulders, legs, and arms.

The local Pakistani cricket team was actually supposed to be playing against a team from India, but the Mumbai attack had put a stop to that. Instead, it was now a visiting team from Sri Lanka that suddenly became the target of violence.

After a few minutes, the driver, Mehar Mohammed Khalil, saw an opportunity to escape and, while under fire, he floored it and drove the quarter mile from the roundabout to Gaddafi Stadium, where the team was supposed to be warming up for the day's match. From there, the athletes were evacuated in a Pakistani military helicopter.

Six officers, a driver, and a civilian were killed in the attack that Tuesday morning.

The perpetrators escaped, but witnesses and amateur recordings from the roundabout made it clear that they were dealing with ten to twelve young men.

That the cricket players got away with their lives, and that the mission immediately appeared to have been a fiasco, did nothing to change the fact that in its execution it was a nearly perfect terrorist attack.

The method was similar to the attack in Mumbai just three months earlier. The men wore backpacks, were young, had powerful weapons, appeared out of nowhere, and fired without hesitation.

Another thing was that Lashkar had previously condemned cricket in a fatwa, as it was—according to the group—"an evil and sinful" sport, which for many Pakistanis had become "a new religion" that prevented them from fulfilling their religious responsibilities.

"The British gave Muslims the bat, snatched the sword, and said to them: 'You take this bat and play cricket. Give us your sword. With its help we will kill you and rape your women,'" Lashkar wrote in an article. They continued:

"It is sad that Pakistanis are committing suicide after losing cricket matches to India. But they are not sacrificing their lives to protect the honour of the raped Kashmiri women. To watch a cricket match we would take a day off work. But for jihad, we have not time!"

The day after the attack, the director of the FBI, Robert Mueller, came to Pakistan to discuss the Mumbai attack with Pakistani authorities.

Headley wasn't far from the attack on the roundabout. Lahore was his hometown, and he followed the details in the news and on the Internet. The man who had brought terrorism to India now saw his own city as the scene of a similar attack.

He was convinced that the whole thing had been put into motion by the Indian intelligence service, the Research and Analysis Wing—known as RAW—but probably carried out by local Pakistanis or other agents.

"The logical conclusion is fucking India. (Forgive my French.) It benefits only them," he wrote in an email.

"One look at this operation and it is evident that these guys were not Mujahideen, if they had been, the SL [Sri Lankan] team would have been dead. But one very small point gives me pride. The Indians with 600 commandos and 2000 cops were unable to protect their guests and got people killed from all nationalities in Mumbai but we, on the other hand, by the Grace of God, were able to protect the lives of our guests and gave our own lives to protect them."

Then secretary of state Hillary Clinton condemned the men who carried out the attack and called it an "eerie replica" of the Mumbai attack.

But even if there were many shared qualities, the two attacks couldn't be compared, as a well-informed Headley wrote. "I do believe, however, that the guys who brought you Mumbai will bring you some thing 'sweet' in 'incredible' India to avenge this attack, in the near future," Headley wrote, adding that his evaluation was "just a guess or maybe a prayer."

The truth, though, was another story.

Headley himself had been asked to find targets for a new, large attack in India.

The Mumbai attack had shattered relations between India and Pakistan, and all diplomatic connections had been put on ice. But on the other hand, the attack hadn't itself brought about the desired result. There was no war. No escalation of the fighting in Kashmir. No Indian surrender of Kashmir.

And thus, the factions in Lashkar, together with Ilyas Kashmiri, once again had their sights on India. They wanted to take back Mumbai.

This time, Headley was to find several Israeli hotels in India that could be targeted. A house in Goa apparently often used as a vacation spot by Israeli soldiers was also to be investigated as a potential target.

Israel's carpet bombing of the Gaza Strip around New Year's had particularly made Kashmiri angry. He knew that an effective attack in Israel would be difficult to pull off, but the many Indian hotels filled with Israelis would be obvious, easy targets.

All they needed to do was wait for the right moment.

It would be Headley's last mission before going to Denmark.

The words formed themselves into a proper will.

Headley had sat in front of the keyboard at his computer shortly before midnight on the day of the terrorist attack in Lahore. He was in the process of writing an email to "dear doctor" in Chicago.

Headley had thought about it a lot in the last few months, and no longer had doubts about being ready to sacrifice his life. The cause was worth it. He wanted to dedicate himself completely to the struggle against India and the West. That could easily bring certain consequences.

"As I am traveling and things are so bad these days, I would like to leave a few instructions with you in case of my death or in case I am incapacitated for some reason," Headley wrote to Rana.

He predicted, evidently, that he might end up either in a prison or in a coffin.

He was also afraid. Had he already been discovered? Would the Indians be ready to arrest him when he next landed? Would he travel of his own accord right into the lion's mouth and give them the chance to detain him in the airport? It wasn't unrealistic to think he might be subjected to torture.

Headley was aware that the email might be intercepted and read by foreign intelligence services, so he didn't refer to Mumbai, Denmark, or terrorism at any point.

Most important of all were Headley's wives.

"M2"—as he referred to Faiza Outalha, his wife from Morocco— would be taken care of in particular should Headley himself no longer be able to.

"Please get her to Canada as soon as possible. Till that time comes send her 350 dollars per month thru Pasha. Communicate with her thru him and dont give her your numbers, even if you call her, as the number doesn't show up on card calls. When she does get the visa give her Canadian 6000 dollars and ticket and instructions," Headley wrote.

"M1"—his wife Shazia, in the secret apartment in Chicago—was another story.

"Sit with her and decide whether she should return home immediately, or after 1 year, or after 2 years. We will play this by ear if I am incapacitated, if I die then use your best judgment," wrote Headley, giving detailed instructions about his children.

"I would like my sons to get into Aitchison after their Hifz, so if you can swing it, great, and if not then whatever is the next best option."*

He also weighed his accounts to determine precisely what he owed to various people and instructed Rana as to how he should ensure that, among other things, Headley's investments in some shops in Dubai could continue without problems.

Some of the shop owners owed Headley significant sums of money, and even if he was dead or in prison, Headley wanted these matters taken care of. Shop by shop, he indicated the amount of the rent and when it had last been paid.

The last point in his will was his father's house in Pakistan, of which Headley said he owned 60 percent.

"I want my sons to keep that house at ALL costs . . . I want this issue settled as soon as possible as I fear the other heirs of my father may have a change of niyyat [heart] after my departure or incapacitation," Headley wrote, finishing with these words: "That's all, my old friend. Salaamun alaikum wa rahmatullah wa barakatuh."

May Allah's peace, mercy, and blessings be with you.

---

* Aitchison College is a tradition-rich and prestige-filled boys' school in Lahore. *Hifz* is Qu'ran school.

* * *

Exactly one hundred days after the Mumbai attack, Headley landed once again in India.

Even though he was behind the country's worst terrorist attack in recent history, there was nobody waiting for him in the airport in the capital, New Delhi.

It was pure routine.

Headley moved around by bus, train, and airplane to investigate different spots said to be popular vacation destinations for Israelis. He kept far from Mumbai and his two friends, Rahul Bhatt and Vilas Varak.

At one point, Headley came across a funeral ceremony in the city of Pushkar. While there he got to talking with a Jewish couple and their friend. Over a group breakfast, Headley got a travel tip for a good Jewish hotel in Goa. Shortly thereafter, he traveled to Goa, stayed the night at the place, and added it to his list of potential terrorism targets, though he noted that it was far from optimal.

Headley's hate for the Jewish people and the state of Israel was enormous. He doubted the Holocaust, and if it really had happened, then no more than six thousand Jews lost their lives, according to Headley.

"This seems to be the best thing that ever happened to them. They are milking it till today. They justify all their murders and bombings and 'pre-emptive' actions in the name of the Holocaust. I have to say had all those Jews been alive today, they and their offspring would only have compounded our misery. They would probably have needed some additional Muslim lands to accommodate their population."

An article in the Israeli newspaper *Haaretz* had at one point described a tradition in which Israeli soldiers received a T-shirt upon completing a sniper training course. "One shot, two kills," it said on the T-shirt beneath an illustration of a pregnant Muslim woman framed in crosshairs. Another T-shirt showed a woman in a hijab kneeling next to her child, who lies on the ground before her, bleeding from his head—again seen through crosshairs. Here, the caption was "Better use Durex"—a well-known brand of condom.

The fact that a majority of Israelis had done military service was for Headley one more reason that it was legal to kill "any Israeli, anywhere in the world."

"That's why I feel so much happiness when any of them is beheaded. Nobody deserves it more. I feel no sorrow for their kids or their old and feeble. They are all the same to me," Headley wrote, explaining that he wasn't speaking in the name of Islam, but with his own "cheap feelings."

"Have you seen any Muslim 'terrorist' or other organization or group or country from any sect, Shia or Sunni, ever celebrating the killing of Infants? Or seen the using of any religious text, Gita, Talmud or Bible, as toilet paper, as the Danes did with the Quran last year and Israelis continue to do and post it on the net? There is no comparison between the lofty ideals of Islam and these gutter religions. Now personally I pray that God would give me the opportunity to catch one of these bastards and cut their throats open, to please Him."

In New Delhi, Headley also investigated the national defense academy and a residential area for aspiring officers known as Raksha Bhavan. A bus filled with soon-to-be officers traveling on a daily route between the two locations had "minimal security measures" and would be a "very vulnerable target," Headley noted, filming both the bus and the route.

Headley was particularly enticed by the idea of striking the Indian soldiers. He guessed that a well-coordinated attack against the bus and the academy would cost more Indian officers their lives than all the wars between Pakistan and India together.

The Lashkar people already had a man from Rawalpindi in Pakistan in mind for an attack on the Indian military. But the man had had his Indian visa application denied because he had a long beard.

"Shave your beard and try again," came the message from Lashkar. That's how it would have to be.

Back in Pakistan, Sajid Mir had bad news.

Several people with Lashkar connections had been arrested, and now the terrorist organization was under pressure to keep a low profile. Sajid Mir and his cohort feared that an attack on Denmark would require far too many resources and quite possibly would be discovered while planning was under way.

There was no option but to put Copenhagen on hold, perhaps forever, he explained to Headley at a meeting in Lahore.

Pasha's prediction had been right. When it came down to it, they didn't have the guts.

Headley was angry. Cowards, that was what they were. Attacking Denmark was the most important thing they could do, he thought. There wasn't even a choice; it was a damn responsibility. Sajid Mir knew that full well.

Sajid Mir was, on the other hand, furious about Headley's trip to India. Sajid hadn't approved it, and he didn't care for elements in Lashkar using Headley without his approval. Not even if it was to plan an attack in India that would be greater than Mumbai.

Sajid Mir was also mad to learn that Headley had spoken of his participation in the Mumbai attack to a man by the name of Haroon, who was later arrested in Pakistan.

And it certainly didn't make things better that a Glock pistol that Sajid Mir had once given Headley had, in a roundabout way, come into the possession of this Haroon, who possibly used it in a murder or a kidnapping attempt.

You must leave Lahore, he'll rat you out, and then they'll come after you, Sajid Mir warned.

Major Iqbal, Headley's connection to the Pakistani intelligence service, showed up at the house in Lahore. He was deeply worried.

Kasab—the one survivor of the "boys" from the Mumbai attack—had revealed far too much, Iqbal explained.

Pack everything up that has the slightest connection to Lashkar and leave your house for a while, he ordered. Don't contact me. I'll contact you.

Altogether, it was a big mess.

Headley decided to remain quiet about the trip to Waziristan and his new connection to Ilyas Kashmiri. It was hardly the time to talk about that.

13

CUT THEIR HEADS OFF

Northern Pakistan
May 2009

American unmanned drones could frequently be spotted or heard in the sky over North Waziristan.

Headley looked up.

With small cameras, the drones carefully scanned through bazaars, caravans, and villages in search of the slightest trace of wanted terrorists from Taliban, al-Qaeda, or Lashkar. Sometimes, they were successful.

One early morning, unmanned aircraft had fired two missiles at a religious school in the village of Daande Darpkhel, near Miranshah. Seven Taliban insurgents were killed when the bombs razed two buildings with a resounding bang. At least three women and two children also lost their lives.

The death toll was reported to be as high as eight children dead and eighteen injured.

It was like that with nine out of ten attacks, Headley noted, remarking ironically that "anti-American feelings are a little over a 100%."

Headley had driven to Miranshah after the incident with Sajid Mir. Now he saw the refugee camps for the displaced Afghans who had lived in the area since the war with the Soviet Union ended, twenty years earlier. And he saw how life was in the poverty-stricken Pakistani tribal areas.

Headley had no issue identifying himself with the global jihad, which was represented in the Miranshah bazaar by Chechens, Uzbeks, Tajiks, Russians, Bosnians, some people from a few EU countries, and of course, the Arab brothers.

He estimated that roughly every third inhabitant of the town was a foreigner who had come to fight.

"The foreign fighters, I was told, come here for some R&R—rest and relaxation—while waiting to join the fight in nearby Afghanistan," Headley wrote in his notes from the trip. "Drones can be seen and heard almost constantly overhead and people have learned to live with it. These are a very Independent minded and fearless people."

Officially, the Pakistani army was at war with the Taliban, but it seemed to be a halfhearted effort, Headley noted.

The people in the region weren't afraid of the Pakistani soldiers. On the contrary, they laughed at them. During the trip, Headley himself had seen many checkpoints that had been abandoned by the army. When a military convoy drove by, he had seen the angst in the soldiers' eyes.

The actual front must be over a hundred kilometers away, Headley thought.

The real threat was the small drones in the sky. They were controlled remotely by young American soldiers sitting in safety and drinking cola while they killed freely, using the small buttons on their joysticks.

It was yet another sign of the Americans' cowardice and another reason that Americans were so hated by the locals, Headley thought. Several thousand had been killed by these invisible machines of death—and many of them were innocent civilians.

On the other hand, a thorough investigation cited in the Pakistani media had shown that people in the area were most afraid of the holy warriors, and thus welcomed the Americans with open arms.

"Such a statement can only come from some soft idiot, totally oblivious to this culture and divorced from reality, writing from the safety of his air-conditioned office, far, far away," Headley thought.

He wrote many emails about the trip to his old classmates. But at no time did he reveal the real reason for traveling in the volatile region: he had come to meet with the one-eyed Ilyas Kashmiri for the second time. He wanted to be a soldier in Brigade 313.

During the long trip from Lahore to Miranshah, Headley had stopped in the city of Banu to switch his rental car's license plates for stolen ones as a security measure.

Before meeting Kashmiri he went down to a gun shop in the city where locals bought and sold rifles, ammunition, and handguns.

Kashmiri arrived in Miranshah in his military jeep, surrounded by a number of heavily armed men. He greeted Headley and the two went into the same house where they had met a few months earlier when they first spoke of an attack on *Jyllands-Posten*.

Now, the house was filled with suicide vests. They were for "an operation," Headley learned.

The men spoke of the drones in the sky above them. Headley said that they would never escape them. If they should manage to shoot a few down, the Americans would just build ten new ones. They had the money for it.

But Kashmiri had an answer for that, too.

He dreamed of attacking Lockheed Martin, the world's largest producer of weapons, and killing the American company's director, Robert J. Stevens. Among other things, Lockheed Martin was behind the Hellfire missiles used by the drones in Pakistan. Kashmiri figured that killing the director would frighten the company and make it stop delivering to the American military.

The terrorist leader told Headley that he had men in the United States who had already begun the initial assessments of Lockheed

Martin's headquarters in Bethesda, Maryland, just a half-hour's drive from the White House. Perhaps Headley could help with those plans at some point, Kashmiri suggested. They'd have to see about that.

The two men agreed, however, that the most important thing right now was an attack in Denmark.

The men discussed the possibility of a more "generalized" attack in Copenhagen. They could attack Copenhagen Central Station or other public places where there were lots of people. It would send the same signal as an actual attack on *Jyllands-Posten*'s offices, which were more difficult to access.

They wanted to attack the official Denmark. As prime minister, Anders Fogh Rasmussen had refused to apologize for the cartoons. Headley considered that to be among Denmark's crimes. Recently, Rasmussen had been elected secretary general of NATO. That was how the West rewarded the man who had refused to intervene against the drawings. That was offensive.

Kashmiri revealed a secret to Headley: over the course of several years, he had been working on building a network of faithful Muslims who had already been placed in Europe as "sleeper cells." These were people with steady jobs, residence permits, and in some cases, even passports and new citizenships. But they were people who were still loyal to him, nonetheless.

Headley could get in touch with some of these men, who had "money, weapons, and manpower" to carry out the suicide attack, if he could just provide a good attack plan.

Kashmiri revealed that the men lived, among other places, in Great Britain and Sweden. The men in Great Britain came from the Kotli district on the border with India—where Kashmiri himself had lived. They could be trusted.

Kashmiri gave Headley some phone numbers so he could contact them and bring them on board. He also needed to make clear to them that they needed to make martyr videos before the attack.

They need to know that this is a suicide mission, Kashmiri declared.

* * *

Al-Qaeda had been working for years to refine the plans for a new attack in Europe.

In 2009, a high-ranking member of al-Qaeda authored a document entitled "Future Works," which was a collection of loosely organized thoughts about possible spectacular attacks in the West.

Among the suggestions was the hijacking of a cruise ship on the open ocean. Hostages would be dressed in orange prison outfits—like those worn by prisoners at Guantánamo Bay—and then be filmed as they were executed over the course of several days. The killings would stop only if the local authorities could convince the Americans to release specific, predetermined prisoners. The Americans would hardly be willing to give in, but that didn't mean much—the attack would create fear and confusion. Westerners would realize that their governments didn't want to save them even if they were given the chance.

Other plans concerned things like simply repeating the Mumbai attack in a large European city, causing the most damage possible. It was cheap, and it would work.

Documents containing these plans were found in 2011 on a memory card that a twenty-two-year-old Austrian citizen had smuggled to Germany from Pakistan, hidden in his underpants. In a file containing a pornographic film by the name of "Kick Ass," there was embedded an encrypted file called "Sexy Tanja." When the German intelligence service succeeded in cracking the encryption, they gained access to a wealth of information concerning concrete terrorism plans.

Al-Qaeda planned all its attacks based on an analysis of the most likely reactions in Western media. It wasn't just about killing. It was about making the attacks so violent and savage that TV broadcasts and front pages of newspapers would be devoid of anything else for weeks. The goal was to scare the Western countries' citizens into demanding their militaries return home. The Western troops would crawl out of the Middle East and never return.

Kashmiri had been thinking along the same lines for the attack in Copenhagen.

Jyllands-Posten's employees couldn't just be killed and left dead in their offices. When they had been shot or stabbed to death, their heads would be cut off, and the severed heads would be thrown out of the windows onto the street in front of Kongens Nytorv, King's New Square.

Kashmiri predicted that this macabre detail would draw the greatest possible "attention" from the authorities, and likely millions of Western TV viewers who would follow the attack live as breaking news.

Danish special forces would presumably be superior to their Indian counterparts, so during planning and execution, everyone had to be aware that they would surely not have three full days to fight, as they had in Mumbai. There might only be twenty minutes for the operation.

Kashmiri reasoned that the severed heads would force the special forces to storm the building. The Western self-image simply could not tolerate the killing of hostages and the defacing of their bodies while their elite soldiers looked on from a safe distance and tried to negotiate with the hostage takers over the phone.

They would be forced to attack—which would result in a violent bloodbath in which the Muslim suicide soldiers would emerge as true martyrs.

The beheading of the *Jyllands-Posten* employees spoke to Headley. That was the right way to kill people, he thought.

Ilyas Kashmiri himself had decapitated an Indian soldier, an act that had brought him great honor. Omar Sheikh's killing of the journalist Daniel Pearl had brought him great honor too.

Headley recalled an episode a month earlier when a forty-two-year-old Polish geologist by the name of Piotr Stańczak was kidnapped in the Pakistani city of Attock. The kidnappers guaranteed that they would send Piotr Stańczak back to Poland alive if the Pakistani authorities freed a number of Taliban prisoners. But that didn't happen, so they beheaded Stańczak, broadcasted the video recordings of the killing, and threw his body into the street.

The killing of the Pole was a hot topic among Headley's Pakistani friends, the majority of whom earnestly distanced themselves from both the result and the method.

But not Headley.

He maintained that it was "great" that the man had been killed, as nobody could know if the man had really been a spy, an engineer, or a journalist from the *Wall Street Journal*.

"After all a Mossad or RAW agent is not going to be wearing a name tag stating his rank in that organization," Headley explained. "So in the absence of this information you need to be balanced in your comments," Headley wrote to a colleague who had denounced the beheading.

"If innocence or guilt is irrelevant to you, and it's the violence that is abhorrent to you, than please feel free to also vent your outrage on other atrocities as well, like the recent Gaza massacre. Let us know how you feel, when you see little limbless children lying in hospitals or fathers burying their kids with tears in their eyes, or old folks sitting under the sky next to their demolished houses," he wrote.

Headley went on to make reference to his detailed insight into the local conditions, arguing that the presence of 1,400 Polish NATO troops in Afghanistan had created a situation in which traditional Muslim hospitality couldn't be expended on "Poles or other Europeans." He explained that the many spies in the area who were identifying targets for drone strikes or exchanging other information for cash justified the slaughter. "So when your brothers catch these gentlemen, they cut their throats open and air the videos to discourage this behavior. Is that so hard to understand?

"As far as beheadings go, this is a punishment reserved for those who help Predators with Target Acquisition and relay the whereabouts of the Mujahideen to the Occupying Crusaders and their Murtadd allies. These folks have a lot of blood on their hands. It seems appropriate."

Headley claimed that, in reality, beheading wasn't barbaric at all; it was a rather fine method of killing people.

"Execution by beheading is our culture and really is less painful and more respectful than hanging or electrocution. The lethal injection method is really appropriate for a dog or a horse or a cat by 'putting them to sleep' but, in my opinion, it is demeaning to kill a human being that way. The best way for a man to die is with the sword. Our beloved Prophet SAW preferred this method himself."

Kashmiri thought they could use for three or four armed men to keep the whole second floor of the *Jyllands-Posten* office in Copenhagen under control. Headley agreed.

They needed to move quickly, Kashmiri said. He let on that "the elders"—the leaders of al-Qaeda, among them Osama bin Laden—had been fully briefed on the plans and had approved of the method in a secret meeting.

"The elders" were very impatient, though, and required from Headley that the attack must take place "as quickly as possible."

Headley received about 85,000 Pakistani rupees, the equivalent of around 800 US dollars, along with the message to go to Copenhagen and make new video recordings, draw up new plans, and collect new details.

Now it was Headley's mission.

14

THE EUROPEAN CELLS

Derby, England
July 2009

The British intelligence service had been keeping an eye on two Muslim men in the city of Derby for some time. These men had connections to several fundamentalist groups in the city, so their telephones and Internet activities were monitored.

In early summer 2009, agents discovered that the men were expecting a guest from the United States. There wasn't much information on the guest, though, other than that the Muslims called him David, and he was apparently American.

The intelligence service shared this information with the FBI, but there wasn't enough information to be of use to them. There are over three million Americans with the first name David.

Based on the profile the men in Derby had, the American intelligence officers thought that the man must have contacts in Pakistani terrorist groups, perhaps Lashkar, perhaps Ilyas Kashmiri's Brigade 313, perhaps al-Qaeda. But they weren't sure about anything.

On July 23, the FBI requested the help of US Customs in identifying the man. Besides the details of his name and nationality, they knew that he was traveling from the United States to Europe soon. There weren't many tracks to follow, but they had access to one effective tool not known to many in 2009.

After the terrorist attacks on New York and Washington, DC, on September 11, 2001, European countries—more or less against their will—gave American intelligence services access to data on all passengers buying tickets for flights to and from the United States.

Regardless of whether a transatlantic ticket was purchased on the Internet, by telephone, or through a travel agency, the system automatically created a so-called Passenger Name Record to be logged in a special registry, which is today managed by the Department of Homeland Security. The registry contains data on several million people's planned and canceled trips and can be used to sniff out suspicious travel activity—both before and perhaps after a terrorist attack. Sorted by airline and booking method, each and every search of the database can give access to an array of sensitive personal information concerning passports, credit cards, and private addresses.

US Customs typed in the sparse details they had: David, American, traveling across the Atlantic—and immediately received several hundred possible candidates. That would take far too long to sort through.

Shortly thereafter, though, British intelligence officers were able to supply the Americans with yet another otherwise innocent detail: the guest would be flying Lufthansa.

That was the missing piece of the puzzle. Now the analysts had just one name on the screen: David Coleman Headley. American citizen. Passport number 097536400, issued March 10, 2006, in Washington, DC, valid until 2016. Born June 30, 1960, in Washington, DC.

The man had previously flown in and out of the United States, often headed to the Middle East. Most recently, he had arrived in New York from Pakistan, around June 10. There, he switched to a JetBlue Airlines flight to Chicago, where he landed on June 11. Now he was in possession of a ticket that would take him to Manchester around July 26.

But who was this Headley? And why would he be meeting with two fundamentalist Muslims in Derby?

From an office in Chicago, a team including FBI special agent Lorenzo Benedict was put on the case. They called it Operation Black Medallion.

Derby is like most other central English cities. It's foggy, industrial jobs are on their way out, and one of the city's prides is beer. Derby is also the home to the company behind the popular Tomb Raider series of computer games. One of the main streets in the city center is even named Lara Croft Way.

Derby also has a sizable Muslim population, a portion of whom have ties to the most extremely radicalized circles on the planet.

One of them was Umrad Javed, who took part in a protest in front of the Danish embassy in London not long after the publication of the Muhammad cartoons.

Javed was captured on video yelling things like "Denmark, you will pay—with your blood, your blood," and "Bomb, bomb Denmark." Several of the more than 450 people who took part in the protest held signs with messages like "What do you do with these people? How do you kill them? Cut their throat!"

After the protest, the police raided Javed's residence. There they found a leaflet titled "Kill Them by the Sword Wherever They Are," which encouraged terrorism. Javed later received a four-year prison sentence for inciting violence.

Parviz Khan—also from Derby—was convicted in February 2008 of planning the beheading of a British soldier. He was so committed to this that he taught his five- and seven-year-old sons how to carry out the beheading.

"How do you want to deal with these people? How do you want to kill them? Cut their heads off!" he told his children while his home was under audio surveillance by the British police. When he asked his children who they loved, they answered loudly: "Sheik Osama bin Laden." For his murder plans, Khan was sentenced to life in prison.

Derby—which is about the size of Buffalo, New York—was also the home of Albanian-born Krenar Lusha, who in 2008 was caught red-handed in his home downloading instructions on how to prepare a suicide bomb. In his cellar, he had almost twenty gallons of gasoline, together with books and videos about time bombs. And on his computer, police also found several videos of long, graphic recordings of beheadings carried out by Islamist groups. He was later sentenced to seven years in prison and then deported.

Headley was going to England to visit men like these.

On July 26, 2009, Headley landed in Manchester and drove the sixty or so miles southwest to the city where Ilyas Kashmiri had his contacts.

The two Derby men went by Bash and Simon, and at first glance, they lived a life just like that of many other Pakistani immigrants in the area. They attended the local mosque in the city and mostly kept to themselves. They also had connections to people in the city's fundamentalist circles, which was the reason the intelligence service had them under surveillance.

But only a small, closed group knew that Bash and Simon were considered friends of one of the world's most wanted terrorists.

At this time, there was a $600,000 reward for details on Ilyas Kashmiri, which was later raised to $5 million. It hadn't been long since Kashmiri showed up at number four on the Pakistani Ministry of the Interior's list of their most wanted criminals.

Bash and Simon were born in the Kotli district in northeastern Pakistan, on the border with the part of Kashmir under Indian control. It was there, under the names Basharat and Sufiyaan, that they had come into contact with Kashmiri, who now considered them "his men" in Europe.

Both Headley and Kashmiri had had problems getting in touch with the sleeper cell in Derby by telephone. But now Headley stood face to face with Bash and Simon.

Headley told them about the attack. About the possibilities for breaking into the *Jyllands-Posten* offices. About the importance of the operation. He also passed on Kashmiri's message that the men were to supply weapons and 10,000 pounds for the plan. And that they were to produce martyr videos.

They likely wouldn't survive the mission, Headley explained. That wasn't part of the plan.

Bash and Simon replied that *Jyllands-Posten* and Denmark had earned the black mark of retaliation—of that there was no doubt. But they were lukewarm about the plans for the attack and made Headley aware that their loyalty to Kashmiri was no longer unconditional, which resulted in a heated discussion between Headley and the two men.

Bash used the harshest words. He claimed that Kashmiri's son had misused a large sum of money designated for jihad for private purposes. He would not put his life into the hands of such a man.

Simon was more receptive, but he expressed doubts about the possibility of carrying out the attack. He'd consider it further, but first he had to travel to Pakistan to hear more details from Kashmiri himself before he finally made a decision.

The men also had to acknowledge that they had no weapons. Nor did they have immediate access to them. Sure, they could help with money, but not 10,000 pounds right there and then. Headley got 2,000 pounds, cash in hand. That would pay for a few plane tickets, but it was hardly enough for a terrorist attack.

Headley left Derby disappointed and continued to the next person on Ilyas Kashmiri's contact list.

The apartment in Stockholm, Sweden, was right by Vanadislunden, one of Stockholm's largest, nicest parks, and just a minute's walk from Stefanskyrkan, a hundred-year-old church with a crucified Jesus in relief over the arched window.

But in the seventh unit on Döbelnsgatan Street, neither the park nor Jesus was of any particular interest. Here lived a forty-seven-year-old Swedish-Moroccan by the name of Farid Lamrabet.

Headley had heard about Farid a few times through his connections in Pakistan. He knew, among other things, that Farid could be "of great assistance," since he "happened" to be "in the same branch as us," and that he had "contacts in the north."

Farid was from Casablanca in Morocco and had come to Sweden in 1985, where he first tried his hand in the hospitality industry and then in a variety of different businesses. Among other things, he imported Moroccan artisan crafts, which he sold in central Stockholm.

Farid Lamrabet had immediately integrated himself into Swedish society, and although he spoke perfectly good Swedish, he politely ended many of his sentences with a "*förstår du?*" [do you understand?], to make sure that his message had gotten through. In 1993, he became a Swedish citizen.

In the more radical Muslim circles of Sweden, they knew another side of Farid. Here, he occasionally went under the name of Abu Umar and had close ties to international terrorism, sectarian killings, and brutal violence.

Among Farid's friends was Mohamed Moumou, who for several years had had a c/o address at Farid's apartment on Döbelnsgatan. Like Farid, Moumou was born in Morocco, and he too had come to Sweden in the eighties, later becoming a citizen in the nineties. Moumou was part of the innermost circle tied to a controversial mosque in the suburb of Brandbergen, south of Stockholm, and in March of 2004 he had been detained and questioned by the Swedish Security Service, or Säpo, for potential involvement with the terrorist attack in Madrid that same year.

When Moumou was released, he traveled to Denmark. His purpose for this trip is still unknown. But by all accounts, Moumou was free for only a short time: he was arrested during a large-scale police operation at a furniture warehouse in Ishoj, Denmark, a small municipality with a large immigrant population, after Moroccan authorities had issued an international arrest warrant. They demanded that he be extradited for judicial proceedings pertaining to his role in the bombing attack in Casablanca in 2003, which had cost several people their lives.

Mohamed Moumou sat behind bars in Copenhagen for one month—before the Danish Ministry of Justice reached the conclusion that the Moroccans' charges were so poorly supported by the evidence that he couldn't be extradited. Moumou was instead released and sent home to Sweden.

In May 2006, Moumou was wanted once again. The US State Department wanted him on the UN list of terrorists and people with close ties to al-Qaeda. That would, practically speaking, forbid him from traveling outside of Sweden, and all his assets could be frozen.

"Cable 77969" was sent from the State Department to a number of American embassies in the Northern Hemisphere.

In Oslo, the question was what the Norwegians' reaction would be if the very controversial radical Islamist Mullah Krekar ended up on the terrorist list. The embassy in Norway replied that the government wouldn't officially have anything to with his addition to the list, but apart from that, it was just fine. Shortly thereafter, Krekar was added to the list.

The write-up also arrived, marked with the word "SECRET," at the American embassy in Casablanca. What would happen if the Americans asked to have both Mohamed Moumou and Farid Lamrabet added to the list of potential terrorists? From Casablanca, intelligence officer Douglas Greene replied that the embassy "does not object to the proposed designations of Moroccan nationals Mohammed Moumou and Farid Lamrabet."

In a confidential reply sent to the State Department on the evening of Friday, May 26, 2006, the embassy said it didn't expect any trouble from the local authorities and, on the contrary, expected that the Moroccan authorities "would support these designations." This got Moumou added to the UN terrorist list a few months later. Farid didn't end up on it, but he was added to a special observation list maintained by American authorities some months after.

Mohamed Moumou, who was now a wanted terrorist, was never captured. Not in Sweden, nor in Denmark, nor in any other place.

But there's much that points to him having stayed in Copenhagen in May 2006 and having flown thereafter to Damascus in Syria, and from there, probably quickly on to Iraq. Here, he became second-in-command to terrorist leader Abu Mus'ab al-Zarqawi, in al-Qaeda's feared Iraqi division, which was responsible for several suicide bombings in those years.

It was also from his new base in Iraq that Moumou began recruiting volunteers for suicide bombings in Denmark. That is, until he was killed in a firefight against American forces in the Iraqi city of Mosul. Shortly thereafter, he was proclaimed a martyr.

While Moumou was escaping to Iraq, Farid's business was raided by Ekobrottsmyndigheten, the Swedish Economic Crime Authority, which in addition to evidence of tax fraud discovered a can of tear gas and two credit cards with fake magnetic stripes.

Headley didn't know the whole backstory when he left Derby in 2009 and traveled via Zürich to Stockholm to visit Farid. He knew only that Farid was a man he could trust.

The two men met in Stockholm. Headley was like a giant to the short Farid, who had a long, black beard and slicked-back hair. The meeting was apparently very short. Farid knew he was under intense surveillance from Säpo, so he could only decline to participate in Headley's operation.

"I'm sorry, brother, but I cannot help you," he told him.

Pass the task along, was what Headley replied.

A few days later, on a busy Friday, the last day of July, Headley boarded a train from Stockholm to Copenhagen.

The central train station in Copenhagen was filled with people. A younger man was standing with his green backpack in a group that was soon to be boarding a train. A woman in a red sweater with a large briefcase was about to buy a ticket from a vending machine, with her daughter.

And Headley stood with his camera, about to take new recordings and gather information for his terrorist attack. He filmed the busy train yard inside and outside with the built-in camera of his Sony Ericsson mobile phone and made sure that there were plenty of good shots of the main train station's construction, with McDonald's and other fast-food restaurants in the background.

He went down through the popular Strøget pedestrian way and past the shops, stopping as he reached Kongens Nytorv, King's New Square. He filmed some more here while speaking from behind the camera—as if he were just an ordinary American tourist adding commentary for his family back home in Chicago.

"This is the famous concert hall, build in 1748, Kings Square . . . And Hotel d'Angleterre," Headley said as he panned from the Royal Theatre across the grand square to the exclusive hotel, where the façade, with its large windows and fluttering Danish flag on top, became part of the film.

The roofs of the hotel and the Royal Theatre were among the positions Headley expected the police's snipers to occupy during the attack.

Bus number 15 drove past Headley, who now stood not far from the entrance to the King's New Square subway station.

"Cars. Really busy. And besides the roads, bicycles," Headley said as he aimed the camera so that *Jyllands-Posten*'s offices were clearly visible in the background.

Headley noticed a yellow tourist bus parked on King's New Square not far from *Jyllands-Posten*. That looked promising as far as the plans to drive a vehicle filled with explosives up to the building were concerned. It seemed possible, at any rate.

The three-minute-long film ended with yet another sweeping motion across King's New Square. "It's full of ice in the winter, so people can ice-skate," Headley said, almost laughing.

At 12:45 p.m., Headley stood outside a hair salon on Store Kongensgade, which leads through King's New Square right between the Hotel d'Angleterre and *Jyllands-Posten*, which Headley had observed in the video. The recordings showed the Danish Royal Life Guards on their way down the street.

"Here are the guards from the palace. They are changing the guards or something," said Headley, allowing the camera to follow the marching soldiers as they passed him.

Headley followed the guards up Gothersgade to the nearby Life Guard Barracks at Rosenborg Castle. Here, he struck up a conversation with a captain by the fence that leads into the barracks. The captain told Headley that their weapons were always loaded with live ammunition.

"Why are they loaded? There doesn't seem to be any threat around here," Headley said.

"You never know," the captain replied.

Headley nodded. Inwardly, he was about to explode with laughter.

In one of Headley's scenarios, someone would throw a hand grenade into the midst of the soldiers, grab the dead ones' weapons, and then, armed with them, storm *Jyllands-Posten*. This plan had a couple of elegant advantages. One, they got access to loaded weapons in the middle of Copenhagen; and two, it would send a clear signal to the Danes and the rest of the world that not even the queen's personal guards can feel safe from global jihad.

In Copenhagen, Headley also looked for places where he could buy weapons. He wasn't successful, but that wasn't an unsolvable problem anyway. There were enough weapons in Europe, Headley thought. He had a connection in Germany who would probably be able to procure weapons that could then be smuggled over the border. Headley himself had traveled across the border in January, and there had largely been no security. It would be easy.

A few days later, with rain pouring down, Headley returned to film the Life Guard.

"They march like this every day," he said on the recordings.

On another evening, he was at King's New Square yet again.

"This is the French embassy," he recorded himself saying as he walked up to the neighboring building, *Jyllands-Posten*'s offices, where he filmed through the windows to get further details.

"Here you are," he said coolly.

The Jewish synagogue in Copenhagen lies well hidden behind a tall fence on a narrow street.

Headley visited the synagogue on Krystalgade, observed it from outside, and took pictures as he—just to be safe—added it to the list of possible targets in Copenhagen.

In the evening, he read the book *How to Pray Like a Jew*, a guide to Jewish traditions, as he considered how he could get close to Flemming Rose.

Like the rest of Lashkar, Headley was still convinced that Rose was a Jew. This belief had gone viral on several Islamist websites, apparently after someone had found a photo of a smiling Rose with a large nose. A radical Islamist group claimed they could even prove that Rose was actually born in Ukraine and worked as an agent for Mossad. Even his name was suspicious to the conspiracy theorists. And a 2004 interview with the American historian Daniel Pipes, who was critical of Islam, was presented along with Rose's translation of the presumably pro-Israeli Russian ex-president Boris Yeltsin's memoir *Against the Grain* as definitive proof of Rose's hidden Jewishness.

As for *Jyllands-Posten*, the paper's six-pointed logo was often compared to the Star of David—which in Islamist circles, of course, documented the paper's Jewish affiliations.

On the evening of Saturday, August 1, Headley sent an email to Rana in Chicago asking him to check a telephone book for Copenhagen to find the numbers and addresses of "any" editors for "the newspaper I plan to advertise with." He also asked Rana to check the website of the *Jyllands-Posten*'s publisher.

Headley knew they it wasn't likely that they would find the editors' private addresses, but he asked Rana to try anyway. Rana was unsuccessful.

While Headley was in Copenhagen, *Jyllands-Posten*'s leadership was working on their final plans to move the paper's offices from King's New Square to its current building near City Hall Square, which previously housed the newspapers *Politiken* and *Ekstra Bladet*. The move would take place later in the summer.

It's not certain whether Headley knew the precise details of the planned move, but during his time in Denmark, he made at least one video recording at City Hall Square of the then-future offices.

On a rented bicycle, Headley rode around Copenhagen searching for alternate targets. He ended up with thirteen videos, which he thought would be relevant to the plans for a successful attack.

Headley packed his bag and left the hotel in Copenhagen.

It was Wednesday, August 5, 2009, and his second trip to Denmark was coming to an end. He had been more alert now than on his first visit to the country in January. That time, his communication had been sparse, and he hadn't written to any of his old classmates in Pakistan. This time he was more relaxed.

He had sat inside the hotel by the front desk a few days earlier and written to Rana while it was raining outside. And he had also sent a number of emails to Pakistan. Everything was going well.

"I am a little busy now, but would like to respond . . . if I may, later," he wrote one evening to a friend, without revealing his stay in Denmark. With others, he continued the seemingly endless discussions about Islam.

"If we sit down and count to see which religion rates #1 in the killing of innocents since its inception till today, Christianity would win with a huge margin. No other religion, Muslim, Jew, Hindu or Buddhist, can even come close," Headley wrote from his keyboard in Copenhagen.

From the hotel, Headley took his luggage down to Terminal 3 of Copenhagen Airport. He allowed himself a certain amount of freedom. On his first trip, he had traveled across Germany to avoid being noticed or added to some sort of list. He wasn't worried about that this time. Nobody was watching him, he thought.

He checked into Delta flight 69 to Atlanta. From there, he would fly to New York, and then home to his family and Rana in Chicago.

Headley went through the security checkpoint, the duty-free area, and onward to gate C28, where the white Boeing 767 was ready to take off at 11:25 a.m.

It was good-bye to Denmark for now.

But Headley hadn't bought just one ticket. He would be back again. In his inbox was an order confirmation for a return ticket to Copenhagen, just three months later.

On October 29, at 6:15 p.m., he would once again leave the United States to arrive in Denmark after 8:10 a.m., local time.

Then everything would be in place.

15

THE SUSPICION

Hartsfield-Jackson Atlanta International Airport
Atlanta, Georgia
Wednesday, August 5, 2009

Headley was pulled aside. Delta 69 had landed not long before at the enormous Hartsfield-Jackson airport in Atlanta with Headley on board. After the ten-hour flight from Copenhagen, he was tired. It was a warm afternoon.

The routine at customs was nothing new for him.

As a former heroin smuggler, Headley was on the list of people who frequently got pulled to the side in airports. It had happened fairly regularly over the last twenty years: in 1993, 1996, 2001, 2002, and 2007. This time, he was taken to a small room, where his luggage and personal possessions were searched. The customs official took particular interest in the contents of Headley's suitcase and wasted no time on small talk.

"What were you doing in Copenhagen?"

Headley explained that he had been in Denmark to set up the local office of an immigration business operating out of Chicago. He was working as the manager of the European branch, and he had been taking care of various steps preliminary to establishing the Danish branch.

Yet among Headley's entire possessions—his carry-on baggage, his suitcase, and his jacket—the officer couldn't find a single document remotely suggesting that Headley was starting a business on the other side of the Atlantic. No draft rental agreements for the office, no paperwork describing the company, no receipts for purchases or the like, no clever slogans on stickers. Just some very nondescript business cards.

The officer found Headley's explanation suspicious and asked more questions about the trip, which Headley answered as best he could. But the story didn't hold together.

Yet Headley's effects didn't point to anything particularly criminal either, and with an American passport there wasn't evidence enough for anything other than to welcome the man back to his homeland, close up his bags, and send him on his way through the airport.

After his flight from Atlanta to Chicago, Headley wasn't questioned any further by the authorities about the purpose of his trip to Denmark.

He was probably aware that his activities were close to being found out that afternoon in the airport. Unusually for him, he hadn't gotten all the details of his cover story straight. He may have thought things would go more smoothly the next time around. On his subsequent trip to Copenhagen, his suitcase would have all the right documents.

What he didn't know was it was too late already.

When Headley had gone to Derby back in July of 2009, British intelligence agents were tracking his movements. His meeting with Bash and Simon had been monitored. All indications are that Farid was right when he told Headley in Stockholm that Säpo was hot on his heels.

But it's also clear that, during his first trip to Denmark earlier in the year, Headley had both arrived and departed without the police suspecting anything. In all tranquility, he was allowed to visit *Jyllands-Posten* in Copenhagen as well as in Viby. At no point during his two stays in Denmark were there plans to arrest him. If it were otherwise, the Copenhagen police would have been brought into the situation at some point. They weren't.

In the US, the FBI was now keeping close tabs on David Headley.

When Headley landed in Atlanta, his visit with the customs officer was no coincidence. It had been planned by American authorities, who were then able to piece together a preliminary assessment of the situation: Headley was planning an attack on *Jyllands-Posten* in Denmark.

It wouldn't have been the first attempt on the lives of the paper's employees, but this one was more comprehensive and more professional in nature.

In the US, wiretaps of Headley were now being monitored intensively at the highest levels. At nearly daily meetings between FBI director Robert Mueller and the attorney general, Eric Holder, Headley was a set agenda item during August and September 2009. Often they would meet with legal advisors and the president's own counterterrorism advisor at the JCC—the command center at the Department of Justice, about a mile from the White House—to review the details of the top secret operation. Where is the situation today? What do we know? Should we intervene?

The surveillance didn't become any less intensive when the FBI realized that David Headley and Daood Gilani were one and the same—a man whom American authorities had previously sentenced to prison on two occasions for drug-related crimes. And a man who had previously been a DEA agent.

After the September 11 attacks, a commission had concluded that American authorities had been sleeping on the job, so to speak. A group of Islamists with connections to al-Qaeda had entered the country and received pilot training—without ever being questioned or arrested. The government didn't want to risk that sort of thing happening again.

FBI agents in Chicago were now monitoring Headley around the clock, and they quickly discovered that he often was in contact with a man by the name of Tahawwur Rana, a Canadian citizen who wasn't in their databases and didn't have any prior conviction. What was his role?

Rana was added to the wiretaps, and on several occasions both men were followed by FBI agents, who knew exactly when Headley stepped through the door of Rana's office on West Devon Avenue and when he left it again. One day, he went into the office and stayed for thirty-five minutes. Another day, an hour and eight minutes. Then thirty-seven minutes. It was all thoroughly recorded.

And then, one day, one of the agents walked through the front door of Rana's office. The agent visited under a false pretext, observing everything in detail, and soon after wrote an extensive report about the place: three small rooms on the west side, four small rooms on the other. Lots of computers. Lots of people. No bombs or weapons immediately visible.

At Rana's slaughterhouse in Kinsman, south of Chicago, the FBI began constant monitoring, for fear that Headley and Rana might have a bomb or other similar device hidden somewhere in the elaborate building complex. Most of the time, they saw only sheep and goats standing around and chewing their cud.

The authorities also broke into Rana's white BMW to install microphones. The FBI was not at all reassured by what they heard being discussed in the car.

16

A Desperate Man

Chicago
Saturday, August 22, 2009

There's nothing like a phone that doesn't ring. Or a letter that never arrives.

No news is bad news.

Headley stayed in his secret apartment in Chicago; he was back from his trip to Europe, and now he was waiting for a response from Pakistan. He had delivered a small portion of his observations in Denmark to a contact with Ilyas Kashmiri, but he had a lot more to report and he was still hiding the video recordings from Copenhagen Central Station, *Jyllands-Posten*, and several other locations in Copenhagen on a USB drive in the apartment. Sending the videos over the Internet would be far too risky.

But there was nothing from Kashmiri.

And even more frustrating, one of Kashmiri's contacts in Derby had apparently been driven into hiding. Simon had previously promised Headley that he would travel to North Waziristan and discuss the attack on *Jyllands-Posten* with Kashmiri, but now there was no getting hold of him in either Derby or Pakistan.

It had been more than two weeks since Headley returned from Denmark, and when he asked people in Pakistan if there were any signs of life from Simon or Kashmiri, the response was simply no.

Headley's funds were also about to run dry. He didn't have a job, and if something didn't happen soon, the plans for an attack in Denmark would come to a standstill.

On August 22, Ramadan came for Muslims around the world. A month during which, according to the prophet Muhammad, heaven is open and the gates to hell are closed. That August day, Headley called Pasha in Pakistan, and as always, the conversation took place through both agreed-upon and improvised codes, intended to make it impossible for the FBI or others to figure out exactly what it was the two men were talking about.

"First tell me—have you spoken to Dr. Ahsan?" asked Headley.

"No friend. There is nothing," replied Pasha on the phone from Pakistan.

"Contact?"

"Nowadays, there is no contact."

But Headley wanted an answer so he could move forward with his plans.

"If you're not able to get in contact with him, then what to do about the business: to start it or . . . ?"

"See, I am try, try, try, try, trying. Inshallah."

Headley had a plane ticket for two months from then, and he very much wanted the go-ahead.

"So for now, do it? Delay it? Give priority or put at the end? What is this arrangement?" Headley asked.

He could hardly hide his apprehension over the phone. Pasha's emphatic declaration that his missions were divine, and that Allah's "meter" for good deeds was running high when he was in Denmark, did little to put Headley at ease.

"The bicycle that you rode—its meter is noted by him," Pasha said.

"Yes, it is so. But I need money. To me, I mean, I want my account be filled with money, you see," said Headley.

"*Inshallah, inshallah*," Pasha replied.

"I do not only need a credit meter. I need, I mean there must be something."

"Yes, yes."

"I have put money, built gardens. They should flourish as well. Also bear some fruit. They must also be seen that these are going to ruin just by standing there. A ruined garden. While you are watching the meter to see, if it's running or not."

"No, no, in this, that is the thing, this is, this is the thing, sir. You have invested in the business, and after that you must show patience, which is necessary."

Things went well for some days before Headley's impatience and anxiety began gnawing at him again. He spoke with Pasha and asked him to tell Kashmiri what he had already told to Pasha. Just to be safe.

"Didn't you convey to him everything whatever I had told you, about him? Or still, it has not been conveyed to him at all?"

Pasha sighed into the telephone.

"No. There is absolutely nobody. Look, from there, from there . . . it has been completely cut off."

"But, ah—it is okay, never mind."

"No, unable to find it out. It is not like I am just sitting here. I am trying my best for it," Pasha assured him.

"Right," Headley replied.

From Chicago, Headley had been working to revive an old plan. During the discussions with the leadership in Pakistan, the plan had had several names, but Headley usually spoke of it as "plan B." It involved a focused, targeted killing of Flemming Rose or Kurt Westergaard. Or perhaps both at the same time. That would be more efficient and easier, as Headley thought now.

And the plan had another advantage built into it: he could take care of it himself if everything else went down the drain.

"I like the option B. I can do it on my own, that is. I do not need any help of anyone else. I'm on my own," Headley said to Pasha.

Headley was angry. And he wasn't shy about letting Pasha hear it, although he packaged his message in coded language about accounts, marketing, and profits when he meant killings, suicide videos, and religious rewards.

"I am qualified. I have studied accounting. I have taken two semesters in college; I could do accounting myself. I can do marketing myself. I do not need anybody's help. The salary that you will give to someone, I take it myself. And I can do it easily, with no problem at all," Headley said.

"I see."

"Yeah."

It was about time, thought Headley. Now.

"I want this project from the bottom of my heart," he declared.

Headley's impatience grew from a realization that had been forming for a good while: neither Lashkar nor his connections in the Pakistani intelligence service, ISI, had the will to carry out the mission in Denmark. They preferred for him to prepare new attacks in India, and though his hate for the Indians was by no means sated from the killings in Mumbai, Headley thought it was a waste of energy.

When you got down to it, Lashkar and ISI were both weaklings. They'd give in to the Pakistani government's wishes for them to hold back.

Major Iqbal had declared back in March that he wouldn't be in touch with Headley any longer, out of fear that he would become implicated in the Mumbai investigation.

"This idiot is the biggest coward," Headley told Pasha angrily during a phone conversation.

"They would say, once it has happened, now again . . . They would never do business without Mr. Bala's company," said Headley, referring to Major Iqbal and ISI.

"They do not have the guts to start investment or business without Mr. Bala's company, because Mr. Bala's people will beat them up."

Pasha tried to calm his friend, and the two agreed to meet in Pakistan in one month's time. That way, Headley would have the opportunity to speak with Kashmiri before his third trip to Denmark.

"*Inshallah*, one month, approximately thirty-five days from now, God, if I am still alive . . ."

The thought of a visit to Pasha lifted Headley's spirits.

"In person, we could bring out a calculator and we will total where the properties, land, and all that. Do it all."

"Yes, yes."

"Instead of being on the phone."

On some days, Headley seemed willing to cut his ties to Lashkar entirely. On other days, he praised the group and planned new projects for it. But Headley had decided one thing for sure: the mission in Denmark was too important to leave up to them alone.

In the future, they would be his backup plan if for whatever reason the mission couldn't be carried out with Kashmiri. Not the other way around.

That's why Headley hadn't told the Lashkar people he'd been to Denmark that summer. Only now did he mention it for the first time, in an offhand way, in an email to Sajid Mir.

Headley wrote that he was working as the "manager" at a restaurant in Chicago owned by Rana. And: "Last week they sent me to Germany to buy some Butchery equipment and guess where else I went for three days—just for a vacation— :) on Dr. Rana's expense?"

Sajid Mir had no problems decoding Headley's message about a visit to Denmark and wrote back, asking about the trip.

"We bought some animal butchery equipment," Headley wrote. "I did get you something. The same gift I got for you last time I was there."

That was code for new video recordings from Denmark.

Sajid Mir wrote a defeatist reply.

"What ever I am saying, I know, deep in my heart, is futile. Because it's you."

"I don't understand, what is futile?" Headley wrote.

"Futile are my advices, because you do what you feel like. Matter and situation is not clear," Sajid Mir wrote, saying that he hoped Headley would take care of himself.

From Chicago, Headley wrote back that he certainly did not just do whatever he liked.

"That's why I always tell you everything," wrote Headley—who certainly had not told Sajid Mir everything.

"I have very few friends left in the world, maybe Dr. Rana and you."

But from Pakistan, some good news came later.

Pasha had found one, perhaps several, potential suicide soldiers who could help Headley with the attack in Copenhagen. He communicated this via code on the phone.

Headley, though, was more and more dejected. One day, he said outright that Rana's and his own morale and esprit de corps were "screwed up." And that it had been that way since right after he came back from his trip around Europe.

"Why?" Pasha asked.

"Especially your cousin's friend, we had high hopes for him," Headley said, referring to Farid in Stockholm, who had refused to help Headley with the attack.

"Okay friend, when you come, if you, God willing, if you came, one more, there, I will give you another. . . . I mean for investment, another person, I found another person there."

Pasha had seen to it that Headley got a new contact in Germany: "You know . . . this place, where we went for the office, office . . . where you, you know . . . the car, you rented it?"

"Yes, yes, yes."

"I met a local person of that place."

"Okay. When Ramadan is over, I will come over there. Then you can tell me all this. Anyway . . . your friend, from where I took the car . . . I mean, in what respect he can do it?"

"Yes, no, he . . . if you talk with him or meet him . . . then only is it possible, because it is not possible to have a detailed conversation over the phone."

"No. When I come return, then I will meet him. I'll go straight to him."

"Okay, that is fine, that is fine. Then I will give you some of the details, and then we will do it."

Rana's white BMW headed south down the road, away from Chicago. With him were Headley and one of Headley's children, who was strapped into a child seat in the back. In the front, the two men sat and discussed the situation as they drove toward Rana's farm in Kinsman.

Headley was worried that his contact from Derby might have been arrested. It wasn't his health or the possible loss of a fighter in Europe that worried him the most. It was the fear that the man from Derby might have talked and revealed Headley's name.

It only made him more paranoid that Pasha couldn't get in touch with Kashmiri.

"Even when I brought my report to Pasha . . . Pasha hasn't even been able to deliver that report to him. It has been a month. A month, yes. It's difficult, you see. They are scared over there. Today after a long time, there was an attack by a drone. . . . There had not been one for a month. And it is also taking place in the north where he lives," Headley said.

"I see," said Rana, ever a man of few words.

"In any case, I don't know how much Gud will help," came Headley's reply.

"Whatever happens, hope it is for the best."

"Yes."

"When you know that he received the notes, then . . ."

"God willing, he'll find a solution."

Headley was in a talkative mood, and even though the men were alone in the car with one of Headley's younger children, they continued to speak on and off in code, while Headley enumerated his four future terrorism targets.

"Denmark, Denmark," he said several times.

"You mean?" Rana asked.

"Denmark," Headley repeated, then naming the Somnath Temple in the Indian state of Gujarat, which he had previously discussed bombing.

"Yeah," Rana replied.

"And Bollywood, so three, and fourth is Shiv Sena," Headley said.

Headley then gave his friend a rather surprising promise: "After this, if I ever pray for any other action, then let me be sentenced to the same punishment as a thief."

In other words: his hand was to be cut off.

"Okay," Rana replied hesitantly.

"May Allah help me complete this task," Headley said.

The conversation was a continuation of a discussion that the two friends had had a few days earlier. Rana had warned Headley that he was getting to be too old. Too slow, too inattentive. He offered Headley a job on the farm instead, where he could take care of the chickens or slaughter sheep in peace.

But Rana knew full well that Headley wouldn't want to retire. Even if all four terrorist operations were successes. If Headley got his plans carried out, he'd just come up with new ones. There was no end to his mission.

Headley, too, knew this well. That's how he was made.

On September 13, Headley made contact once more with Pasha, who had just returned home from a trip to Karachi. Headley was excited to learn the news.

"Okay. Karachi, then you met doctor in Karachi or not?"

"No, sir. Met with doctor? No."

"Did you find out anything, any news, how is his health?"

"Uh, no, friend, uh, there . . . there is some news, that he has gotten married there."

"What has he done?"

"Married. He has gotten married."

"Married?"

"Yes. That is the news. He has gotten married. Don't know, don't know exactly . . . don't know exactly."

"Okay. So he wasn't before?"

"You don't understand."

"Huh?"

"I said, you don't understand," Pasha repeated.

Either Headley had forgotten that the word *married* was code for "killed," or he was simply too shaken to comprehend the message right away.

"I don't know when. . . . The news is arriving, but it's not . . . confirmed."

"Okay, friend, this is . . ."

"Are you all right?"

"Yes, fine . . . that's . . . okay, anyway . . ."

Headley said he hadn't heard about it on TV, but Pasha explained that the "wedding" probably had been mentioned only on the Internet. Headley spoke casually about Rana and life in Chicago, but he was apparently confused or overwhelmed by the news from Pakistan. After a few sentences, he collected himself and returned to the subject.

"So it means our company has gone into bankruptcy then."

"No . . . that is . . . that doesn't happen like that. God willing, there won't be bankruptcy. These things will continue. . . . Anyway, let's see, in a few days."

"So then the projects and so forth will go into suspension for the time?"

"No, no, why? Why, sir? Projects will continue. What difference does it make?"

"Okay."

Headley tried to reassure himself that the new contacts in Sweden and Germany would still be of use.

"I have become very depressed."

"No, no, don't become depressed. One should be even more—one should move forward."

"I hope that the foundations on which our company has been formed . . . those are all okay, right?"

"No, those . . . those are . . . You'll know once you arrive here."

The conversation lasted eleven minutes. And exactly three minutes after he hung up, Headley typed "Ilyas Kashmiri" into the search field on Google. He had to know more.

Headley had promised Pasha that he wouldn't say anything about Kashmiri's death to Rana until the details had been confirmed. Nevertheless, he called his friend later that evening to ask Rana to pray for Kashmiri's health.

"It's just a rumor for now, not confirmed. That maybe he got married."

"I see," Rana said, but in a tone that suggested to Headley that his friend didn't quite understand.

"Pray that he didn't—because he's already a married man."

"Yes, yes."

"If he is marrying again, then it will disrupt his already married life."

"Okay, if you are free one minute?"

"Yes. You come over, man. Everyone is sleeping. I'm sitting alone watching football."

The two men discussed the situation that evening, but while Rana went to work the next day, as he would have done any other day, Headley sat down to scour the Internet. A few days later he found an article that he sent to Rana.

"International media reports have confirmed while citing US intelligence sources the death of the HuJI leader Ilyas Kashmiri along with Nazimuddin Zalalov, alias Yahyo, a top al-Qaeda leader belonging to the Islamic Jihad of Uzbekistan. The two died in two separate drone attacks conducted on September 7 and September 14, 2009. . . . Ilyas Kashmiri died after the Predator targeted a car carrying five suspected militants in Khushali Toori Khel village."

The article's conclusion was particularly disheartening:

"The trouble-stricken Waziristan region has become the new battlefield for the Kashmiri militant groups which are increasingly joining forces with the pro-Taliban elements to fight the NATO troops from Afghanistan."

The front had moved. Everything was falling apart.

In the following days, Headley stayed in close contact with Pasha, hoping to hear news about Kashmiri. Some of the conversations took place in the middle of the night while Headley's family was sleeping in the adjacent room.

Pasha advised Headley to get over the loss of Kashmiri quickly.

"Let it go, my friend," came his advice over the phone. "Sometimes a little loss occurs. A little bit."

But Headley didn't want to let it go.

"No, buddy, this is not a small loss, this is very gigantic. . . . This is a very gigantic loss."

"No, buddy," Pasha was said, having now become tired of listening to Headley's complaints.

"Whenever any loss takes place, you get upset right away."

"This is not a small one."

"But this happens."

"I am concerned also that he worked very hard for all those projects, the farmhouse . . . that he wanted to establish . . . the one he mentioned to me and you as well," Headley said.

"He could not see the success of that project. We have not even started doing marketing for that. . . . The poor chap could not see that either, now that he has retired from the company after getting married."

In Chicago, Headley was having a hard time seeing any sort of future for his attacks. Without Kashmiri's financial backing, the project had come to a grinding halt, so he was basically willing to sign up under any old flag. As long as it led to an attack in Denmark.

"Main thing that I have an income. . . . Make some money. I don't care that if I am working for Microsoft or I am working for General Electric or Philips, I don't care. As long as I am making money, I don't give a shit," Headley said, explaining that, "The main thing is the business must go on."

But Headley had a hard time seeing as a solution that they would once again turn to Lashkar only to wait an eternity, like snails, for an attack.

"When somebody takes a risk, then he can get success, too. However, they do not even want to take any risk either and, above all, want to get famed as well," Pasha said of Lashkar.

Perhaps everything would be just the same with them, Headley suggested: Lashkar was about to be broken.

"Based on all these circumstances, it looks like within six or eight months . . . the bankruptcy is evident. My assessment is that within six to twelve months all companies will be descended."

"Well, when one company goes down, one new company arises. These things will keep on going," he said.

Headley was distraught, though. Lashkar was on the brink of dissolving, Kashmiri was dead, and his contact network in Europe was uncertain. Indeed, maybe it didn't exist at all.

Headley had stopped taking the oblong white Lipitor pills he would have otherwise used for his high cholesterol. Now instead, he was running in the streets of Chicago to vent his frustration and get his body where it needed to be. And to collect his thoughts. His pulse would reach 160 when he ran. He could maintain an average pulse of 148 for about half an hour.

Headley began considering more seriously the possibility of moving on to his own plan B.

"This life is temporary anyway, whether we go out in savage splendour or whether we go out in an Old Folks' Home in Florida. And I am not the one saying the Mujahideen will win, God Almighty is," Headley confided to an acquaintance.

He also became paranoid. Sajid Mir had offered Headley a trip to Pakistan where he could relax with another training stay with Lashkar. That would be a good opportunity to get away from everything for three months. But it got Headley to thinking: maybe Sajid Mir was out to kill him, and the stay with Lashkar was just a pretext to lure him to

Pakistan. Sajid Mir wanted to eliminate a man who knew everything about Lashkar's inner structure. Wouldn't he himself have considered that possibility, if he were Sajid? Headley knew too much.

Meanwhile, in the United States, Headley had a very pressing problem. He had tried to get Shazia and the childrens' residence status approved, but that would require a meeting with the immigration authorities. And he feared the authorities might have discovered that, besides Shazia, he was also married to Faiza, and he would be convicted of bigamy.

"I hope they don't put me in jail, while doing all this," Headley said to Rana.

"That is very much possible," his friend replied.

A third problem was that Headley's cousin had also run into difficulties with the authorities. This cousin had bought Headley's chain of video stores in New York and Philadelphia, but the scams that had become an integral part of the business's operations had become a bit too obvious. On several occasions and apparently without reason, customers were billed up to $305 in false charges on their credit cards, and the authorities had also discovered that many of the DVDs in the stores were pirated copies. The business had to close, and the cousin was charged with organized fraud. Now Headley feared that the investigation into that case would sooner or later find their way to him.

He called US Cellular and presented himself as Adeem Kunwar Aziz—the name of the deceased Pakistani who was registered as the owner of both his mobile phone and the Chicago apartment. "Adeem Aziz" explained to the phone company that he would like a new number.

"I have given my phone number to too many people," he explained and requested that the new number be hidden when he called others and that he no longer wished to be listed in phone books or search engines on the Internet.

Headley did everything he could to ensure that nobody found a way to him. He did, however, make sure that Pasha got the new number.

He used it two days later:

"Buddy, the reports that are coming in. . . . By the grace of God, he is doing well!"

"*Inshallah*. . . . You mean the Doctor?"

"Yes, yes!" Pasha nearly yelled from Pakistan.

It was September 21, eight days after Pasha had first told Headley of Kashmiri's death.

Now he had been resurrected.

"If this is true, I will say a hundred prayers, a hundred prayers! And also keep the fast!"

"I don't know . . . but the matter over there has complicated. It is confirmed. Yesterday I had two . . . I received two confirmations yesterday, that he is all right."

"Yes!"

Headley called it "a great blessing."

Later, Pasha explained that he it was "absolutely confirmed" that Kashmiri was unharmed.

Swear on it, Headley demanded.

"I swear: I am telling the truth," Pasha said.

"So, then, I will be able to meet him upon returning?"

"Absolutely, right, and he—just today—was asking about you."

Headley called Rana.

"If I give you good news, what reward will you give me?"

"Whatever you want, sir."

"Pir Sahib is alive," Headley said.

"Which Sahib?" Rana asked.

"Our Pir Sahib!" Headley blurted out.

"Wow! Great! Great!" said Rana, finally understanding the miraculous contents of the message.

Headley was happy. With the message of Kashmiri's resurrection and possible new contacts in Europe, the plans for an attack in Denmark suddenly became very relevant. Not plan B, mind you, but a proper attack. Soon, he'd return to Pakistan, show them his video recordings and notes—and finish the planning together with Ilyas Kashmiri.

Hidden somewhere in the mountains in South Waziristan, Kashmiri confirmed in mid-October that he was, indeed, alive. He made it known in an interview that he certainly understood the Americans' attempt to kill him.

"They are right in their pursuit. They know their enemy well. They know what I am really up to."

17

SACRIFICE EVERYTHING

Copenhagen
Friday, October 2, 2009

Barack Obama was just twenty-six years old when he visited Denmark for the first time. Back then, he was an adventure-hungry young man from Hawaii with a backpack and on his own for a few weeks in Europe. In summer 1988, he ended up in Copenhagen and met random youths in the city.

Now, Denmark was closing its airspace and the greater part of Copenhagen as President Obama landed at Copenhagen Airport early one Friday morning in October 2009. The American president stepped out of Air Force One in a sharp suit and red tie, and with a clear mission for his short visit: to secure the Olympic Games for Chicago in 2016.

Barack Obama had sent his wife, Michelle, his friend Oprah Winfrey, and his personal advisor Valerie Jarrett in advance to do some boosting for Chicago. But they hadn't succeeded in convincing the members of the International Olympic Committee, which was gathered in the Bella Center at Amager, to designate Chicago rather than Madrid, Tokyo, or Rio de Janeiro. So, at the last moment, the president decided that he himself would fly to Copenhagen.

At the Bella Center, Obama told the Olympic committee that as a young man, he had had a hard time finding a place where he felt that he really belonged.

"And then I came to Chicago. And on those Chicago streets, I worked alongside men and women who were black and white; Latino and Asian; people of every class and nationality and religion. I came to discover that Chicago is that most American of American cities, but one where citizens from more than a hundred-thirty nations inhabit a rich tapestry of distinctive neighborhoods," Obama said.

He called Chicago the city that glorifies the diversity of its citizens. And he had lived there for nearly twenty-five years. He thought he knew his city pretty well.

Later, Obama met with Queen Margrethe and Prince Henrik, and in the prime minister's office there was laughter and friendly handshakes with Prime Minister Lars Løkke Rasmussen in front of the press, while Obama, in a moment of seriousness, thanked Denmark for its contributions in the war in Afghanistan.

"Denmark and the US are close friends, long-term allies. We share values, we share interests, and the bonds are not only strong between our two governments but between our two peoples," Obama said.

On local TV stations in Chicago, clips of the president in Denmark were shown again and again in the early morning hours as the city's residents crossed their fingers and hoped the president's appearance in Copenhagen could secure an Olympic future for the city.

But somewhere in that large, multicultural city, there was a man who found the way the president had embraced the Danes degrading and filthy. And the way Obama left Denmark again after barely five hours, and then Chicago was rejected as an Olympic city in the very first round, while Obama was still on Air Force One headed back to the US—that only made the humiliation greater. Headley was full of anger.

"Your president was on a visit there today," Headley said the next day, during a drive with Rana in the BMW.

"Oprah had also gone?" Rana replied.

"We left . . . we left your place disgracefully," Headley said.

"I have said this."

Headley had tickets for a flight to Philadelphia later that day. From there, he would travel on to Pakistan to meet Pasha, Sajid Mir, and Ilyas Kashmiri, who had yet to see the latest videos from Copenhagen. And at the end of the month, Headley would return to Denmark again and make the final preparations for the attack.

During the trip, Rana and Headley also discussed a covert system that would let them send confidential emails to each other while Headley was away.

The method would be one they had used before: they'd create a free email account with Gmail. This time, they'd name it liaqatwing—after the wing they shared at the military academy in Pakistan—with the number 11: liaqatwing11@gmail.com.

"After two or three times—when I will ask you, obviously—you will create it, because you are in America," Headley explained. "The person who is in America will create it. But you will change the number eleven. We will create a formula every time. For example, multiply eleven by two and then minus two. Like this: Multiply by two minus . . . this is twenty-two minus two. This will be the email ID. And the third will be forty minus two, thirty-eight."

Rana was confused by Headley's somewhat unclear demonstration of his own code.

"Minus two?"

"It will not."

"But minus two?"

"What?" Headley asked.

"First multiply by two, then we will multiply by three. It is eleven. First it was multiplied by one, so it remained eleven?"

"Yes."

"No, rather it is nine," Rana said, about ready to give up on the calculations.

"No. We are saying two. First multiply by two, and then minus two," Headley replied, now himself having a hard time following along.

"But you multiplied eleven by two to get twenty-two?"

"Yes."

"Then multiply eleven by three, and subtract two. The remainder is thirty-one?"

"This is all right."

"Then multiply by four and result is forty-four. Minus two and the remainder is forty-two?"

"Well, eleven. Multiply two and then minus two. Right? Then multiply three and then minus three. Later multiply four and then minus four," Headley finished.

"It is minus two all the times," Rana corrected him.

"What? This is all right. Right. It is two."

The email would also have a password, and Headley decided there wasn't any reason to complicate things any further. They were running behind on their agenda for the day, so Headley chose one of the various derogatory expressions he often used to refer to President Obama: Coconut. Dark on the outside, but white on the inside.

Later that day, Headley left for O'Hare International Airport in Chicago, about a twenty-minute drive from his secret apartment. It was a cool Saturday.

He had packed his clothes in a plastic bag and placed the bag in his suitcase along with the items his colleagues in Pakistan were expecting: a small SanDisk memory stick with thirteen short video clips of, among other things, Copenhagen Central Station and both day and evening recordings of *Jyllands-Posten*'s office in Kongens Nytorv.

Headley had also brought a copy of the *Jyllands-Posten* front page from August 1, 2009, showing Denmark's former prime minister Anders Fogh Rasmussen wearing a tight blue tie under the headline: "Anders Fogh Demands Increased Solidarity in NATO."

That front page was from Fogh's first day as the secretary general of NATO. Headley had gotten his copy during his most recent visit to Denmark, and for him it was further proof that *Jyllands-Posten* was glorifying the man who as prime minister had refused to apologize for the Muhammad cartoons.

Headley checked into his flight to Philadelphia—the first stop on the way to Pakistan—and went through the security checkpoint and into the airport.

Meanwhile, he was being monitored by the FBI's JTTF agents in Chicago.

Special Agent Lorenzo Benedict was responsible for Headley, and the day before, he had delivered sixty-five dense pages of information about the case. Pages that all presented arguments as to why it was time for the FBI to intervene.

"The evidence gathered to date by the government's investigation establishes probable cause to believe that Headley participated with others in a conspiracy to commit terrorist acts involving murder, kidnapping, and maiming outside the United States, including in Denmark," Benedict wrote.

Arlander Keys, a judge for the federal court in Chicago, had stamped the document and approved the FBI's intervention, including raids and arrests, should they be necessary.

An agreement had been reached at the highest levels that this case was not to be let go. If Headley left the United States and suspected there was an investigation, it was reasonable to believe that he might never return. Nobody wanted to take that risk.

When Headley was about to board the plane to Philadelphia, a few agents stepped toward him and asked him to follow them.

He didn't resist.

The arrest took place so peacefully that only a few people in the line even noticed that the FBI had just detained one of their fellow passengers.

Headley was driven from the airport to an FBI office in downtown Chicago under intense police protection. There, he was placed in a simple room with video surveillance that had white walls, a small table, a few chairs, and a group of FBI agents.

Special Agent Douglas Seccombe, who after the September 11 attacks had participated in the investigation of the wreckage from United Airlines flight 93 in a field in Pennsylvania, was tasked with investigating Headley's property, as the head of the FBI's evidence department.

Apart from the clothing in the plastic bag, the front page of the newspaper, and the video clips, he found Headley's copy of *How to Pray Like a Jew*, which Headley had apparently thought might come in handy when he was to visit Denmark again in August. Among his things, there was also a map of the Inner City in Copenhagen.

Additionally, Seccombe found a series of handwritten notes that Headley had scribbled on some sheets of paper with a letterhead from a hotel in Europe. These turned out to be his notes after the first meeting with Ilyas Kashmiri's contacts in England and Sweden.

Finally, the FBI found a small, yellow, lined notebook filled with Headley's notes. In it could be found, among other things, a multipage list of more than forty telephone numbers for all of Headley's closest contacts and friends: Major Iqbal, Pasha, Rahul Bhatt, Vilas Varak. And a number, 313-417-6233, for Wasi, the cover name for Sajid Mir.

Altogether, the FBI had so much evidence in wiretaps, emails, documents, and objects that it would take a good bit of work to go through all of it.

"You'd better be careful, because we know a lot more than you think we know," one of the agents said to Headley in the interrogation area.

Headley had his rights read to him, including the right to remain silent, and the accompanying explanation that his words could be used against him in judicial proceedings, should he choose to speak.

"Having these rights in mind, do you wish to talk to us now?" asked one of the two agents.

Headley had previously ratted out his drug contacts, but he had kept his contacts among the world's most wanted terrorists to himself for nine years. In fact, he had often mocked the Muslims who caved in to the pressure and ran their mouths off with details about friends, family, and their religious brethren.

"A Muslim never turns over a fellow Muslim to a Kafir EVEN if he is guilty, and gives his brother help against his enemy and gives him shelter when he needs it and makes ease for him in difficulty and in return Allah will make ease for him on a very difficult day," Headley explained in an email to his old classmates.

Headley explained that the lack of unity among Muslims was worst in Pakistan, where the government had on several occasions turned Muslim captives over to the United States. It was another story with Afghanistan, an example of a state that completely understood what was at stake: "The Taliban refused to turn over even one person to the Crusaders and preferred losing their government rather than violating one Islamic principle."

Headley also thought that such important battles as the one at Karabala in the year 680, during which several of the prophet Muhammad's closest family members were killed, had an important message for Muslims that they would do well to take to heart:

"In my very humble and ignorant opinion, that is one of the main lessons of Karbala: To be prepared to sacrifice everything, including your family, for the Honour of the Divine Faith."

The punishment for failing one's Muslim brothers should be the highest, Headley concluded.

"As far as executions of folks go, who support Kuffar against Muslims in ANY way, I support it, regardless if they are Shia, Deobandi, Salafi or Barelvi, whether they have a beard or not or if they are punctual in their prayers or whether their names are George or Abdullah."

The majority of the jihadists in American custody had stood by that code. Hoping to either die martyrs or gain respect from their religious brethren in their home countries, they spat on their interrogators, went on hunger strikes, or refused to say a single word. Among them was the Pakistani-born Khalid Sheikh Mohammed, who refused to speak when he was arrested in March 2003. He was then waterboarded 183 times before being sent to Guantanamo.

David Headley observed the agents in the room.

It had been half an hour since he had been arrested. Half an hour since he had been on his way to Pakistan to visit one of the most wanted terrorists in the world—to complete the plans for a large-scale terrorist attack against the West.

And then he started to talk.

What followed was described by FBI Director Robert Mueller as the most significant revelation of terrorism-related intelligence the American government had received in at least half a year. The information was so crucial that in a short time it had been sent directly on to the White House and likely also to president Barack Obama personally. Dianne Feinstein—the powerful leader of the Senate's often very secretive intelligence committee—was briefed thoroughly.

Headley spoke for more than a week. In long, eloquent sentences, the forty-nine-year-old explained how he had been in touch with Lashkar-e-Taiba for nearly nine years. He talked about his stays at training camps in Waziristan and the plans for kidnappings, counterfeit money, and murders. He told them about the current plans for a large attack in Copenhagen, targeting *Jyllands-Posten*'s offices specifically but also with the goal of killing a great many random Danes. Perhaps even members of the queen's Royal Life Guards, if they got in the way.

He talked about the men in Derby, about his meeting with the Islamist Farid Lamrabet in Stockholm, and his contacts in Pakistan.

The FBI agents knew much of this beforehand. They had been focusing on the attack on *Jyllands-Posten* for a good while. But as they sat now with his passport in their hands, seeing the many stamps from the Mumbai airport, it became clear that he could also be tied to the attack in Mumbai.

Yes, said Headley. He had planned that attack in detail. He had visited and chosen several locations.

He had produced fifty hours of video recordings.

The 166 deaths were partially his responsibility.

After that, he named all the people in the control room in Karachi, and he drew and told of their internal connections to each other. For each of his contacts—Sajid Mir, Pasha, Major Iqbal—he gave detailed information: unusual characteristics, the way they spoke, their psyche, their background, their weaknesses, how he contacted them.

He described in detail the manner in which the terrorist organizations communicated in code. He named specific targets the American and Indian governments weren't aware of and was able to point out specific weaknesses in the American government's surveillance of terrorists.

Headley also revealed details that are still classified, which the American government will likely keep secret forever.

Every day, Headley was brought to the small place in Chicago, with his back to a wall and behind a table with bottles of water and food, and in this way, the "interrogation" of the free-talking detainee proceeded: Headley went detail by detail through his trips to Pakistan, India, and Denmark; the training camps; contacts; and the preparations for the attack in Mumbai. The sessions often went on for eight to ten hours at a time.

Headley also signed a declaration that gave the agents the right to examine the files on his memory stick, and he gave them the password to his email accounts, and access to his computer.

Soon it became clear to Headley what he personally could expect to be charged with: acting as an accomplice to the murders of six Americans during the Mumbai attack; plans to kill, bomb, and give support to the attack in Mumbai; supporting a known terrorist organization; and planning killings in Denmark and supporting those plans.

The case would immediately go to trial in an American court with American judges, and it was clear that in the worst-case scenario, Headley would be sentenced to death in Chicago. The agents also made Headley aware of an important detail: the case—or perhaps part of it—might end up before a court in India.

Prisons in India are not known for their high standards. Especially not for terrorists. And by no means for a jihadist who acknowledged being behind the planning of an attack where 138 of the 166 who were killed were Indians.

Headley understood the message.

"I know I'll never come back if I'm sent to India," was his conclusion.

And so he began playing the game he had played so many times before: a hunt for the greatest possible reduction of his sentence, despite starting with no good cards in his hand.

Headley needed a guarantee that he wouldn't be sentenced to death, and he demanded that neither India, nor Pakistan, nor Denmark be able to request his extradition for judicial proceedings or punishment. In return, Headley was ready to help the American government capture some of the people to whom he had otherwise sworn eternal loyalty.

Headley pursued three concrete plans, in particular. He tried to help the FBI with information that could lead to the capture of his weapons contact in Germany.

He offered to travel to North Pakistan and arrange a meeting with Ilyas Kashmiri. Headley suggested that, during the meeting, he could present Kashmiri with an antique sword as a gift. The sword would contain a hidden GPS unit that would make it possible for American drones to find Kashmiri and send him a Hellfire greeting from above.

The third plan was to lure Sajid Mir out of Pakistan and to a more cooperative country, where the Americans could then arrest him and send him to Guantanamo, or wherever they liked.

One afternoon—after eleven days of questioning—Headley was getting impatient.

"You have any plans to nab these guys? Or are there no plans?"

"You know there are some things we can't share with you," one of the agents replied.

"No, I understand that. I'm not saying what plans, I mean: Are we working on this thing or not?"

"Always working."

"Okay, good," Headley said, rocking back and forth on the chair in the place. "That would be a plus for me . . . and for you," he said, smiling as he stretched his hands out toward the FBI agents.

"David," said one of the agents, "You've provided useful information so far. You cooperated."

Headley lifted his right hand for a high-five.

But the FBI agent's words hadn't appeased him. The following day, he sat once again in the interrogation place wearing the same gray shirt, black jacket, and light pants.

"I want some . . . I mean, I would like—it doesn't matter what I want. . . . But from my . . . I want some busts to happen. . . . I don't wanna keep on . . . I know you have plenty of evidence against me, but really I'm just providing you more and more evidence against me, and we are not making any arrests," Headley said, emphasizing his worries with some nervous gestures.

"We understand."

"We have to make some. I mean—"

"We understand."

"That's why I was thinking about this thing with Sajid. Maybe something happened? If nothing works out then all of this stuff is gonna be sitting there. . . . And I'll be the only person that you've got. Do you know what I mean?"

"We understand completely."

"Yes."

In Pakistan, it must have slowly become apparent to the Lashkar people that something hadn't gone quite according to plan.

Headley didn't show up as arranged in Pakistan. Even though he sent explanations by email, it must have confused them that he had previously insisted on getting to Pakistan so quickly to meet Kashmiri so that the details for the Copenhagen attack could fall into place—yet now a week had passed and he still hadn't shown up.

Nor did Rana, in Chicago, know that Headley had been arrested.

Thursday morning, October 8, 2009—five days after Headley's arrest—Rana went to gmail.com and created the liaqatwing11@gmail. com account, as they had agreed. He believed that Headley was in Pakistan, and with help from the authorities, Headley did everything he could to ensure that Rana remained convinced of this.

Before his departure, Headley had been talking about an investment in a construction project in Karachi that would secure apartments for veterans from the Pakistani army. Headley had access to some land that could probably be resold for a significant profit; he now offered Rana the opportunity to invest in the project. While Headley was sitting in daily interrogations in Chicago, Rana informed him that he would be happy to put $11,000 into the project.

Headley also sent a fax to Rana's office, which was currently in the process of helping Headley's wife get a residence permit in the United States.

The FBI agents became increasingly interested in this Rana. But Headley refused to tell on his friend. He lied about Rana on several occasions. No, Rana hadn't participated in the terrorism plans. Headley readily discussed his childhood with Rana, their friendship, and their work together in the immigration business, but under no circumstances would Headley talk about Rana's connections to terrorism, fearing that his words would be misinterpreted, distorted, and used against his friend.

"If . . . my wife knows something or Dr. Rana knows something . . . it's just because of their closeness to me. . . . And I don't feel that they should be targeted . . . for that," he said, during one of the first interrogations.

"Does your wife know what you're doing?" asked FBI agent Jeffrey Parsons.

"I don't wanna say that."

"Okay. Fair enough."

"But if she did . . . which I'm not saying that she does . . . but then it would be the same thing as for . . . Dr. Rana. That if he . . . it would be like they wouldn't know, if they did know."

"Mm-hmm."

"Which I'm not saying that they did."

Every day, the questioning resumed where it had left off the previous day. And every day, the agents began by explaining that Headley needed to tell about Rana.

Headley was silent. Instead, the FBI's investigators began to dig through Rana's past. They wondered about, among other things, how he had earned at least $475,000 from his activities in 2008, but only paid about $37,000 in taxes. For income at that level, a tax rate of about 8 percent was definitely not normal.

One of Rana's wife's telephone conversations had also piqued the FBI's interest. She talked about Headley's and Rana's friendship and declared that the two gradually began thinking the same way: "They talk nonsense all day, idiots. That's not how Islam spreads! . . . Such as, 'kill him, he is not practicing like us—kill him, do that to him, do this to him, he is like this—look, how that woman is'—is this how Islam spreads? . . . Hatred spreads like this, not Islam," she said.

Mayor Mark Harlow was used to very little happening in Kinsman on a Sunday. Or, for that matter, on any other day of the week. The little town has one hundred residents and fourteen small streets, three of which don't even have names. There's a church, a post office, and a small bar. But there's no gas station, no shops, no police station. The city is divided down the middle by a railroad where trains carrying goods rumble through uncontested with an endless hail of cars. When the train has passed, the city is still once again. Just as it was that Sunday morning, October 18, 2009.

In the distance, though, the town's residents could make out a rumbling sound that quickly transformed into the unmistakable sound of rotor blades, and when the helicopter appeared, the sight of snipers with raised weapons quickly followed. Simultaneously, some one hundred agents rolled noisily through the city in their FBI cars.

The police had been monitoring Headley and Rana's visits to the farm on South Kinsman Road for several months. Now they wanted to know just what was really going on in there—apart from the slaughter of a few hundred goats per day.

They went through the building with a fine-toothed comb searching for evidence, and the people on the farm—Doctor Syed Hamed, for example, the fifty-one-year-old head of the business—were quickly detained and barred from going into the small shed where he normally both slept and stayed. The authorities confiscated, among other things, a computer, which they had been following from a distance for some months. A computer from which Headley and Rana had sent emails to Pakistan.

The agents remained silent about the reason for their visit to Kinsman.

"What are they doing? We don't know. Are they making bombs? We don't know," stated Mayor Harlow, who couldn't find out anything from the local sheriff either. The sheriff could say only that he had been aware of the plans for a raid for "several weeks." The FBI is in charge of everything, he offered.

Nor could the local TV stations explain the presence of a huge police force in a small, almost unknown town in Illinois a few hours' drive from Chicago. The massive police presence became a local mystery.

While the Kinsman farm was being raided, the Rana family was simultaneously awakened at their private address in Chicago. Without resisting, Rana was led out of the house and driven away. In the house, the agents found among other things the DVD with recordings of the burning Danish embassy that Headley had acquired in his time in Pakistan. Rana's immigration office was raided that same morning at 8:00 by a team of FBI agents.

The FBI also showed up at Headley's secret apartment, warrant in hand. Since his arrest, Headley had been in almost daily contact with Shazia, but he hadn't shared the whole truth with his wife, either.

While the FBI agents turned the apartment inside out, Headley spoke with Shazia over the phone to calm her, and later that day she was allowed to visit him at the FBI office, together with their four children.

It'll be okay. I'll be out again in a few months, Headley explained, and fed her another lie, that the FBI would try to get her an American passport. He just needed to set some things straight for them.

The FBI's goal in the comprehensive operation was to obtain an answer to one question in particular: did Rana know about Headley's terrorism plans to such a degree that he could be considered an accomplice? Was there something at one of those three addresses that could support that theory?

In the small interrogation space, Rana spoke in broken English; he was eager to explain himself and went on interrupting himself and stumbling over his words. It was often difficult for the FBI agents to understand what he was saying. But the man spoke for six hours straight without asking for a lawyer.

First, they talked about Headley. Yes, he had told Rana about his connections to Lashkar, ISI, Ilyas Kashmiri, and about "running around" in some camps. And maybe there were weapons, sure; in Kashmir province a liberation war was being fought, so that would make sense, Rana said. But on the other hand, Rana hadn't thought much of it. It was just talk.

"I say okay. He makes up those stories and tell them with a lot of love and passion, and I said well, yeah, okay. . . . Friends are talking, loose talk, good talk, bad talk. Yeah, but I don't specifically would say that at this very day, he did some training or that," Rana said.

He used Headley's dog, Tyson, as an example of Headley not always doing what he said he was doing. After all, he claimed to follow a literal interpretation of the Qur'an. But a true orthodox Muslim cannot own a dog.

That's how it often was with Headley, Rana explained. You couldn't always trust him.

The FBI agents also shifted the discussion to the Muhammad cartoons. He had never seen them, Rana said.

But he had heard Headley say that the men behind them would have been sentenced to death "in the perfect world, in the prophet's time." They had spoken about the cartoons for hours and were upset about the artist, but more than anything about the ones that did nothing to stop it. Editors, journalists, newspaper owners, and Denmark's prime minister. They were the real villains.

"How do you feel about those cartoons?" FBI agent Parsons inquired.

"There's a resentment in the whole world. He should not have done that. That's a very bad idea," Rana said, apparently unaware that Kurt Westergaard was not the only artist.

"Why is it a bad idea?"

"In Islam, you shouldn't make a picture of the Prophet. Shouldn't do that."

"Would you ever support the company that sponsored those?"

"No, no, no. I wouldn't have my ties with anybody, something like that."

"Okay, well, the company that published those, the newspaper was the *Jyllands-Posten*."

"*Jyllands* . . . ?"

"The *Jyllands-Posten*."

The FBI agents were trying to lure Rana into a trap. If he was familiar with the drawings, didn't care for them, and wouldn't support a business that printed them—why had he personally answered an email from a salesperson from *Jyllands-Posten* regarding advertising prices that Headley had inquired about during his visit to Denmark earlier that year? Why would he even consider running an ad in *Jyllands-Posten*?

Rana thought a bit about the question. "Okay, first of all, can you help me to . . . Is this in Denmark, this newspaper?"

"Yes, it is."

"Okay, okay . . . You know those Scandinavian countries are like a block to me," Rana said, who perhaps had smelled a rat by that point. At any rate, he denied having noticed the coincidence between Headley's visit to Denmark and the newspaper that was behind the cartoons.

In another life, perhaps Headley had become friends with Patrick Fitzgerald.

Both were born on the East Coast in the 1960s, they played sports in their youth and were good at it (Fitzgerald played rugby; Headley played cricket), and both were extremely focused in their efforts.

But their lives had each gone in their own direction.

Headley was convicted for purchasing heroin in New York in the 1990s—Fitzgerald, as a state prosecutor in New York in the 1990s, contributed to convictions in such cases. Headley was involved with some of the world's most dangerous terrorists and glorified Osama bin Laden—Fitzgerald put terrorists behind bars and was at one point part of a secret group that traveled around the world to find evidence against Osama bin Laden.

While Headley planned a terrorist attack on Denmark, Fitzgerald had governor Rod Blagojevich arrested for attempting to sell Barack Obama's seat in the Senate to the highest bidder.

The two men crossed paths now. As a state attorney for northern Illinois, the case registered as number 09CR83 was officially Patrick Fitzgerald's responsibility, and in these October days in 2009, he often stopped in at the white interrogation space to check on the status of David Coleman Headley's questioning.

On October 23, Headley was once more transferred from his cell on the eleventh floor of the Metropolitan Correctional Center—the federal prison located in central Chicago—to the FBI's interrogation space.

But that day—after twenty days of questioning—Fitzgerald had come with an ultimatum for him: If you want to have any hopes of an agreement, you're going to tell us everything. And you'll do it now.

"You cannot refuse to talk about anybody," Fitzgerald said, clearly referring to Rana.

"Okay. Let me fill in some of the gaps," Headley said, having signed an agreement a few days earlier that he could tell them the whole truth without risking a stricter sentence. He now revealed that he had closer ties to Ilyas Kashmiri than he had first admitted to. In fact, he had visited Kashmiri several times and received money from him. And he had sworn allegiance to al-Qaeda.

Headley spoke of his knowledge of the assassination of Ameer Faisal Alavi, a two-star general and leader of the Pakistani special forces who was shot and killed by three men in Islamabad on November 19, 2008—exactly one week before the Mumbai attack. And Headley revealed that he had secret notes from his stays in the training camps hidden in the house in Pakistan. In that same house, there was also a GPS he had taken with him on his trips to Mumbai. The FBI might be able to find some evidence on it.

Headley received a piece of paper and a ballpoint pen.

Think hard and write down the names of all the targets you've heard discussed in connection with your terrorist activities, the agents said.

Headley didn't think for long.

The hotels in Mumbai, *Jyllands-Posten*'s offices in Denmark, a nuclear power plant in India, Jewish *chabad* houses in four Indian cities, and India's national defense academy. Headley readily jotted down the locations, and when he set the pen down shortly after, the agents counted thirty-four potential targets in all.

"Do you want to make any more corrections?" they asked Headley.

"No," he replied.

Shortly thereafter, the agents followed up with a series of focused questions about Rana to pressure Headley. And he changed his story. Yes, Rana did know about his activities. He might not have known all the details and all the attacks, but he was an accomplice; he had helped with the terrorism plans.

All the other participants were at large and in Pakistan, Headley said. There wasn't anybody else to arrest in the United States.

With those words, the prosecution had yet another man to bring a case against. Headley had done it again; it had become a pattern for him to turn in his accomplices. But it seems nonetheless that he had scruples about ratting out his best friend.

"I acknowledge that I made a fool of him. He should be released. The poor fellow is stuck in this thing for no reason. It was my fault," Headley later said.

Come late October 2009, all the documents in the case were still confidential, and there were still no journalists who could explain why a man had suddenly been arrested in O'Hare International Airport on October 3 or what sort of basis there was for the raids in Chicago and Kinsman.

But with Headley's latest revelations, the FBI gave up on their efforts to lure other terrorists out of hiding. That is, additional details of the case were now shared with other entities, including the Danish intelligence agency, which up to that point had played a lesser role in the investigation.

In Denmark, the Danish Security and Intelligence Service (Politiets Efterretningstjeneste, or PET) began a broad inquiry. Had Headley found any Danish contacts or like-minded folk during his two trips to Denmark? PET also sent a number of agents to the United States to follow the investigation from close up. With FBI support, the Danish agents questioned Headley in Chicago. They took their findings back to the investigation in Copenhagen.

PET and the Ministry of Justice also briefed the prime minister's office on the case. Lars Lokke Rasmussen reacted angrily when he learned of the plans to behead Danes in Copenhagen. It was cowardly, he thought.

Late in the afternoon of Friday, October 23, 2009, the first in a series of so-called talking points, and then a draft of a press release, were sent from the Ministry of Justice to the prime minister's office, and thus on to Prime Minister Lars Løkke Rasmussen. All the emails were sent with the words "SECRET SECRET"—marked in all capitals several times, with a "high" priority.

On Monday, the Ministry of Foreign Affairs was also briefed, while the Ministry of Defense likely received the news on Tuesday, October 27. That same day, the judge in Chicago approved publication of the indictment.

"Two Chicago men have been arrested on federal charges for their alleged roles in conspiracies to provide material support and/or to commit terrorist acts against overseas targets, including facilities and employees of a Danish newspaper," read a press release sent out by the American authorities that day.

Not long after, PET sent out a press release with the headline: "FBI og PET afdækker terrorplaner mod Danmark" ("The FBI and PET uncover terrorism plans against Denmark").

The *Jyllands-Posten* leadership received a special briefing about the case.

The leading media outlets in the United States and Denmark ran the story as a feature soon after, and in the Danish government the coverage was followed intently. What would the revelation mean for the security situation?

The same day, PET's Terrorism Analysis Center (Center for Terroranalyse, or CTA) published a new analysis of the terrorist threat against Denmark. Even though it was noted in the evaluation that "the risk of becoming a victim of a terrorist attack in Denmark or in other countries is still very limited," it was also possible that "terrorist attacks can occur without any visible intelligence-related indications. Without warning, in other words."

David Headley wasn't a crazy man acting on his own, the CTA believed. Quite the contrary, he was the expression of something new in the global terrorism picture.

"The experience from recent years in Denmark and other European countries shows that the majority of militant extremists are young men, born and raised in the West. They've often gone through a process of radicalization, where the Internet, established extremist ideologists, and charismatic people, in combination with friends and personal networks along with travel to foreign countries have all played a significant role."

Even though neither the FBI nor PET revealed that day that Headley was the brain behind the Mumbai attack—that detail was initially kept secret—CTA drew a direct comparison between the attack in Mumbai and the current threat against Denmark:

"Simple attacks against unprotected or lightly protected symbolic and political targets, including individuals, is an established type of attack for terrorists without a comprehensive support system. That sort of attack can be carried out with few resources, along with limited planning and training. Terrorist groups constantly seek to learn from earlier attacks while developing new, surprising, and thereby difficult-to-predict kinds of attacks, as seen in connection with the terrorist attack in Mumbai in November 2008."

In Folketinget, the Danish parliament, all parties strongly condemned the terrorism plans, which were called "shocking" and "absurd."

"This shows that there are powers on this planet that have values that are completely different from ours. It's a very serious issue. Denmark is among the countries that are in focus here, but I don't intend to reshape my life. If we change our lifestyles because of this, then we'll have given in to those who wish to stomp all over our values," said Lars Løkke Rasmussen.

The Social-Democrat opposition leader, Helle Thorning-Schmidt, felt one could not repeat too often that "They must not succeed in making us nervous or in any other way challenge our freedom and democracy." Among Headley's old classmates in Pakistan, there was considerable worry. One of them—a high-ranking official in the Pakistani education ministry—wrote on a closed forum for their circle of friends:

"This is extremely sad for all of us. We tried to drill sense into them and obviously failed. Terrorism in all its manifest forms is absolutely abhorrent and to be condemned in every possible way. Half my time is now spent worrying about security, for my children, for the schools, and for the universities. We are building walls, hiring security guards, and taking steps to protect ourselves from these maniacs who are trying to destroy us from within. Money that could be used for scholarships, equipment, etc. is going to buy barbed wire. Damn these people who have brought this misery on us."

At a hastily called press conference in the Søborg headquarters, PET's leader, Jakob Scharf, said that the terrorism issue was "very serious."

He explained that the unveiling of Headley occurred after "close cooperation" between PET and the FBI, and that PET had put into place "a long series of investigative measures"—though neither PET nor other Danish authorities were named a single time in the eight-page-long press release from the American authorities. Instead, the Americans had chosen to praise the local police in Chicago. In the press release, it stated that—after having exposed Headley—information was "shared" with "our partners in foreign countries."

In Søborg, Jakob Scharf continued: "There is every reason to direct special thanks to the American federal police, the FBI. Without their very great efforts—especially on the part of the FBI's team in Chicago—we would hardly have gotten as far as we have now in our endeavors to thwart the planned terrorist attacks in Denmark."

Scharf repeated this message later in English to a TV station in New York: "We are very grateful," he said.

Several times in the course of the thirty-minute press conference in Søborg, Jakob Scharf emphasized that the attack against Denmark had not been "imminent."

"It's important to emphasize that the risk of becoming a victim of a terrorist attack in Denmark is still very small. This case, however, shows that Denmark is facing a serious terrorist threat, and that's something we all have to take into consideration," Scharf said.

He repeated several times at the press conference that the terrorist threat for that specific attack had been "minimized" by the arrests of Headley and Rana. But it was a delicate subject. Because despite the arrests, the long series of investigative measures, and the heightened security in several locations in Denmark, there was still one detail that had made the American and Danish governments deeply concerned.

A detail that was best expressed in one simple sentence, which first disappeared from a draft of the press release a few days before a communications worker for PET pressed "send" on the email to the Danish press. "It is, however, currently not possible to say whether or not the terrorist attack has been successfully thwarted."

Headley's video recordings and plans for an attack in Denmark were still out there.

18

FROM STOCKHOLM

Järfälla, near Stockholm
Late in the evening of December 23, 2010

Most of Sweden had already gone to bed. For a small few, it was time to wrap those final Christmas gifts or prepare tomorrow evening's Christmas ham.

In a fifth-floor apartment on Frihetsvägen in the city of Järfälla, half an hour by car from Stockholm, two men sat over cups of tea and quiet music, addressing entirely different challenges.

Forty-four-year-old Mounir Dhahri, a Tunisian citizen with permanent resident status in Sweden, went once again through the plans he and his friend, thirty-seven-year-old Sahbi Zalouti, had been discussing. They would drive to Denmark, attack *Jyllands-Posten*, and kill as many as they could.

It would be an attack just like what Headley had wanted.

It would happen soon, Mounir Dhahri explained. Very soon, certainly before the new year. There was a week, at most, to get all the details sorted out.

The attack was sanctioned from an Islamic point of view, so there was nothing to worry about in that regard. As long as they didn't kill women, they were in their full rights to kill all the employees at *Jyllands-Posten*'s offices in Copenhagen, Dhahri explained.

"You may kill as many of the people you find as you can. I hope there's only one survivor left," Dhahri said.

One witness who could later tell the world what happened.

He compared the plans for an attack in Copenhagen with the Chechens' attack in the Dubrovka theater in Moscow in 2002, where 129 hostages were killed during the Russian special forces' violent attempt to put an end to the attack. An operation that lasted several days. Even though that attack was genius, the Copenhagen attack would be put together differently.

We aren't like the Chechens, Dhahri said. "They prolonged the release of a number of people, you see, and drew the whole thing out."

The Chechens had given the commandos plenty of time to mobilize and come up with a plan to storm the theater. In accordance with Headley's plans, Mounir Dhahri would not give his enemies time.

"We'll do it the way we must. Even when we're on our way out, you must kill the people you come across. We don't have a demand that would make it possible for them to buy time. We just need to be careful of snipers—that's what's most important."

Zalouti, who, like Dhahri, was of Tunisian background but who now held Swedish citizenship, asked inquisitive questions about the operation.

"And then what?"

"You get rid of them as you like. All the ones you find before you must die, except the women," Dhahri answered.

These kinds of discussions were nothing new for the men in the apartment. They had had many such discussions in the last days, the last week. They tested each other, experimented with ideas, and convinced each other once again that as long as there were people in Denmark who were killed, the mission was valid and good.

The men also made plans for what they would do if they couldn't force their way into the newspaper. They could try attacking a completely ordinary house in Copenhagen.

"We aren't guaranteed to get into the newspaper. We might break into a villa—one of those villas where there are lots of people," Dhahri said.

"Far from people, far from the police. After all, people are celebrating Christmas Eve and New Year's Eve in their homes," Dhahri said.

Zalouti was curious about the details of the plan again. If he saw women in the house, should he kill them?

"My God, don't kill them. You break in, masked, and you go your way when the operation is complete. But if we can go for the newspaper, that would be best."

The two men in Järfälla had never been in direct contact with David Headley. But they knew his name, his story; they had read about him on the Internet; they had visited the same areas with militants in Pakistan; they had at least one common contact in the Middle East; and their plan, as it were, had been thought out by Headley.

The men from Sweden, too, dreamed of chopping off the heads of journalists and random Danes in the building on Kongens Nytorv in Copenhagen.

And the cell in Sweden had two advantages: they had weapons. And they could get into Denmark without problems. They lived just a few hours away by car and could take their car to Copenhagen without being stopped and asked to show their passports.

Dhahri and Headley were similar in many ways, not only because they were middle-aged and enjoyed women and brand-name clothes. Like Headley, Dhahri had a complicated past with Islam. He, too, was a former apostate who had since found his way back to the true faith.

Like Headley, Dhahri had a past with the sale and heavy use of drugs.

Like Headley, he had a violent temper: in 2004, Dhahri was convicted of throwing a roommate against a wall. The year before, he had threatened the lives of two employees in a 7-Eleven in Stockholm after they refused to let him use a telephone.

Like Headley, he was stuck between two worlds—his Tunisian background and his modern life in multicultural Sweden.

Like Headley, in his later years Dhahri became a fervent Islamist with a great hatred for *Jyllands-Posten* and Danes in general after the publication of the Muhammad cartoons.

Dhahri was also trained in the Islamist interpretation of war and jihad. In the two years leading up to autumn of 2010, Dhahri had suddenly vanished from the watch of the Swedish authorities. Part of the time he was most likely staying in a terrorist training camp in Pakistan, and he had contacts for the city of Miranshah, where Headley had met with the terrorist leader Ilyas Kashmiri.

When Dhahri came back from Pakistan, he traveled secretly, first to Athens and then to Brussels. Here, Sahbi Zalouti gathered him up in a car, and the men drove north to Denmark.

In Copenhagen, it became apparent that *Jyllands-Posten* had moved its offices to a new address at City Hall Square since Headley had made his plans. The two men ate, among other things, a burger at a restaurant in the Fisketorvet shopping center before they drove on to Stockholm.

It's unclear if Dhahri and Zalouti had already begun planning an actual attack on the office by that point, but it's a known fact that Dhahri had received a message from Pakistan: "Attack."

In early December 2010, Dhahri called a certain phone number in Miranshah eighty-eight times; it was a known communication channel between Westerners and Islamic fighters. Here, he asked for Marwan or Rabani, and created the email addresses "pushpushzz@yahoo.com" and "pullpullzz@yahoo.com" for his terrorist contacts in Pakistan. But the men's true identities remained a secret.

However, Headley and Dhahri had at least one mutual acquaintance through their contact network in Pakistan: Farid Lamrabet—the man Headley met with in Stockholm who had refused to participate in the Copenhagen attack because he was on Säpo's watch list.

On the evening of December 6, Mounir Dhahri called Farid Lamrabet three times, and in late December he called the controversial Swede-Moroccan again from his mobile phone.

What their conversations were about is not known. But it's certain that a few days later, Dhahri sat himself behind the wheel of a silver-gray Toyota Avensis with three passengers in the car, heading toward Denmark.

The men had been told in advance that they were to escape after the attack. And if that didn't succeed, they were to be ready to sacrifice their lives.

"God willing, martyrdom lies at the end of this operation. What you are to do is clear: you call your family shortly before the operation and then you leave," as Dhahri explained to one of the men.

Munir Awad took apart his mobile phone. The twenty-nine-year-old Lebanese-Swede usually did so when he traveled out of the country. That was his way of ensuring that nobody could track him in the car on the way to Denmark.

And the authorities had good reason to keep an eye on Munir Awad. Of the four men in the car, he was the most openly fundamentalist Muslim, and on several occasions he had drawn attention to himself with his views and opinions in the press. His mother-in-law, Helena Benaouda, was also known throughout the country: she was the spokeswoman for the Muslim Council of Sweden—an umbrella for the largest Muslim organizations in Sweden.

Together with his girlfriend, Munir Awad traveled to Somalia in 2007, but he was arrested at the border between Somalia and Kenya, suspected of wanting to fight for Somalia against Ethiopia. He remained in prison for three months in Addis Ababa before Säpo and the Swedish foreign ministry managed to get him out of the country. The situation received a good amount of coverage in Swedish newspapers at the time.

In 2009, he was arrested in a bus on the way to a suspected terrorist training camp in Waziristan, together with, among others, Mehdi

Ghezali, who was known in Sweden as the "Guantanamo Swede" after spending two and a half years in the controversial prison in Cuba. Here, too, the Swedish authorities helped restore the men's freedom and get them back to Sweden.

"We know that Säpo has gotten us home, and we're very grateful," he said to a newspaper at the time. In December 2010, the roles had shifted.

Behind the rented Toyota Avensis traveling south through Sweden toward the bridge to Denmark was another car, containing Säpo agents.

As terrorist planning had become more and more sophisticated, Säpo's agents had also intensified their surveillance. They had installed hidden microphones in the Järfälla apartment and observed who went in and out of the door. And now, they followed the Toyota all the way to Denmark. And Säpo was there too when the fourth man in the car—the thirty-year-old Omar Abdalla Aboelazm—had been in a Swedish home improvement store called Bauhaus to buy two hundred plastic zip ties for 398 kroner.

The zip ties would be used as handcuffs. They would make it easier to behead people at *Jyllands-Posten*'s offices.

Omar Aboelazm was the outsider in the car. He was born and raised in Sweden but had lived in Egypt in his early childhood and in the religious city of Fez in Morocco in recent years. He had been previously convicted of a series of sexual offenses against both girls and women and had also been diagnosed with Asperger's syndrome.

Omar Aboelazm was, broadly, unstable. But he had a connection to Sahbi Zalouti, who was the link between all four of the men. It was Zalouti who had organized everything, so Säpo was surprised by what happened partway through the trip to Copenhagen.

In Jönköping, the car suddenly pulled over and stopped at Statoil gas station that rented out cars. Here, the car's rental contract was edited so that Sahbi Zalouti's name no longer appeared on the papers.

It seems he had chosen to back out at the last moment. What exactly happened before then in the car was impossible to say. Säpo hadn't installed any microphones in the Toyota that the four had rented shortly before departing.

The car traveled on without Zalouti, who began to walk the long road back to Stockholm.

Not that he ever considered warning the authorities about the attack in Copenhagen. Instead, he walked on and thought about his shoes. It was almost 14°F, and he wasn't excited about going home with wet feet.

The Danish authorities noted the time precisely. The Toyota rolled through the tollbooth, and at 2:02:42, on the night of December 29, 2010, three men crossed the Øresund Bridge, at which point they were on Danish soil. Säpo ended their surveillance and entrusted their colleagues from PET to keep an eye on Dhahri, Omar, and Awad.

The car rolled over Amager, past a local gas station at Sydhavnen, where the three asked for directions. From there, the trip continued on to Tivoli, where the three met a man whom PET had already been monitoring.

The man was an Iraqi refugee living in Denmark who had access to an apartment on Mørkhøjvej 82 in the Copenhagen suburb of Herlev. Zalouti had arranged for them to stay in the apartment with the Iraqi, and before he left them in Jönköping, he had given the men a handwritten note with the address on it. But he had written the street name "Mørkhøjvej" without the first J—which was apparently what had caused the men to stop in Sydhavnen to ask for directions.

The man from Iraq quickly disappeared after he let his three guests into the apartment in Herlev. The three took off their clothes, prepared three mattresses on the floor, and lay down to sleep.

A few days before, PET had been in the apartment. They had installed cameras and microphones, so they were now able to follow each and every word, each and every movement.

In all, the Danish and Swedish intelligence services performed 5,233 interceptions, wiretaps, and so on—resulting in 20 gigabytes of data—during the operation.

In the building's parking lot, PET agents obtained access to the silver-gray Toyota with the license plate number JXH 965. Here, they found a laptop, the two hundred zip ties, thirty-six rounds of live ammunition packed into a gray sweater, a magazine with thirty-six live rounds hidden in a checkered shirt, an automatic pistol, and a silencer.

The PET agents carefully closed the trunk.

The men in the Herlev apartment woke up, washed themselves, and prepared for the first of the day's five prayers.

Apart from the weapons in the car, the men in the apartment had a 9mm pistol and thirty-six rounds. Dhahri also had a large sum of cash, $20,000, and 2,106 euros. The money most likely was to be used if they managed to escape after the attack.

They discussed driving into Copenhagen to have a look at *Jyllands-Posten's* new offices at City Hall Square. Maybe just to observe the place. And maybe to attack the Find of the Year, which was to be held in an event space in the cellar beneath the paper's offices that same day. Several hundred people would be participating. Among them happened to be Crown Prince Frederik.

Dhahri had explained to one of the men earlier: "We're hoping for the best. When we go in, we'll keep our heads away from the windows. Because in just about twenty minutes, they'll have us surrounded. A paper like this one has many locations, but . . . kill everybody. If God has decided that someone's going to be killed by a sniper, that's what God has decided."

The men crouched and prayed together for a blessing that they might kill the infidels.

The men quoted from the Qur'an: "When you meet the infidels, cut their heads off! The actions of those who are killed for God's sake will not be forgotten." It was 10:44 a.m. In just a few seconds, the door was broken down, and the Police Special Task Force stormed the apartment in full armor with masks and raised weapons. "Get down, get down!" they yelled, grabbing the men. One resisted but was quickly subdued. Shortly after, all three men were lying on the ground, yelling loudly. In the apartment in Järfälla, Sahbi Zalouti was also arrested. The terrorist attack had been thwarted.

19

THE TRUTH

Federal court, Chicago
Monday, May 23, 2011

He sat calmly in the chair at the witness stand.

"Do you solemnly swear or affirm that you will tell the truth, the whole truth, and nothing but the truth?"

Headley carefully raised his right hand as he was sworn in, leaning forward to the microphone and nearly whispering his answer.

"Yes."

Though he hadn't done all that well with the whole truth thing. He had lied, manipulated, and torn reality to shreds for most of his life. That was what he was good at.

The truth? All too often, it had merely stood in the way.

It had been a good six months since Headley was arrested in the Chicago airport and driven away. A lot had happened since then. The men from Stockholm had tried to attack *Jyllands-Posten*. Osama bin Laden had been killed. Headley's children were growing up and had begun asking questions about their father.

Behind bars, he had turned fifty. His hair was cut short, and behind the witness stand, he fidgeted uncomfortably with his sneakered feet.

This trial was actually of Rana, and Headley had just been called in as a witness in a case that would otherwise be best described as a journey through Headley's own life.

On several occasions, the judge had to ask him to speak loudly and clearly. Headley didn't care much for it. But once he got started, there was no stopping him.

Over five days, he spoke of the military academy in Pakistan. About the drug dealers. About the lecture with "the Professor" that had incited him to jihad. About the training with Lashkar. About the trips to Mumbai. About the meeting with the young woman in Denmark. About the visits to *Jyllands-Posten*'s offices in Copenhagen and Viby J. About the conversations with Ilyas Kashmiri. About the beheading plans. About the trips to England and Sweden.

On the other side of the closed doors in the courtroom, the FBI remained on high alert. Bomb-sniffing dogs had inspected the nineteenth floor courtroom several times, and everyone present had gone through at least two security screenings before gaining access to the courtroom.

The case was intensely covered by media from India, Pakistan, the US, Canada, and Denmark.

The prosecutors attempted to prove that Rana was aware of Headley's plans in detail.

"There were only a few people in the world who knew what David Headley was really doing in Mumbai. One of them was Tahawwur Rana," said prosecutor Sarah Strecker, who denied that Rana could claim in any way to be free of guilt.

"One cannot say that Rana has killed anybody. But he has helped, so it could have easily happened. Rana knew that when Headley traveled outside the country, there were people who were going to die," Strecker said.

Rana's team of lawyers, on the other hand, called Headley a master of manipulation, and pointed out, among other things, how Headley had lied to the FBI on several occasions, including after his arrest.

He was like a chameleon, able to change colors, personalities, and languages in just a few seconds.

While working at various times for Lashkar-e-Taiba, ISI, Kashmiri, and the American authorities, he had maintained several marriages at once. He lived several lives, and lied to everyone he came across.

"The matter will show that David Headley is trying to take all of us for a ride," said Charlie Swift, one of Rana's lawyers, in court.

Headley's past had taught him that it always pays to snitch, and now he had wanted to rat out an innocent friend who had done nothing wrong—just so he could evade the death penalty, the defense lawyers explained.

Charlie Swift posed a simple question he felt could prove Rana innocent: In the many emails and wiretapped phone calls, it was clear that Headley, Pasha, Sajid Mir, and the men behind the terrorism plans in Denmark all referred to the plans as "the Mickey Mouse project," "the northern project," or variations on these same themes. But despite nearly three months of intense surveillance and wiretaps, the authorities had never heard Rana use these descriptions. How could that be, if Rana was as involved as the prosecution claimed? Was the truth really, perhaps, that Rana had just been used? That he, too, had gotten everything but the truth from his friend?

Since his arrest, Rana had denied his guilt in any and all matters of terrorism or murder. He maintained that if he had ever helped Headley in any way, he had been cheated by his smooth-talking, charismatic friend. Had the wool pulled over his eyes in a web of white lies, double lives, and stories of terrorism that Rana had come to take as nothing more than boasting. Rana's defense claimed, among other things, that Rana had never even seen Headley's videos from Denmark and that that in itself was proof that he wasn't in the inner circle that planned the operation.

For the first thirteen months, Rana sat in isolation in the federal prison in central Chicago, and he rarely came out into fresh air. For a long time he didn't have a clock, and therefore he didn't know when he should pray. That took a heavy toll on him. One day, he collapsed on the floor in his cell and lay there, crying, until, after seventeen hours, he was attended by a doctor. It turned out that he had had a heart attack.

Rana's family offered to pay one million dollars in bail so he could be released until his trial came. That was rejected, as the court feared that Rana would try to flee.

Now, Rana sat in court in Chicago. His hair had turned gray, and with his index finger resting on his lip, he listened to Headley while looking up at his old friend at the witness stand through rimless glasses. With his right hand, he wrote page after page of notes.

Only when he entered and exited the courtroom did he smile reassuringly at his wife and daughters, who had come to sit in the gallery and follow the case. In the courtroom, his focus was constantly on Headley. As if he was trying to understand him.

Rana himself didn't speak at the trial.

One late Friday evening, Ilyas Kashmiri was drinking a cup of tea in an apple orchard outside the city of Wana in South Waziristan.

The one-eyed terrorist leader was surrounded by a number of his fighters, and through the evening they likely discussed the case against Rana, which had been going on for twelve days, six thousand miles away, in Chicago. The Pakistani media covered the cases of Headley and Rana intensely, and now, for the first time, it had been disclosed that Headley had offered the American authorities help to kill Kashmiri.

Officially, Kashmiri's name was also on the indictment in the case in Chicago, but the Americans hadn't managed to get hold of him. After Headley's arrest, Kashmiri, for his part, had continued on undeterred with his plans for an attack in Europe.

Kashmiri had been the cause of terrorism warnings in Germany, France, and the UK in 2010 and 2011. It was also Kashmiri's plans that caused American authorities in October 2010 to explicitly discourage

Americans from vacationing in Europe. It may be that he had some connection to the men from Stockholm.

In the al-Qaeda network, Kashmiri took on the role of manager for the planning of attacks on the West. It had been only a few weeks since he had thought out a sophisticated attack on Pakistan's fleet in Karachi, during which eighteen soldiers were killed.

The FBI had placed Kashmiri on the list of the world's most dangerous men, and a week earlier, Secretary of State Hillary Clinton had delivered a short list to Pakistan with five names. The five were terrorists whom the US expected Pakistan to help find and kill.

Kashmiri was on the list.

That Friday evening, June 3, at 11:15 p.m., two missiles began descending from a drone somewhere in the sky, high over the tea party in the apple orchard.

The explosions that followed shortly afterward rattled nearby building; flames shot up everywhere. Two more missiles followed.

Ilyas Kashmiri and six or seven others were killed then and there.

"On behalf of Harkat-ul-Jihad al-Islami, 313 Brigade, we confirm the fact that our leader and commander-in-chief Mohammad Ilyas Kashmiri, along with other companions, have been martyred in an American drone attack," as the statement from Brigade 313's spokesman Abu Hunzala said the following day.

"And *Inshallah*, the present pharaoh America will see our full revenge very soon. Our only target is America."

Kashmiri's body has never been found, and parts of the Indian intelligence agency are still convinced that Kashmiri survived the attack. The UN considers it "overwhelmingly likely" that Kashmiri was killed in the American drone attack.

The journalist behind the only lengthy interview with Ilyas Kashmiri, Syed Saleem Shahzad, was found dead in a canal in Pakistan just four days after the drone attack in the apple orchard. A connection between the two killings has never been documented, but the journalist had told close friends shortly before then that he feared for his life and that the Pakistani intelligence service, ISI, was out to kill him. Less than two weeks before his death, Syed Saleem Shahzad had published a book with detailed information about Ilyas Kashmiri.

In Chicago, Rana's trial was coming to an end. During his closing remarks, prosecutor Daniel Collins brought up an email on a large screen. The email was from the advertising salesperson at *Jyllands-Posten*, who had written to Headley in good faith after the visit at Kongens Nytorv in January 2009.

"Thank you for your visit at Jyllands-Posten Friday last week," it said on the screen.

"Think about that. They wrote him a thank-you," Daniel Collins said, raising his voice. "If the newspaper had known what the accused knew, they would not have said thanks. They would have said: Oh God, get out of here! What happened in Mumbai was disgusting, and the plans against Denmark were disgusting. The poor people at *Jyllands-Posten* said thank-you for the visit of a trained terrorist who sought after death and destruction in Denmark! They could have been beheaded."

Collings looked at the jury, making eye contact with them one at a time.

"The innocent people in Mumbai, and the many people at the newspaper deserve justice. Use your reason, dear jurors. This man knew that his friend was a terrorist. He helped him. And when you recognize this truth, you will do what is right. And you will find him guilty," said Collins, sitting down.

In Chicago, the jury took barely two days to reach a verdict. And before it was read, it was decided that the jurors' names would remain secret. For their safety. The jury found Rana guilty of being an accomplice to the terrorist plans against Denmark and of providing support to Lashkar-e-Taiba.

He was, however, acquitted of providing direct support to the attack in Mumbai, and it was also the jury's finding that nobody had lost their lives as a result of Rana's involvement in Headley's terrorist activities.

The judge in the case, Harry D. Leinenweber, declared during the sentencing in January 2013 that it was beyond any doubt that Rana was a loving man with a large family of which he took good care.

"It is, however, difficult to understand how Rana became involved in this cowardly plan to attack the offices of a private newspaper because of one artist's work. The mere thought of it goes against what people say about Rana's personality. It is difficult to comprehend."

Rana was sentenced to fourteen years in prison for his support of David Headley's terrorism plans. Through his lawyers, Rana explained that under no circumstances did he wish to speak to Headley again. Their friendship was over.

As prisoner number 22829–424, Rana is now serving his sentence at Terminal Island prison in Los Angeles, where, among other things, he sits together with a member of the eco-terrorism group Earth Liberation Front, which planned to blow up a dam in California in 2007.

Rana is expected to be released on December 28, 2021, fifteen days before his sixty-first birthday. He will thereafter be deported from the United States. There is still no known evidence showing that Rana sought to incite terrorism—except in Headley's company.

David Headley, since his arrest, has helped the authorities to unravel several terrorist plots. It is his defense attorney's judgment that Headley's help has saved "hundreds, if not thousands" of human lives. The contents of Headley's revelations remain closely guarded secrets, but his cooperation is described by the American authorities as the most comprehensive ever provided by a top terrorist.

The prosecutor, Patrick Fitzgerald, called the information Headley provided "a valuable insight into terrorist leader Ilyas Kashmiri's thought process and plans. . . . We need that kind of information. The Indian authorities need information. The Pakistani authorities need it. And the Danish authorities need it," Fitzgerald said.

Through his close cooperation, Headley avoided a lengthy trial that likely would have gotten him the death penalty, due to the killing of six Americans in Mumbai. He also ensured that he will never be extradited for judicial proceedings in India, Pakistan, or Denmark, either now or at any time in the future.

Danish authorities have never requested that Headley be put on a plane for Copenhagen, while India, on the other hand, is still fighting to get its hands on the highest-ranked terrorist currently behind bars for the attack in Mumbai.

Most recently, India has suggested that David Headley be extradited for one year, after which he will be sent back to the US. The American authorities categorically refused this suggestion, but Headley did—via video link—briefly participate as a witness in a trial in Mumbai in February 2016.

When Headley's sentence was finally decided in January 2013, one of the survivors of the Mumbai attack spoke. Linda Ragsdale, from Nashville, Tennessee, found herself at Tiffin Restaurant in the Oberoi-Trident Hotel during the attack, with a group of friends, including Alan Scherr and his thirteen-year-old daughter Naomi, both of whom were killed.

"I saw the carnage of war in a place where moments before friends and families were enjoying their meals," Linda Ragsdale told the court.

"I know what a bullet can do to every part of the human body. I know the thick and sweetening—sickeningly sweet smell of gunfire and blood. I know the sound of life leaving a thirteen-year-old child. These are things I never needed to know, never needed to experience."

Linda Ragsdale emphasized that she did not wish for Headley to die. Only that he remain eternally silent, isolated in a cell.

"I don't know you. I know you only from the testimony in this courtroom. In this light and understanding, I would not kill you, nor would I send other people to kill you, nor would I train others, nor would I come back in thirty years and attack an arbitrary location in Pakistan to kill innocent people as retribution for your actions," Linda Ragsdale said, explaining that her hope was that Headley might one day dare to be a man "and not bargain away the life of others for your own salvation."

Headley today claims that he regrets what he has done.

In a letter to the federal court in Chicago from January 2013, he wrote that he now "believe[s] in American values and way of life, and certainly wish my children to be raised that way." He also claims that he has reread the religious texts Lashkar showed him at that time, and now sees that the texts were taken "out of context."

"Your Honor, I request clemency and another chance to redeem myself. I am capable of change, and feel I can still make some positive contributions—even in this late stage of life," Headley wrote in a letter to the judge before his sentencing. Judge Leinenweber was of another mind.

"I don't have any faith in Mr. Headley when he says he's a changed person and believes in the American way of life," Leinenweber said, declaring that for his actions, Headley deserved life in prison without any doubt.

But his cooperation with the authorities meant that, instead, the judge had to set the sentence at between thirty and thirty-five years.

Leinenweber gave Headley thirty-five years in prison without any further thought.

"It is my hope that this sentence will hold Hedley under lock and key for the rest of his life," he said.

With the current rules and the time he already had served, Headley will be a free man shortly before his seventy-ninth birthday in the summer of 2039.

In the summer of 2013, the White House reported that the tracking and arrest of David Headley succeeded with the help of one of the highly controversial surveillance programs run by the National Security Agency. However, the American government has never put forth any evidence for this claim, which is strongly doubted by international experts.

The convictions of Rana and Headley have not caused American authorities to close the investigation into the planned terrorist attack on Denmark. Federal authorities have acknowledged that they should have exposed Headley far earlier.

Headley has said that he wishes to perform religious work when he eventually gets out of prison—to set straight all the misunderstandings about Islam that abound in the media. He feels he's the right man for the job.

Today, Headley is prisoner 39828–066 in a top secret prison at a secret address "somewhere in the US," as part of the FBI's protection of criminal witnesses.

He is allowed to watch TV and regularly follows the news, but in letters from the prison, he has recounted that the authorities deliberately make his life difficult, and letters to and from him are thoroughly vetted for hidden codes and messages. Sometimes, they're delayed for up to five months for the same reasons.

Several family members, as well as many friends, have turned their backs on him, but it's not known if Headley is still in direct contact with his children and his wife Shazia, or if she followed Headley's advice in his will and has traveled back to Pakistan. Shazia was never indicted in the case, despite her documented knowledge of Headley's terrorist activities.

Headley has sworn on the Qur'an that he will no longer make contact with his other wife, Faiza. She herself has said she hasn't heard from him since his arrest.

Behind bars, Headley remains a devout Muslim, citing in a letter the Qur'an verse sent to him from Pakistan when his father died: "And we will surely test you with something of fear and hunger and a loss of wealth and lives and fruits. But give good tidings to the patient, who, when disaster strikes them, say, 'Indeed we belong to Allah, and indeed to Him we will return.' Those are the ones upon whom are blessings from their Lord and mercy. And it is those who are the rightly guided."

In prison, Headley—on the advice of a Muslim scholar—has begun learning the Qur'an by heart, and he still believes that "everything that has happened to us, or will happen in the future, has been predetermined by Allah, mighty and majestic."

He once again signs his letters as Daood.

AFTERWORD

The Danish Security and Intelligence Service (PET) has in recent years been involved with several terrorist cases in Denmark but as of 2016 still sees the Headley case as among the most serious due to its international reach.

At PET's Center for Terrorism Analysis (CTA), it is said that the matter of the cartoons has given Denmark the status of a "high-priority terrorism target" and that this status is cemented in the militant Islamist state of mind. Indeed, Denmark is still considered a "legitimate" target by al-Qaeda and other militant Islamists.

Indeed, the threat of a revenge attack for *Jyllands-Posten*'s Muhammad cartoons is higher than ever, according to PET.

The number of cases where one sees "concrete planning of attacks and/or attempted attacks against Denmark or Danish interests in other countries" as a result of the cartoons "has increased in the 2010–2012 period," and is now higher than in the first period, after the drawings were published (2005–2008) and after their second printing (2008–2010), according to CTA.

"This development emphasizes the continued focus on Denmark among militant Islamists, and that there is still a serious terrorist threat to Denmark. CTA considers that this trend will continue in coming years."

And the threat is not just empty words. In February of 2015 a twenty-year-old male with roots in Palestine killed two Danes and wounded five police officers in a terror attack in central Copenhagen. The terrorist was shot dead by Danish police late at night.

Hafiz Saeed—the leader of Lashkar-e-Taiba—remains a free man. "The Professor" has on several occasions called for new attacks and declared that "one Mumbai is not enough." Today, he lives in a restricted area in a residential district of Lahore, surrounded by armed guards, but claims that he is not worried by the bounty placed on his head by the Americans. "My fate is in the hands of God, not America," as he said to the *New York Times* in 2013, when he encouraged political solutions instead of violence.

Lashkar-e-Taiba is still considered one of the most active and most professional terrorist organizations in Southern Asia. According to experts, Lashkar today has a larger network in Europe than it did before the Mumbai attack, but it is uncertain whether its network is capable of being used for major terrorist attacks.

Sajid Mir, Pasha, and several others with connections to Lashkar-e-Taiba are still at large, and they likely remain based outside Pakistan. Unsurprisingly, American authorities consider them "dangerous." They are still wanted for the planning of the terrorist attack on *Jyllands-Posten*.

Al-Qaeda continues to directly threaten Denmark, despite Osama bin Laden having since died. Their threat was renewed, among other times, in January 2013, when the group promised an attack described as "violent, serious, alarming, like an earthquake, shocking and terrifying." On a known Islamist web page, the group wrote: "Where will the next strike by al Qaeda be? The answer for it, in short: The coming strikes by al Qaeda, with God's Might, will be in the heart of the land of non-belief, America, and in France, Denmark, other countries in Europe."

The rise of the terrorist organization ISIS and the attack in Paris, France, in 2015 against the satirical magazine *Charlie Hebdo* has done nothing to ease the fears of a major attack against *Jyllands-Posten*.

Mohammed Ajmal Amir Kasab, the lone survivor of the ten attackers from the Mumbai attack, was sentenced to death by a court in Mumbai.

"To be hanged by the neck till death," said Judge Tahaliyani, adding that Kasab had lost any right to "humane treatment." The majority
of death sentences handed down in India are commuted to life imprisonment, and though more than four hundred sit on India's death rows,
before the Mumbai attack only two death sentences were carried out in
the previous fifteen years.

On November 12, 2012, Kasab secretly received word that the
authorities would soon be carrying out his death sentence. Kasab didn't
write a will, or any letters, and he had but one wish: that his mother in
Pakistan receive word as soon as possible that he had been hanged. The
following week, Kasab was moved from his maximum-security cell in
Arthur Road prison in Mumbai and secretly sent to Yerwada prison in
Pune. There, he was hanged at 7:30 a.m., Wednesday, November 21,
2012, just a few days before the four-year anniversary of the Mumbai
attack.

Nobody had requested that his body be delivered, so Kasab was
buried on the prison grounds. The hanging took place in secret to
avoid protests or celebrations. Later that day, the public learned for the
first time of Kasab's death.

"The majesty of the Indian justice system has been upheld. We
have done better than the Americans, who could not try Osama bin
Laden and had to liquidate him. But we went through the due process
of law," said Prithviraj Chavan, political leader of the Indian state of
Maharashtra that same evening.

The remaining nine attackers from Mumbai were buried secretly—
and only after several months since the attack, as local Muslims initially
refused to bury the men in sacred grounds. Their burial places are still
kept secret.

Major Iqbal—Headley's connection to the Pakistani intelligence
service, ISI—has never been identified. Headley himself claims he
never heard Iqbal's first name. The Americans remain convinced,
though, that Iqbal continues to work in Pakistan with ISI's approval.
Officially, ISI has no knowledge of Iqbal.

Jyllands-Posten no longer has offices or any other connection to Kongens Nytorv. Extra security at the new City Hall Square office, and at the Viby J headquarters near Aarhus, has cost them "significant sums," but the precise amount remains a secret. JP/Politikens Hus reveals that currently, "about 1.5 million dollars per year" is spent on security. The paper has, since Headley's plans became known, retained a former PET agent as the head of security.

Kurt Westergaard, the man behind the drawing of the prophet Muhammad with a bomb in his turban, was sent on vacation by *Jyllands-Posten* a few weeks after David Headley's plans were revealed. After his vacation, he retired from his position as a permanent artist at *Jyllands-Posten* after twenty-eight years. The original cartoon of Muhammad is "hidden safely away," Westergaard says.

Today, Westergaard calls the Muhammad drawings "catalysts in a necessary process" in the debate on freedom of expression—a debate that could just as well come up about a film or a novel, but "now, it happened to be my drawing." He regrets nothing, though he continues to receive death threats and will likely have to live with police protection for the rest of his life. In January 2010, Mohamed Geele—a twenty-eight-year-old man of Somali background—tried to kill Westergaard. Geele broke into Westergaard's home armed with an axe. The artist probably survived only because he sought shelter in his bathroom, which had been converted into a safe room. Geele was sentenced to ten years in prison and will be deported afterward.

Kurt Westergaard continues to give talks about his experiences with the drawing.

Flemming Rose left *Jyllands-Posten* after sixteen years in 2015, deciding to use his time to write books and debate free speech all over the world. He published the book *The Tyranny of Silence* in 2010, in which he gives his personal take on why it was he who ended up in the spotlight, so to speak, after the Muhammad cartoons.

"I've become a widely controversial figure, one whom many people love to hate, and one whom some people even wish to kill. I've racked my brain to find an explanation for an apparent paradox: I'm no provocateur, I'm not on an endless hunt for conflict for the sake of conflict, and it does not satisfy me to see people get upset about anything I've said or done."

Rose describes the course of events surrounding Westergaard's drawing as paradoxical.

"The ones who wanted Westergaard's head said: if you, Kurt Westergaard, claim that some Muslims are violent, we'll kill you. And in that way, every assassination attempt on Westergaard, every plan to murder him, became a confirmation of the drawing's contents. It would have been absolutely hilarious if it hadn't been so scary."

As he left the newspaper, Flemming Rose wrote in an e-mail to all the journalists at *Jyllands-Posten*, saying that liberty was under pressure from the increasing diversity in Europe.

Munir Awad, Omar Abdalla Aboelazm, Mounir Dhahri, and Sahbi Zalouti—the four men from Sweden—were each sentenced to twelve years in prison for their roles in the planning of terrorist acts against *Jyllands-Posten*.

PET has never officially connected the men directly to the Headley plot, but at a press conference after the four men's arrests, PET leader Jakob Scharf said: "It certainly can't be ruled out that there's some connection to the David Headley case."

Farid Lamrabet—the man who met with Headley in Sweden and was in contact with the four men from Sweden—is apparently still living in Sweden. His shops in Stockholm have closed, and he has been convicted for violations of business regulations. He has never been indicted in any of the terrorism cases.

Swedish authorities do not wish to reveal if he has been interrogated in connection with the investigation of the Headley case.

Jesper Bornak is still working in the shipping business, and today has his own company with branches in Denmark, Germany, England, Belgium, and Spain, where he lives with his family.

Since Mumbai, he has participated in his first triathlon. Several of his acquaintances from the Leopold Café have tried to hide the images burned into their retinas, and by no means wish to speak about the attack. For Jesper Bornak, it's the other way around. Since the violent night in 2008, he has returned to Mumbai and eaten the very same dish he did that evening at the Leopold Café. Right next to the bullet holes, which the restaurant has chosen not to plaster over.

NOTES

David Headley's life has been characterized by lies, deceit, and manipulation. That made him the perfect man for the jobs of drug dealer, informer, and terrorist. At the same time, it has not made the task of reconstructing his life and actions any easier.

This book is, first and foremost, based on the many documents, pieces of evidence, and testimonies upon which the trial in Chicago was based. Far from all of the ten thousand documents in the case have been released—and many never will be—but they paint a clear picture of David Headley as a person.

More than three hundred private emails sent by David Headley to his friends in Pakistan in 2008 and 2009 have also played a crucial role in the making of this book. Emails often leave electronic tracks—for example, one's geographic location (via IP addresses), dates, and times. These tracks have been checked and compared with the explanations Headley gave in the trial. They confirm his story.

In other contexts, documents, information, evidence, or other things have been verified in the classical journalistic way. Did he really travel to Manchester? Was he really wearing a tie? Did he really buy those kinds of books? Did it rain that day? Airplane tickets, eyewitness accounts, receipts, and old weather forecasts say yes.

The same, of course, goes for information and accounts from many other people who agreed to be interviewed for this book. Many had the chance to read through their accounts before the book was published. Not all of them have wished to come forward, but all the names used in the book are the correct ones. That is, no aliases have been used.

Certain conversations—for example, with the terrorists in Pakistan who have since been killed—are reproduced entirely based on David Headley's own memory and retelling.

The responsibility for any errors there may be, though, rests with the author of this book alone.

Apart from the American, Indian, and Danish interrogations, Headley hasn't spoken about his criminal activities, and his physical location remains secret for reasons of security.

Through his lawyer, in autumn 2013, Headley presented a number of concrete answers to questions about the plans for the attack in Denmark in connection with the making of this book.

Headley stated that currently he doesn't "feel that he's able" to talk to the press. He hasn't ruled out, however, that at a later time he might answer the last unanswered questions about his life. Headley dreams that one day, his life will become a book. Perhaps even a movie.

Several sources are used in successive chapters and are named here in the first chapter in which they appear. The sources are listed in chronological order, chapter by chapter. Book titles are given in italics.

1. A Beginning
Leaked copy of the Indian intelligence service NIA's thirty-four-hour long interrogation of Headley from June 3–9, 2010. Transcript.
Headley's own testimony in Chicago on May 23, 24, 25, 26, and 31, 2011. Transcript and own notes.

2. Light the Fire, My Brother and 4. In the Control Room
"Fleeing, hiding, dying," *Los Angeles Times*, November 28, 2008.
"Taj Mahal hotel chairman: We had warning", CNN, November 29, 2008.
"Mumbai: City of Death," *Sunday Times*, November 30, 2008.

"Jeg lå og ventet på å få kula" ["I Lay Waiting for the Bullet"], *Verdens Gang*, December 1, 2008. Line Kristin Woldbeck and Arne Strømme still dispute the official story about the Mumbai attack.

"Vengeance through Kindness," *Jerusalem Post*, December 3, 2008.

"Hvad der skete i Mumbai" ["What Happened in Mumbai"], from the blog *Seiersen Science*, December 15, 2008.

"Final Report. Mumbai Terror Attack Cases," Ashok T. Duraphe, Mumbai Police, February 25, 2009.

"Revealed: The Chilling Words of the Mumbai Killers Recorded during their Murder Spree," *Mail Online*, June 27, 2009.

"Secrets of the Dead: Mumbai Massacre," PBS, November 25, 2009.

"Terror in Mumbai," CNN, December 12, 2009.

"Det var skuddsalver, skrik og gjester som ble meid ned" ["There Was Gunfire, Screams, and Guests Being Mowed Down"], NRK, November 26, 2010.

"The Events at the Mumbai Chabad House and the Immediate Aftermath," *chabad.org*.

"26/11 Attacks: Cops Find Voice That Guided 11 Terrorists", *Hindustan Times*, June 26, 2012.

Interview with Jesper Bornak, Benjamin Matthijs, Klaus Seiersen, Line Kristin Woldbeck, and several other witnesses.

3. The Army of the Righteous

"Bombing at Hotel in Pakistan Kills at Least 40," *New York Times*, September 20, 2008.

"PET-medarbejder dræbt ved terrorangreb i Islamabad" ["PET Employee Killed in Terrorist Attack in Islamabad"], *PET*, September 24, 2008.

"Militant-linked Charity Fears Indian Reprisal," Reuters, December 2 2008.

Transcript of Headley's Interrogation, FBI, November 6, 2009.

"The Double Life of David Headley," Channel 4, January 2010.

"Little Progress in Locating 26/11 Terror Commanders," *Hindu*; June 27, 2012.

J. M. Berger, *Jihad Joe. Americans Who Go to War in the Name of Islam* (Washington, DC: Potomac Books, 2011).

Stephen Tankel, *Storming the World Stage: The Story of Lashkar-E-Taiba* (London: C. Hurst, 2011).

S. Hussain Zaidi, *Headley and I* (London: HarperCollins, 2012). "LeT took Headley Seriously," *Asian Age*, July 30, 2012.

"Sex, Drugs & Jihad," *India Today*, February 7, 2013.

Excerpts from more than three hundred emails sent by David Headley in 2008 and 2009.

Several copies of the indictments against Rana, Headley, Pasha, Sajid Mir, and Ilyas Kashmiri.

"The Fighters of Lashkar-e-Taiba: Recruitment, Training, Deployment and Death," Combating Terrorism Center, West Point, April 2013.

5. Burn Denmark Down

"I feel terribly guilty," *Guardian*, November 4, 2004.

"Lærer overfaldet efter Koran-oplæsning" ["Teacher Attacked after Qur'an Recitation"], *Politiken*, October 9, 2004.

"Jeg tør ikke pisse på Koranen—og det gør mig vred" ["I Wouldn't Dare Piss on the Qur'an—And That Makes Me Mad"], *Information*, September 7, 2005.

Prime minister Anders Fogh Rasmussen's letter to Muslim ambassadors, October 21, 2005.

"Fra idé til krise" ["From Idea to Crisis"], *Journalisten*, February 15, 2006.

"May our mothers be bereaved of us if we fail to help our prophet." Words of Osama bin Laden, IntelCenter, 2008.

FBI interrogation of Headley, May 9, 2011.

"David Coleman Headley: Cold, Detached," NDTV, May 25, 2011.

Interview with Flemming Rose, Kurt Westergaard, and several others at *Jyllands-Posten*.

Sixty-six e-mails, tape transcripts, pictures, maps, bills, contracts, telephone lists, video clips, and other materials entered as evidence in the Chicago trial against Rana.

6. The Prince
"A Terror Suspect with Feet in East and West," *New York Times*, November 21, 2009.
"Avoid Daood, Father Said," *India Today*, February 1, 2013.
NDTV interview with Headley's now deceased uncle. Author's own observations from Chicago.

7. A Dream about the Prophet
"The Saga of the Khyber Pass," *Today Magazine, Philadelphia Inquirer*, September 8, 1974.
Letter to Judge Amon from the United States Attorney, Eastern District of New York, September 22, 1998.
Lawrence Wright, *The Looming Tower: Al-Qaeda and the Road to 9/11* (New York: Random House, 2006).
"The Lost Picture Show: Complaints About Closed Video Store," City Room, *New York Times*, June 10, 2008.
"A Terror Suspect with Feet in East and West," *New York Times*, November 21, 2009.
"Terror Suspect Was Drug Dealer, Then Informant," *Philadelphia Inquirer*, December 13, 2009.
Author's own observations in Philadelphia.

8. In Denmark
"Terrorist udnyttede dansk kvinde" ["Terrorist Used Danish Woman"], *Politiken*, November 23, 2011.
"Kronik: Terrortruslen er alvorlig" ["Essay: The Terrorist Threat Is Serious"], Morten Bødskov, Justitsministeriet [Ministry of Justice], November 22, 2012.
Several emails shown in court in Chicago.

Interviews with several people Headley met in Denmark. The young woman did not wish to participate, but her identity is known.

9. The Women
"Newly Discovered Warnings about Headley Reveal a Troubling Timeline in Mumbai Case," Sebastian Rotella, ProPublica, November 5, 2010.
"The American Behind India's 9/11—And How U.S. Botched Chances to Stop Him," Sebastian Rotella, ProPublica, January 24, 2013.
Interview with Faiza Outalha. *ABP/STAR News*, June 2012.
Interview with Faiza Outalha, NDTV, October 11, 2011.
Headley's email to friends in Pakistan.

10. Why This Talk of Death?
Excerpts of emails to and from Headley and his friends in Pakistan.
Interviews with several participants.

11. Brigade 313
"Omar Sheikh's Pak Handler Ilyas Kashmiri Also Handled Headley," *Express India*, November 16, 2009.
"The New Bin Laden," *Newsweek*, October 23, 2010.
Syed Saleem Shahzad, *Inside al-Qaeda and the Taliban* (London: Pluto Press, 2011).

12. The Will
"Pakistan's Jihadists No Fans of Cricket," *Hindu*, March 5, 2009.
"As Human Victims of Terror Attack Are Buried, Nation Mourns the Other Casualty – Cricket," *Guardian,* March 7, 2009.
"Mehar Mohammad Khalil: A Hero Across Borders," *Sunday Times* Sri Lanka, March 8, 2009.

13. Cut Their Heads Off
"Documents Reveal al Qaeda's Plans for Seizing Cruise Ships, Carnage in Europe," CNN, May 1, 2012.

14. The European Cells

"Flemming Rose – A Ukrainian Jew Working for Mossad?" Christopher Bollyn, February 27, 2006.

"This Is How You Slit the Throats of Your Enemies," *Daily Mirror*, February 19, 2008.

"Another City Link to Terror," *Derby Telegraph*, March 3, 2009.

"Man Jailed Over Suicide Bomb Book," BBC, December 15, 2009.

"Mumbai Terrorist, MI5 Spooks and the Link to Derby," *Derby Telegraph*, November 11, 2011.

Magnus Sandelin, *Jihad – svenskarna i de islamistiska terrornätverken* ["Jihad—The Swedes in the Islamist Terrorism Networks"], *Reporto*, 2012.

Interview with Raffaello Pantucci of the Royal United Services Institute and Stephen Tankel of American University.

15. The Suspicion

"U.K. Cites David Headley to Join EU Directive on Air Passengers," PTI, May 11, 2011.

"A Perfect Terrorist," Sebastian Rotella, PBS *Frontline*, ProPublica, 2011.

Speech by Alan Shatter, Irish minister of Justice, about PSR, May 16, 2012.

16. A Desperate Man

"A Shuttered Video Store, with Troubles Still Brewing," City Room, *New York Times*, September 16, 2008.

"Affidavit in Support of Search Warrants," FBI agent Lorenzo Benedict, October 2, 2009.

17. Sacrifice Everything

"Federal Agents Raid Goat Meat Plant," CB2, Chicago, October 20, 2009.

"Massive FBI Raid on Islamic Slaughterhouse Mystifies Tiny Illinois Town," Fox News, October 22, 2009.

Drafts of press releases and several internal emails, Justitsministeriet [the Ministry of Justice] and Statsministeriet [the Prime Minister's Office], 2009, released in 2013.

Press conference with PET, recorded by TV2 on 27 October 2009.

"FBI director Mueller discusses Headley case with Indian Home Minister Chidambaram," confidential diplomatic cable from the American embassy in New Delhi, released by Wikileaks, February 26, 2010.

Lawyer George Jackson III, Chicago.

Excerpts from Rana's immediate interrogation after his arrest. From "Government's objections to the presentence report," January 14, 2013.

18. From Stockholm

"The Terror Tapes," *Copenhagen Post*, April 24, 2012.

"Terrortiltalt: Operationen kan føre os til martyrdom-men" ["Man Indicted for Terrorism: 'The Operation Can Bring Us to Martyrdom'"], *Jyllands-Posten*, February 24, 2012.

"Aflytning afslører tiltaltes mordplaner" ["Surveillance Reveals Accused's Plans for Murder"], *Politiken*, April 19, 2012.

"Danish Newspaper Plotter Arrested Twice Before," *The Long War Journal*, December 31, 2010.

In addition, some information comes from *Jyllands-Posten*'s journalists Jonas Høy Bruun and Carsten Ellegaards's coverage of the hearing in Copenhagen, April 2013.

19. The Truth

Letters from Headley to the organization Aseerun, 2011.

Press release from Brigade 313, translated by *The Long War Journal*, 2011.

"Al-Qaeda Pakistan Chief's Death Likely," Associated Press, June 5, 2011.

Transcript from hearings in Chicago in 2011 and 2013.

Afterword

"Al Qaida truer på ny Danmark" ["Al-Qaeda Threatens Denmark Again"], *Jyllands-Posten*, December 31, 2012.

"Pakistani Militant, Price on Head, Lives in Open," *New York Times*, February 6, 2013.

Transcript of press conference in the White House, June 13, 2013.

Acknowledgments

Special thanks to editor Truels Præstegaard Sørensen at People's Press, *Jyllands-Posten*'s Fond, and my dear Ellen.

Thanks to Jakob Kvist (People'sPress), Jakob Moll (Zetland), and my former colleagues at *Jyllands-Posten*, several of whom have actively helped with this book: Carsten Ellegaard Christensen, Jonas H. Bruun, Thomas Lund Hansen, and Niels Christian Bastholm.

Thanks also to my amazing colleagues all over the world who have dug into the Headley case throughout the last years, each helping in their own way: Sebastian Rotella (ProPublica*)*, Puk Damsgaard Andersen (Danish Broadcasting Company), Morten Skjoldager and Claus Blok Thomsen (*Politiken*), Ginger Thomsen (*New York Times*), Rummana Hussain (*Chicago Sun-Times*), Mayank Chhaya (freelancer), Chuck Goudie (ABC7, Chicago), Magnus Sandelin (freelancer), Sarah Jacobs (NDTV), Sabrina Shankman (PBS/*Frontline*), and innumerable other journalists with newspapers and TV stations in India, Pakistan, the United States, Canada, and Denmark, and terrorism researchers at several international institutes.